URBAN-REGIONAL DEVELOPMENT
IN SOUTH AMERICA

UNITED NATIONS RESEARCH INSTITUTE FOR SOCIAL DEVELOPMENT – GENEVA

Regional Planning

Antoni Kuklinski
Editor

Volume 10

MOUTON · PARIS · THE HAGUE

Urban-regional Development in South America

A Process of Diffusion and Integration

Poul Ove Pedersen
Technical University of Denmark

MOUTON · PARIS · THE HAGUE

Denne afhandling er af det matematisk-naturvidenskabelige fakultet ved Københavns universitet antaget til offentligt at forsvares for den filosofiske doktorgrad.

København,   Morten Lange
30 september 1972   Dekan

Regional Planning

1. Regional Development: Experiences and Prospects in South and Southeast Asia
2. Regional Development: Experiences and Prospects in the United States of America
3. Regional Development: Experiences and Prospects in Latin America
4. Regional Development: Experiences and Prospects in Eastern Europe
5. Growth Poles and Growth Centres in Regional Planning
6. Regional Information and Regional Planning
7. Regional Sociology, Environment and Regional Planning
8. Regional Disaggregation of National Policies and Plans
9. Growth Poles and Growth Centres as Instruments of Modernization in the Developing Countries
10. Urban-regional Development in South-America: A Process of Diffusion and Integration

ISBN: 90-279-7631-7

Jacket design by Françoise Rojare

Printed in Hungary

To Ingrid

Preface by the Director of UNRISD

This comparative study on regional structures in South America was prepared by Mr. Pedersen in the framework of his association with the Centre for Urban and Regional Studies of the Catholic University in Santiago de Chile in the years 1967–68 and of his present association with the Technical University of Denmark.

At the 1969 Lund Seminar on Information Systems for Regional Development, sponsored jointly by UNRISD and the University of Lund, Mr. Pedersen presented a paper on "Innovation Diffusion in Urban Systems". It was subsequently agreed that Mr. Pedersen would adapt his studies on the role of information accessibility and diffusion of innovation in urban-regional development to the UNRISD/MOUTON Regional Planning Series.

The study is based on data for 74 regions in South America around 1950 and around 1960. Part I of the study investigates the regional disparities and the way they have developed. In Parts II–IV the development process is seen from the perspective of innovation diffusion, and a model is developed based on the empirical relationships among measures of information accessibility, regional *per capita* income and selected demographic variables.

The Institute is grateful to Mr. Pedersen for his contribution to the Series. Like other volumes of the Series, this volume has been prepared under the editorship of Mr. Antoni Kuklinski.

Donald V. McGranahan

Foreword by the Editor

The study of Mr. Pedersen is an important contribution in our field. The value of this contribution can be tested not only in terms of pure intellectual curiosity as an attempt to explore the interrelation between information accessibility and urban-regional development but also in terms of policy-oriented research as an attempt to arrive at conclusions which could be directly applicable in policy and planning.

This last point deserves special attention. In the past the instruments of regional policy and planning were applied predominantly to the allocation in space of physical objects, now the new approach to regional development and planning is recognizing the growing role of information flows and the diffusion of innovation. The study of Mr. Pedersen is a most welcome contribution to this new approach. The innovative quality of Mr. Pedersen's study is expressed also in the macro-regional continental scale of his analysis. The integration of interregional and international analytical approaches on a continental scale is opening up new comparative perspectives in our field. I think that Mr. Pedersen's study should be followed up by a research project using – naturally with the necessary modifications – the analytical approach developed by Mr. Pedersen in a comparative study of urban-regional development in Europe and Latin America.

But that is already a problem for the future. At this moment, however, I should like to look back to the past since the volume by Mr. Pedersen is the last volume I am editing in the framework of this series. Let me then formulate my farewell to arms in the following way.

Each of the volumes printed in this series has its own strength and weaknesses and *grosso modo* is an independent unit, but the real value of the series is in the totality of its contribution to regional development and planning as a policy-oriented discipline. Since this series was a direct result of the implementation of the UNRISD Regional Development Programme, we can in this place submit to the competent judgement of scholars and planners involved in the promotion of regional development around the world the following questions:

1. Whether the leading projects were correctly related to the leading issues of regional development and planning today in the developed and developing countries?

2. To what extent the programme generated or promoted new ideas and approaches which could be applied in practical regional planning operations and theoretical studies?

3. Whether by its empirical studies it effectively increased the knowledge of regional development and planning as practised in different parts of the world?

4. Whether the programme served as an efficient channel of communication among regional planners and scholars and was thereby instrumental in the promotion of regional planning in countries or regions where communication barriers have been an obstacle to the application of regional planning?

Geneva, December 1, 1972   Antoni Kuklinski

Acknowledgments

This volume is the final outcome of research initiated during the author's stay from 1967 to 1969 as a Ford Foundation — sponsored visiting professor at the Center for Urban and Regional Studies (CIDU) of the Catholic University in Santiago de Chile. Roughly speaking the study was designed and the data were collected in Chile.

The data were analysed and the manuscript was written while the author was working as an associate professor at the Institute of Road Construction, Traffic Engineering and Town Planning of the Technical University of Denmark.

The author is indebted to many persons at these institutions for help and advice during the course of the study. For advice during the first part of the study period his thanks should go especially to John Friedman and Walter Stöhr from the Ford Foundation mission of advisers to the Chilean Ministry of Housing and ODEPLAN, and to Guillermo Geisse and Ivo Barbarovic from CIDU.

For advice during the second part of the study period, his thanks must go to Professor P. H. Bendtsen from The Technical University of Denmark.

Thomas Reiner from the University of Pennsylvania and Walter Stöhr now at McMaster University (Canada) have read the manuscript and supplied valuable comments on it.

Finally, Antoni Kuklinski has followed the study from its origin in the ideas presented in a paper by Walter Stöhr and the author at the 'Seminar on Social Science and Urban Development in Latin America' in Jahuel, April 1968 (Pedersen and Stöhr, 1969), to the discussion of some of the results at the Seminar on Regional Information Systems arranged by UNRISD and the Department of Cultural Geography at Lund University in Lund, October 1970. He has, especially in the last part of the study period, provided valuable comments on the manuscript and, last but not least, accepted it for publication in this series.

To all who have helped to guide this study the long way from the first thoughts to this volume, the author wants to extend his thanks. For errors and mistakes, of course, only the author can be blamed.

Poul Ove Pedersen

Contents

PART IV. SOCIO-ECONOMIC FEED-BACKS TO THE PROCESS OF INNOVATION DIFFUSION

APPENDICES

CHAPTER 1

Introduction

The South American continent[1] consists of 13 countries, which again are divided into more than 200 provinces, departments or states.

While the division lines between the nations are deep and have often led to tension or even war, the boundaries between the provinces are of less consequence than in most other regions of the world. Regional[2] autonomy is negligable, and in most of the countries more than 90% of all public expenditure is allocated by the national government (Stöhr, 1974).

This picture of the political structure of the continent is almost the opposite of the picture provided by the economic and geographical features. Though the South Americans might themselves see more differences than similarities between their nations, few nations in the world are more alike both in cultural heritage and economic structure than the South American nations, and in few others are the regional differences created by a rough geography more profound than in the South American countries.

This has given rise to some very complex problems of integration and development on the continent.

In discussions of economic development policies in the developing countries such problems of regional (sub-national) development have in

---

[1] Most parts of this work will be concerned with South America rather than with Latin America in its entirety, unlike most recent writings which have generally been concerned either with Latin America or with the Latin American Common Market (LAFTA) countries. The reason for this choice is that we are primarily interested in the interrelation between economic integration and spatial transformation, and increased interaction with Mexico, Central America and the Carribean is not likely to have much impact on the spatial transformation of the South American countries.

[2] The terms 'region' and 'regional' will in this work refer to sub-national units and not to multi-national groupings, as is common in literature on international integration. For South America we shall use the term 'continent'.

2

recent years come into the forefront. One reason for this is that the size of an economy has become an increasingly important factor determining not only total production, but also *per capita* production. In many developing countries both social and regional disparities in development are very large, and large parts of the population are in reality kept outside the national market economy. The lack of social and regional integration, therefore, is a serious impediment to national growth.

During the 1960s, studies of regional development have been made by a number of South American countries, and a number of regional planning bodies have been set up. Also some more or less explicit regional planning measures have in many countries been in existence for some years, *e.g.* industrial location and relocation support, agricultural settlement schemes, mineral resource exploitation projects, and transport plans. The effort so far, however, has only had limited success. First, because the strong tradition of centralized government has been difficult to change; as a result, most regional development efforts until now have been made on central government initiative, with their headquarters in the capital cities rather than in the regions. Secondly, lack of infrastructure, such as transportation, public utilities, and services outside the largest cities has made the decentralization of other activities difficult. Finally, the effectiveness of many regional planning measures has been seriously reduced by the existing national borders.

As remedies for these problems the key policies which have been discussed are (1) urban and social development projects, most dramatically manifested in such growth pole projects as Brazilia and Ciudad Guayana, but perhaps more valuably reflected in a growing general concern for urban and social problems everywhere on the continent; (2) transport and communication plans outstandingly represented by the Carretera Marginal de la Selva, the Brazilian road construction programme and the satellite communications system, and (3) the establishment of international integration and collaboration, which at the regional level, for instance, has resulted in studies of the border areas between Ecuador and Colombia and between Colombia and Venezuela, a development scheme for the La Plata River system, and the Valdivia-Neuquen development project comprising regions in both Argentina and Chile.

All these projects, however, are unrelated. None of the Latin American countries has at present established a regional development policy in terms of which needs and means, costs and benefits can be assessed, and at the international level such a policy of course exists to an even smaller extent.

Before such a continental policy for regional development can be clarified and specified or national policies can be evaluated in continental terms, studies of the regional structure of the continent as a whole are needed; such studies would make it possible to compare regions not only within one country, but also in different countries. The first purpose of this study is to make such a cross-nation analysis of regional differences in South America.

Knowledge of the spatial development processes will also be necessary before effective plans can be established. We must have tools so that we can judge what effect a given policy can be expected to have on the regional structure.

In the last five to ten years a few works have been published, most notably Williamson (1965), in which attempts have been made to evaluate the changes in regional income differences taking place in different countries and at different times. Broadly speaking these investigations indicate that the regional income differences have tended to increase during the first stages of development and decrease again during the later stages.

There are also a number of very frequently cited works, *e.g.* Myrdal (1957) and Hirschman (1958), which in qualitative theoretical terms attempt to explain and predict changes in regional income differences.

However, very few studies have attempted to give a quantitative description of the mechanism which leads to increasing or decreasing regional income differences, and the few studies which do attempt such a quantative analysis mostly use data from the United States of America or other highly developed countries. The reason for this, of course, is clear. In developing countries one need not be very critical of the available data to run into insurmountable problems. In that respect the South American countries are no exception.

In spite of the data problems the second purpose of this study is to attempt to set up such an empirically based model illustrating how the regional income differences might be expected to change over time.

In doing so it will be assumed that information accessibility and innovation are the prime factors of economic development. In his introduction to the *Seminar on Information Systems for Regional Development* (Hägerstrand and Kuklinski, 1971) Hägerstrand writes:

'Regional development should to a large degree be a question of mobilizing information in order to make it work in new environments. How to do this is partly a problem of restructuring the more formal channels for information flow between decision-makers in governments, organizations and firms and of revising the content of messages. A second – no less important part – is to try to understand and make use of the "natural" communication system which is the unplanned aggregate outcome of free transactions between individuals directly and through media.

It seems to be the right moment just now to call attention to the informational aspects of regional development',
and this is what we attempt to do.

To do this it has clearly been necessary to apply data which many researchers would turn down with disgust, because their reliability is uncertain.

The conclusions of the study, therefore, can only be rather general, concerned with average trends and tendencies rather than with specific regions; and even though they are based on empirical analyses, they should be considered hypotheses rather than proven facts. Another limitation of the study is that lack of data has made it possible to include only economic and demographic aspects of development. Political, sociological, and cultural aspects are, therefore, not treated explicitly.

The study is based on cross-section data for 74 regions covering all the South American countries. The data are collected from the population censuses taken around 1950 and 1960. Though the study is basically a cross-section analysis, it compares wherever possible 1950 and 1960 data and could thus be classified as comparative statics. Details of the data are given in appendices A and B.

By including regions from different countries in the same analysis the data problems are of course increased many times over. The consequent loss in the quality of the data is, however, partially offset by the broader spectrum of observations obtained, ranging from almost completely rural areas in parts of Peru and Bolivia to the highly urbanized areas of Buenos Aires, Montevideo and São Paulo.

The study consists of four parts. Part I is a descriptive analysis of the 74 regions and their interdependence, and consists of chapters 2 and 3. Chapter 2 is a factor analysis of census data for the 74 regions around 1950 and around 1960. Three principal factors which explain 63% of the total variance are examined.

The first of these three factors was found to correspond roughly to the physical planner's concept of urbanization as 'a place of living'. Factor 2 somewhat resembles the sociologist's concept of modernization or urbanization as 'a way of life', with the restriction that as the planner's and sociologist's concept of urbanization are highly interrelated while the factors 1 and 2, by definition, are not, factor 2 only covers that part of the sociologist's view which has not already been accounted for by factor 1. Similarly, factor 3 appears to be similar to that part of the economist's concept of industrialization which has not been accounted for by the factors 1 and 2. The planner's, the sociologist's and the economist's views of urbanization are thus oblique factors in factor space.

Finally, an analysis of how regions in the decade 1950–1960 have moved in factor space shows that there is a high degree of correspondence between the structure of a region in 1950 and the way it changed its structure during the decade.

Chapter 3 presents an analysis of data on interregional flows to give an idea of the interrelation of the regions of South America. It shows that while at the time of the analysis, some integration had been achieved on the southern part of the continent, little had been achieved in the northern part.

Part II attempts to view the development of the urban system as a process of innovation diffusion. Chapter 4 reviews the process of innovation diffusion in urban systems and presents some data on innovation diffusion in Latin America, while chapter 5 analyses the relations between innovation and information diffusion and the growth of urban systems.

Rapid diffusion is contingent on effective integration. Integration, therefore, can be seen as complementary to diffusion. Integration is created by increased accessibility among more and more people and activities, and part III, therefore, presents an analysis of the relation between accessibility and regional economic development as expressed in the measurement of *per capita* income. In chapter 7 the variation in accessibility is found to explain about 50% of the variation in *per capita* income between the consolidated regions (with relatively high population density, *i.e.* those regions which load high on factor 3). In the very thinly populated, peripheral regions, on the other hand, accessibility was not correlated with the level of *per capita* income. Here the availability of natural resources and direct capital investments, often in the form of subsidies, appears to be more important in explaining the variation in *per capita* income.

To the extent that regional income differences are determined by regional accessibility differences, changes in the income differences can be seen as a result of changes in the accessibility differences. Changes in the accessibility differences, however, in part result from changes in the distribution of population and its level of socio-economic development so that we really have a circular process. In chapter 8 a type of simulation is attempted in order to show, firstly, how accessibility can be expected to change as a result of urbanization, international integration, and improvements in the transport and communication networks, and secondly, how these changes in accessibility differences can be expected to change the regional differences in income *per capita*. The results of the simulation indicate that the regional income differences can be expected to increase at very low levels of accessibility but decrease at higher levels, a result which is in conformity with most empirical studies of regional income differences.

The process of innovation diffusion not only influences the economy of regions but also their social and demographic characteristics. Migration tends to flow from areas with few economic opportunities to areas with many, and the birth and death rates are influenced by the spread of health services and education. The social and demographic changes can, therefore, be seen as a feed-back from the process of innovation diffusion. These feed-back mechanisms are treated in part IV.

PART I

The regional structure of South America

CHAPTER 2

The spatial structure of South American development

2.1 INTRODUCTION

Concepts such as those of the level of urbanization, economic development, social development, modernization, industrialization, and of centre-
periphery structure are in current literature often used for very similar
purposes, according to the approach of the researcher.

The urban planner or geographer mainly interested in the physical
aspects of development (physical infrastructure, housing, etc.) will most
often describe development in terms of physical urbanization or as a type
of settlement. This is also the definition (urbanization as a percentage of
the population living in urban areas) on which population censuses are
based, and researchers relying on census data, therefore, have to some
extent been forced to apply this ecological concept of urbanization.

The sociologist on the other hand has tended to consider urbanization
as a 'way of life' (Wirth, 1938) rather than as a 'place of living'. He
emphasizes the organizational structure, such as family structure and
economic organization, and the system of values, especially the attitude
towards innovation and change. He claims, that although population
with an urban way of life is found mostly in the urban areas, it is very
common to find both population with a rural way of life in urban areas
(especially in the developing countries) and urbanized population in rural
areas (especially around the largest cities) (Lewis and Hauser, 1965;
Friedmann, 1969).

Finally, the economist has emphasized the division of labour aspect
of urbanization. His viewpoints are represented by the theories of growth
poles and centre-periphery structures. To him development is measured
as *per capita* income and regional income differences are a result of an
uneven distribution of the high and low productivity industries. As the
largest productivity differences are generally those between agriculture
and the urban trades – manufacturing and services – this distinction also
becomes the most important in determining development differences.
In many developing countries, however, not all urban trades are high

9

productivity industries. A large proportion of the urban population is employed in very low productivity handicraft and petty trades, and only large-scale manufacturing and part of services can be counted as high productivity activities. Urbanization as a type of settlement, therefore, is not necessarily identical with the economist's concept of development.

Most of the concepts of development proposed in current literature can roughly be classified in one or other of the three groups described above. In the following pages we shall call them urbanization, modernization, and industrialization.

One of the reasons for the apparent confusion with regard to these concepts is that development is a multi-dimensional phenomenon. Attempts to describe it in terms of a single dimension inevitably create ambiguity, because the number of possible interpretations of the empirical data is infinite.

In an attempt to clarify the multi-dimensional nature of regional development this chapter presents a factor analysis of regional development in South America. This factor analysis has led us first to set up a typology of regions and secondly, to see how the regions in the course of development change structure and pass from one regional type to another.

2.2 A FACTOR ANALYSIS OF REGIONAL STRUCTURE

The basis for the following factor analysis is a matrix of census data for 74 areas covering the whole of South America and each consisting of one or more provinces, departments, or states. The data are collected from population censuses taken around 1950 and around 1960.

The matrix contains 18 variables related to population and employment structure (see Table 2.1). In making the selection of variables consideration was given to the possible rather than the optimal, because the possibilities of obtaining easily accessible, internationally comparable data for subnational areas are very limited. Even when only population censuses are used, there are great difficulties because census definitions vary both from country to country and from census to census. To avoid this all the data used here have as far as possible been corrected to conform to a common set of definitions. Where this has not been possible the data have been excluded, with one exception, namely, the data on urban population which were found so important that they had to be included, even though they are strictly speaking not internationally comparable.

Even if the sample of variables is not optimal it is found that the picture it gives of the social and economic structure of the regions is sufficiently broad to be useful. The worst deficiency is probably that the regional economies are judged from the standpoint of employment structure alone. It might be claimed that this can lead to serious misinterpretation, because some of the sectors, such as manufacturing and services, cover a very broad range of productivity levels from handicrafts and household servants to capital-intensive industry and professional services. The results to be presented below, however, indicate that the sectors depend on one another so that if two regions with the same proportion of manufacturing employment have different proportions of capital-intensive manufacturing and handicrafts, then this difference will show up as differences in some of the other sectors. Even though it would be misleading to judge between the two regions on the basis of employment in one sector alone the structure of the total matrix is therefore still meaningful.

Another important deficiency in the sample of variables is that it does not contain variables directly related to the organizational structure. Only in so far as such structures are reflected in the economic and demographic variables can we get some idea of this important aspect of development.

The resulting matrix characterizes and compares the structure of the 74 areas in South America around both 1950 and 1960. As neither the 1950 data nor the 1960 data exist for all countries the data matrix is incomplete. For 1950, the data exist for 69 areas, and for 1960, for only 56 areas. This means that for some areas we have data for 1950 only, for some areas for 1960 only, and for some areas for both years. In the following analysis all the data available for both years (125 areas) are included so that, as far as the data go, we can at one and the same time compare the areas in both space and time.

By including data for two points in time in the same factor analysis we assume implicitly that the basic regional structure of South America was unchanged between the two points in time, and that the development which has occurred in the regions has resulted from changes within the existing structure. Similarity between the structures revealed by two preliminary factor analyses of the data for 1950 and 1960 respectively indicates that this assumption about stable structure is not unreasonable.

By means of a factor analysis we have reduced the many correlated data included in the large data matrix (containing data for 69 areas in 1950 and for 56 areas in 1960) into a simpler and more comprehensible structure of only three uncorrelated dimensions or principal factors.

The number of dimensions or principal factors extracted from the data has been chosen by using three criteria. First, the dimensions should all be meaningful; secondly, they should represent a sufficiently large proportion of the total variance so that the resulting typology does not become useless; and finally, as the number of groups in the typology increases exponentially with the number of dimensions, the dimensions should be sufficiently few for the groups in the typology to be easily distinguishable and the number of areas in each group to be reasonably large.

The three dimensions which were finally chosen represent 63.4% of the total variance in the data matrix (see Table 2.1).

Table 2.1 *Factor weights for three dimensions or principal factors* of the South American regional structure, 1950 (69 areas) and 1960 (56 areas)*

	1. dimension: Urbanization	2. dimension: Demographic structure	3. dimension: Export-base dependency or economic diversity
1. Percentage of population in urban places	0.81	0.03	0.05
2. Percentage women in the population	−0.03	−0.84	0.34
3. Percentage of children (0–14 years) in the population	−0.40	−0.52	−0.18
4. Percentage of old people (60 years or more) in the population	0.21	0.12	0.75
5. Percentage of the population in the active age group (15–59 years)	0.39	0.92	0.11
6. Percentage illiteracy in the population 15 years or more	−0.76	−0.37	−0.11
7. Percentage active in the population 15 years or more	−0.22	0.54	0.07
8. Child-women relation (0–4 years/women 15–49 years)	−0.51	−0.53	−0.48
9. Population density	0.35	−0.23	0.19
10. Percentage of active population employed in agriculture	−0.74	−0.19	0.08
11. Percentage of active population employed in mining	0.26	0.14	−0.60

* The three factors have been rotated into a simple structure solution by means of a varimax rotation. The three original principal factors have the eigenvalues 7.45, 2.35, and 1.61 respectively.

All computations have been carried out with BMD-programme 03 M.

Table 2.1 *(continued)*

	1. dimension: Urbanization	2. dimension: Demographic structure	3. dimension: Export-base dependency or economic diversity
12. Percentage of active population employed in manufacturing	0.50	0.08	0.68
13. Percentage of active population employed in construction	0.84	0.08	−0.06
14. Percentage of active population in electricity, gas, water, etc.	0.77	0.02	0.21
15. Percentage of active population employed in commerce	0.86	−0.07	0.19
16. Percentage of active population employed in transportation	0.87	0.17	−0.06
17. Percentage of active population employed in services	0.71	0.35	−0.03
18. Percentage of active population employed in other activities	0.64	−0.07	0.23
Percentage of total variance explained	36.6	15.8	11.0
Eigenvalues	6.59	2.85	1.98

2.3 THREE DIMENSIONS OF REGIONAL DIFFERENTIATION

To interpret the three dimensions or factors, the factor weights shown in Table 2.1 and the factor scores shown on Figures 2.1–2.6 have been used. (The factor weights are correlation coefficients between the variables and the principal factors or dimensions, and the factor scores are the coordinates of the regions in factor space.)

The first dimension has high positive factor weights for the percentage of urban population and percentage of employment in the infrastructure and service activities (construction, electricity, water, etc., commerce, transport and services), and high negative factor weights for illiteracy and employment in agriculture. It represents the differentiation between urban and rural areas, and we shall interpret it as a measure of *urbanization*. Indirectly it appears to be related to the physico-economic aspects of

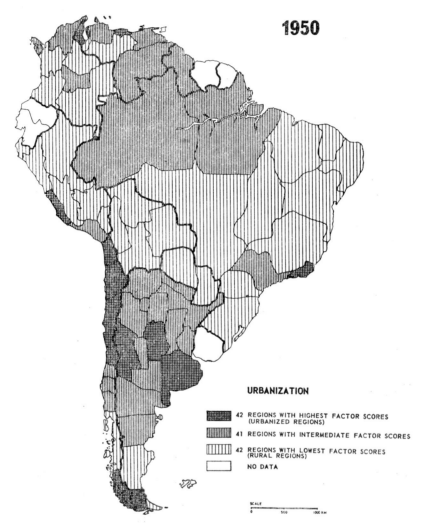

Fig. 2.1. *The geographic distribution of the factor scores for factor 1, urbanization. In the rank-ordered list of regions on which the three groups in the legend are based, the 69 regions represented in the 1950 data and the 56 regions represented in the 1960 data are*

treated as 125 different regions. The maps for 1950 and 1960 therefore should be read simultaneously

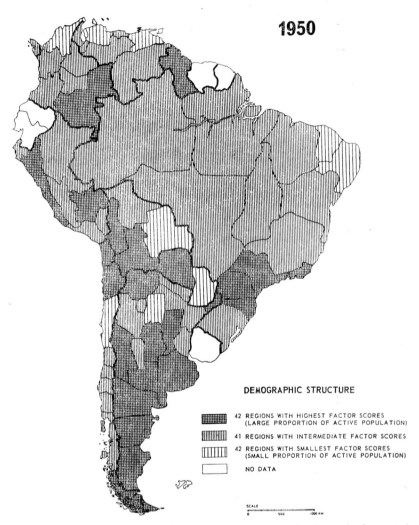

Fig. 2.2. *The geographic distribution of the factor scores for factor 2, demographic structure. In the rank-ordered list of regions on which the three groups in the legend are based, the 69 regions represented in the 1950 data and the 56 regions represented in the*

1960

1960 data are treated as 125 different regions. The maps for 1950 and 1960 therefore should be read simultaneously

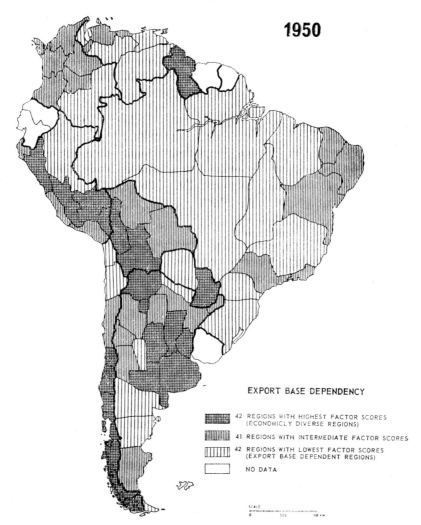

Fig. 2.3. *The geographic distribution of the factor scores for factor 3, export-base dependency. In the rank-ordered list of regions on which the three groups in the legend are based, the 69 regions represented in the 1950 data and the 56 regions represented*

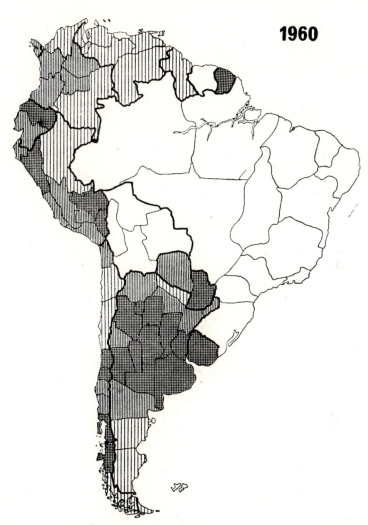

1960

in the 1960 data are treated as 125 different regions. The maps for 1950 and 1960 therefore should be read simultaneously

development: concentration of the population and distribution of the infrastructure and services.

At the upper end of the dimension we find the capital regions and some of the thinly populated but highly urbanized regions, such as the Chilean north. At the lower end we find the north and the interior of Brazil and most of Peru and Bolivia (see Figure 2.1).

The second dimension is basically a *demographic* dimension having high positive factor weights for population in the active age group (15–59 years), high negative factor weights for the percentage of women, and medium-sized negative factor weights for the percentage of children and for the child-women relation. It distinguishes between areas (with high negative factor scores) with a large proportion of dependent population and areas (with high positive factor scores) with a large proportion of active population (see Figure 2.2). This large proportion of active population might be due either to a small proportion of women, as is found in many land-settlement areas with heavy male immigration, such as the southernmost regions of Argentina. It might also be due to a small child-women relation or a large proportion of economically active women, as would mostly be found in urbanized areas, such as the central parts of Argentina. In both cases we are likely to find relatively high educational levels; in the first, because immigrants tend to have an above average education; in the second, because there tends to be a correlation between low birth rate, high female activity rate and educational standard. Correspondingly the second dimension also has a medium-sized negative factor weight for illiteracy.

The third dimension has high positive factor weights for employment in the manufacturing industries and for the percentage of old people (60 years or more). It also has high negative factor weight for employment in mining, and medium-sized negative factor weight for the child-women relation. At the positive end of this dimension we find those regions which have a high level of employment in manufacturing in proportion to employment in mining. These are partly the urban-industrial regions, such as the capital regions, where the manufacturing industry is concentrated, and partly those predominantly rural areas which have relatively large employment in traditional handicraft industries, such as the densely settled Andean regions of Bolivia and Peru. These regions also have the largest proportion of old people, in the urban-industrial regions because the death rate is low and in the traditional rural areas because the out-migration of young people is large.

At the negative end of the dimension we find partly areas with a very high level of employment in mining and partly areas with a very low level of employment in manufacturing. The first group consists of highly urbanized areas with medium-sized manufacturing such as the northern provinces of Chile. The second group consists of rural areas with very little besides agriculture and service employment, such as the Amazon regions (see Figure 2.3).

These natural-resource regions at the negative end of the third dimension are also land-settlement areas. They receive a flow of migrants in the active age group which, even if not very large in proportion to the total South American population, is still sizable in proportion to the small population already living in the areas. The proportion of old people, therefore, tends to be lower in these regions than elsewhere.

The dichotomous character of the third factor – manufacturing contra mining – points towards an interpretation of it as a centre-periphery structure. This, however, is clearly an unwarranted interpretation as our analysis only contains employment data and no data on the interregional organizational structure which is usually considered the main content of the centre-periphery structure. In the centre-periphery structure the centre is usually defined as regions which dominate other regions, and the periphery is defined as those regions which are dominated by the centre. In factor 3 the regions with low factor scores tend to be dependent on a single or a few export-base products and in an economic sense we might well treat them as a periphery. The regions with high factor scores, however, contain both the capital regions, which economically dominate the periphery, and some regions which in the centre-periphery model are usually considered part of the periphery, but which are economically more diverse.

The third dimension, therefore, ought rather to be interpreted as a measure of *export-base dependency or economic diversity*, distinguishing between the peripheral regions in which the economy is centered on the production of a single or a few resources for export (small factor scores), and the consolidated regions which have a more diverse economy and, therefore, are more self-sufficient (large factor scores). The last type of regions are generally regions that were colonized in the last century or earlier and are today relatively densely settled. Their self-sufficiency can be either a result of their predominance over other regions, as is the case of the capital regions, or a result of isolation from other regions, as in the case of some of the Andean regions. The export-base dependent regions, on the other hand, are thinly populated, land-settlement regions. The export-base on which they depend is generally a natural resource, but sometimes government services, such as military establishments or direct subsidy (*e.g.* in the form of free port status) substantially supplement the export-base.

Thus it can be concluded that at least three independent or orthogonal dimensions should be taken into account in distinguishing between regions in South America. These three dimensions can be interpreted as

1. *Urbanization*, distinguishing between more or less urbanized regions;
2. *Demographic structure*, distinguishing between regions according to the proportion of economically active population;
3. *Export-base dependency* (or economic diversity), distinguishing between peripheral and consolidated regions on the basis of the relative importance of the manufacturing and mining sectors.

2.4 THREE CONCEPTS OF DEVELOPMENT

At this point it might be relevant to ask about the relation between the three concepts briefly described in the introduction to this chapter (urbanization, modernization and industrialization) and the three independent dimensions of development found in the factor analysis (urbanization, demographic structure, and economic diversity).

It appears that the urban-rural axis found in the factor analysis is very similar to the urban planner's concept of urbanization as a form of settlement. The two other factors, however, are clearly not identical with the sociologist's and the economist's views of development. The reason is that the concepts of modernization and industrialization as outlined in the introduction are closely related to the concept of urbanization, while factors 2 and 3 of the factor analysis are by definition independent of factor 1. Factors 2 and 3, therefore, must be combined with factor 1, if they are to account for the concepts of modernization and industrialization. Such a combination of factors corresponds to a new axis in the factor space, an oblique factor. By projecting the regions (represented by points in factor space, Figures 2.4–2.6) on this new axis we can obtain the regional co-ordinates on the axis; and by a similar procedure we can obtain the factor weights corresponding to the new axis (see Figure 2.7).

By combining factors 1 and 2 and factors 1 and 3, respectively, we have obtained the new factor weights shown in Table 2.2. The table shows that these two new axes come rather close to the concepts of modernization and industrialization, respectively. The two new axes are in many ways similar to the urban-rural axis. All three have rather large factor weights for most of the original variables, but they emphasize different aspects. The rural-urban axis alone emphasizes the proportion of population living in urban areas and the proportion of the work force employed in commerce, transportation and construction. When it is combined with factor 2 the emphasis shifts towards the birth and activity rates, illiteracy, and employment in the services sector.

Table 2.2 *Factor weights for the principal factor, urbanization, and for the oblique factors, modernization and industrialization*

Variables	Urbaniza- tion (principal factor 1)	Moderniza- tion (combined factor 1–2)	Industrial- ization (combined factor 1–3)
1. Percentage of population in urban places	0.81	0.60	0.61
2. Percentage women in the population	−0.03	−0.61	0.22
3. Percentage of children (0–14 years) in the population	−0.40	−0.65	−0.41
4. Percentage of old people (60 years or more) in the population	0.21	0.23	0.68
5. Percentage of the population in the active age group (15–59 years)	0.39	0.93	0.35
6. Percentage illiteracy in the population (15 years old or more)	0.76	−0.80	−0.62
7. Percentage active in the population (15 years old or more)	−0.22	0.22	−0.11
8. Child-women relation (0–4 years/ women 15–49 years)	0.51	−0.74	−0.70
9. Population density	0.35	0.09	0.38
10. Percentage of active population employed in agriculture	−0.74	−0.66	−0.47
11. Percentage of active population employed in mining	0.26	0.28	−0.24
12. Percentage of active population employed in manufacturing	0.50	0.41	0.84
13. Percentage of active population employed in construction	0.84	0.65	0.55
14. Percentage of active population employed in elec., gas, water, etc.	0.77	0.56	0.69
15. Percentage of active population employed in commerce	0.86	0.56	0.74
16. Percentage of active population employed in transportation	0.87	0.74	0.57
17. Percentage of active population employed in services	0.71	0.75	0.48
18. Percentage of active population in other activities	0.64	0.40	0.62

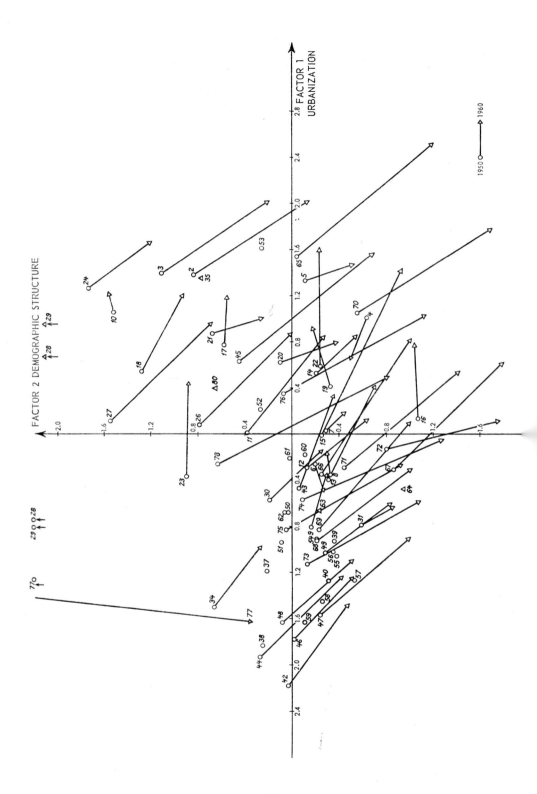

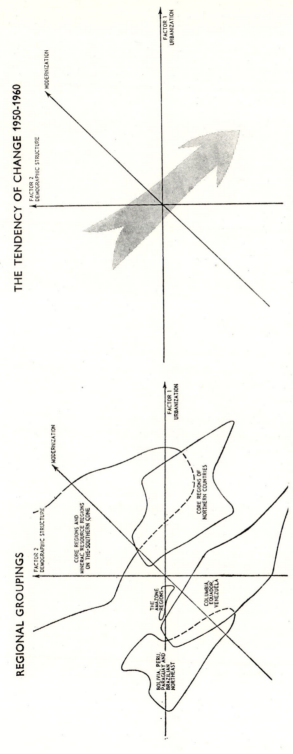

Fig. 2.4. *The relationship between the factor scores of factor 1, urbanization, and factor 2, demographic structure. Each point represents a region. The numbers refer to the list of regions given in appendix D*

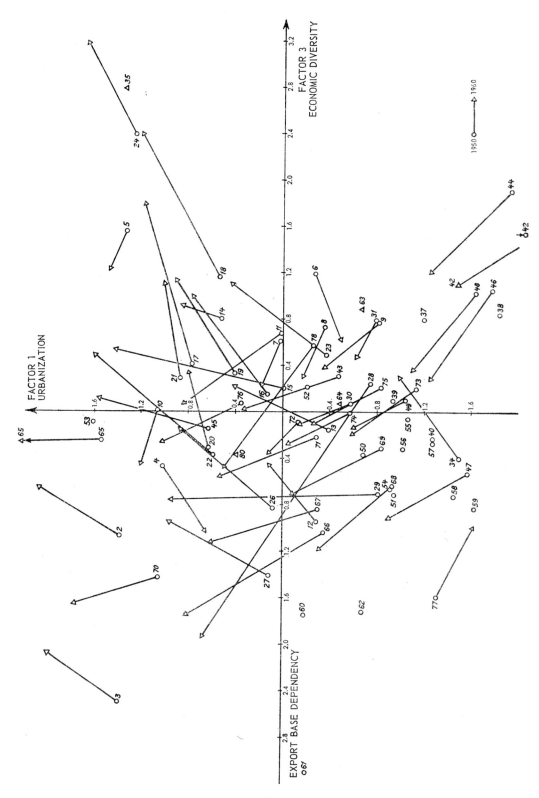

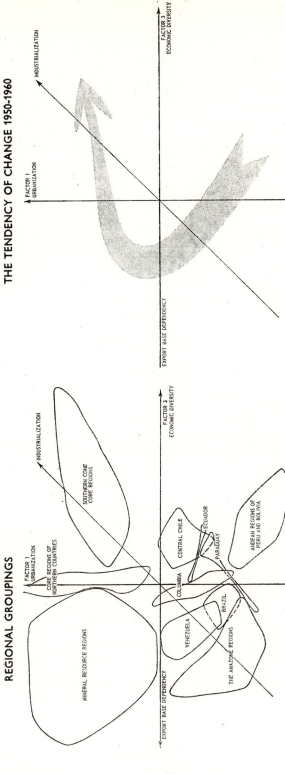

Fig. 2.5. *The relationship between the factor scores of factor 3, export-base dependency, and factor 1, urbanization. Each point represents a region. The numbers refer to the list of regions given in appendix D*

27

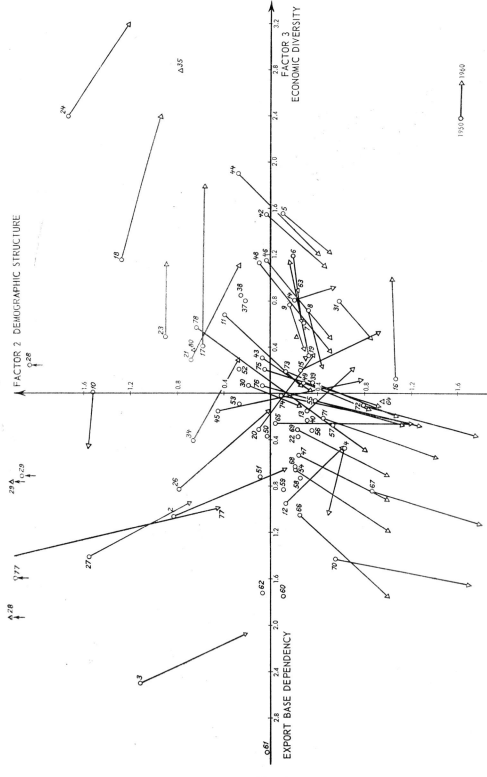

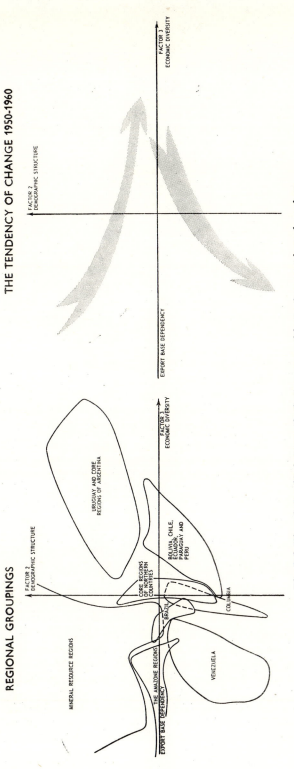

Fig. 2.6. The relationship between the factor scores of factor 3, export-base dependency, and factor 2, demographic structure. Each point represents a region. The numbers refer to the list of regions in appendix D

29

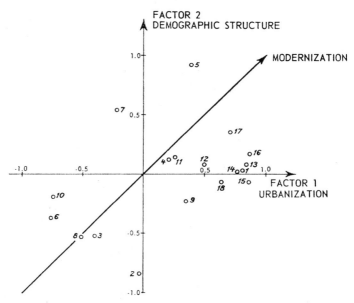

Fig. 2.7. *Diagrams of the factor pattern. Each point represents a variable (see code numbers in Table 2.1), and the coordinates of the points are the factor weights of the variables*

High factor scores for the combined factor 1–2 are a little more con-centrated on the southern cone of the continent than the high factor scores of factor 1; but the difference is not very large (**Figure 2.8**).

When factor 1 is combined with factor 3, the emphasis shifts to the manufacturing sector, and among the demographic variables the new oblique factor emphasizes particularly the proportion of old people (60 years or more). The factor scores for the combined factor 1–3 are especially large in the capital regions and in the central parts of Argentina (Figure 2.9).

This indicates that the two combined factors, 1–2 and 1–3, can be inter-preted as crude measures of the concepts of modernization and industrial-ization described in the introduction, while the two principal factors, 2 and 3, represent only those parts of the concepts of modernization and industrialization which have not already been accounted for by factor 1, the ecological concept of urbanization.

In comparing the three related concepts of urbanization, moderniza-tion, and industrialization as they are represented by factors 1, 1–2, and 1–3, it is interesting to note that the economic sectors, construction, commerce, and transportation are related most closely to urbanization,

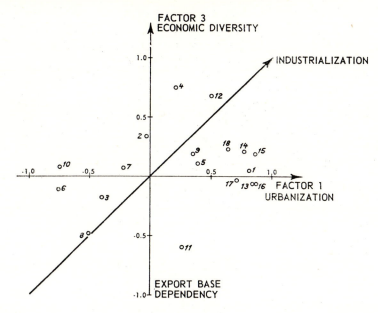

while services are related to modernization and manufacturing to industrialization. Among the demographic variables, fertility (child-women relation) and activity rates are related most closely to modernization, while old age is related to the economic factor of industrialization.

2.5 A TYPOLOGY OF REGIONS

The three dimensions found in the factor analysis constitute a three-dimensional space in which we can represent our 74 areas as points. In Figures 2.4–2.6 we have shown the projection of the points on the three planes made up by the three axes, taken two at a time.

To make a typology of regions we have divided the factor space into sections and let the points located in the same section belong to the same type of regions. Unfortunately the points do not fall clearly into groups on the axes, but are clustered around the middle of the axes. For this reason we have simply divided each of the axes in two halves, thus dividing the three-dimensional space into eight sections and obtaining the eight-group typology shown in the left part of Table 2.3. The division points on the first two axes are the average value 0.0. For the third dimension, the export-base dependency, the division point has been moved towards the periphery end of the axis. The reason for this is that

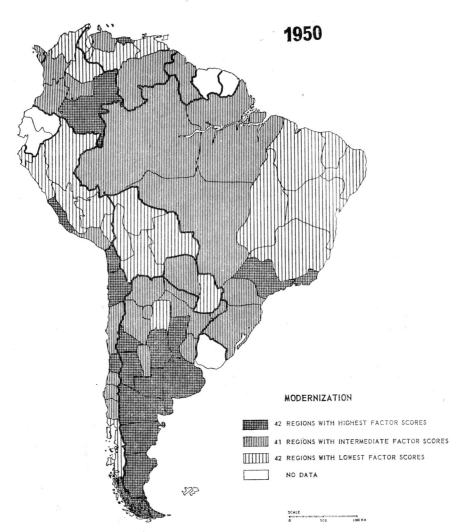

Fig. 2.8. *The geographic distribution of the oblique factor, modernization, obtained by combination of factor 1, urbanization, and factor 2, demographic structure. In the rank-ordered list of regions on which the three groups in the legend are based, the 69 regions*

1960

represented in the 1950 data and the 56 regions represented in the 1960 data are treated as 125 different regions. The maps for 1950 and 1960 therefore should be read simultaneously

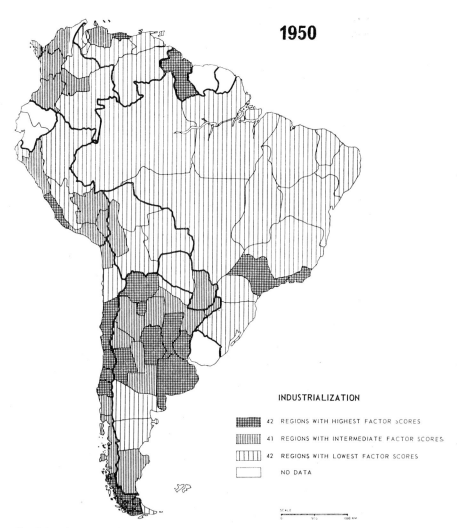

INDUSTRIALIZATION

42   REGIONS WITH HIGHEST FACTOR SCORES

41   REGIONS WITH INTERMEDIATE FACTOR SCORES

42   REGIONS WITH LOWEST FACTOR SCORES

NO DATA

Fig. 2.9. *The geographic distribution of the oblique factor, industrialization, obtained by combination of factor 1, urbanization, and factor 3, export-base dependency. In the rank-ordered list of regions on which the three groups in the legend are based, the 69*

1960

regions represented in the 1950 data and the 56 regions represented in the 1960 data are treated as 125 different regions. The maps for 1950 and 1960 therefore should be read simultaneously

most people would intuitively feel it disturbing to have some of the national capital regions among the peripheral export-base dependent regions.

In making the typology we have, as shown in Table 2.3, found it preferable to start by grouping the regions according to the two basically economic dimensions, urbanization and export-base dependency. On the basis of these two dimensions we get four broad types of economic regions which can be characterized as:

1. *Core regions*, which are highly urbanized and have a diversified economy;

2. *Depressed areas*, which are little urbanized and do not have any export-base;

3. *Mineral resource regions*, which are highly urbanized and highly dependent on an export-base which is often, but not always, a mineral resource;

4. *Agricultural settlement areas* which are rural areas, dependent on some export-base which is generally agricultural.

When the demographic dimension is introduced each of these four types of economic areas are divided into two new regional types: those with a large proportion of active population and those with a small proportion of active population.

The geographical distribution of the eight regional types is shown in Figure 2.10 for both 1950 and 1960. (Areas for which sufficient data have not been available are left white.)

In evaluating the maps in Figure 2.10 it should be kept in mind, first, that the classification of those areas which are located close to the division point on one or more of the axes is rather arbitrary. The maps therefore, should not be read independently of Figures 2.4–2.6. Secondly it should be kept in mind that the areas applied in the analysis are very varied in size. This is unfortunate because large areas with heterogeneous populations will in general have much lower scores than small areas with homogeneous populations; *e.g.* São Paulo in Brazil has a much lower score on the urbanization dimension than one would tend to expect simply because it is located in a large area which also contains a large rural population. Finally, the classification of the regions is based on factors, which represent only 63% of the total variance among the regions. A number of the regions should therefore be expected to fit rather badly into the system.

Table 2.3 *A typology of regions in South America*

Scores on the three dimensions of regional differentiation			Tendencies for change of the scores on the three dimensions			Tendencies for change on the two oblique dimensions	
1. dimension Urbanization	3. dimension Export-base dependency	2. dimension Demographic structure	1. dimension Urbanization	2. dimension Demographic structure	3. dimension Export-base dependency	Modernization	Industrialization
Urban	Diversified economy (Core region)	Active population	More urban	Constant	More diversified	Constant	More manufacturing
		Dependent population	More urban	Constant-more dependent population	More diversified		
	Export-base dependent (mineral resource region)	Active population	More urban	Constant	More export-base dependent	Constant	Constant
		Dependent population	More urban	Constant-more dependent population	More export-base dependent		
	Diversified economy (depressed area)	Active population	More urban	(insufficient data)	More export-base dependent	Constant	Constant
		Dependent population	More urban	Constant-more dependent population	More export-base dependent		
Rural	Export-base dependent (agricultural settlement area)	Active population	(insufficient data)	More dependent population	(insufficient data)	Constant	Constant
		Dependent population	More urban	More dependent population	More export-base dependent		

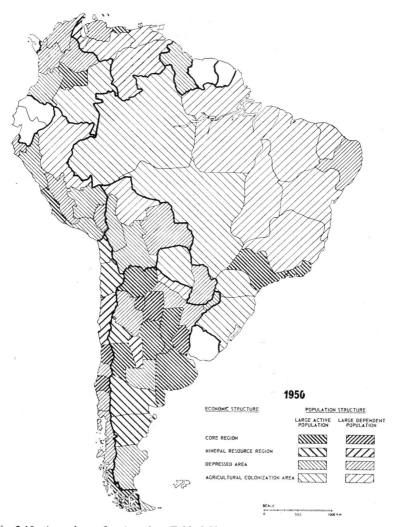

Fig. 2.10. *A typology of regions (see Table 2.3)*

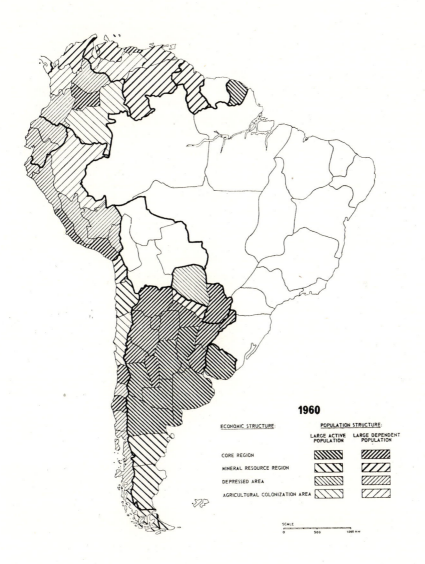

1960

ECONOMIC STRUCTURE:

POPULATION STRUCTURE:

LARGE ACTIVE POPULATION

LARGE DEPENDENT POPULATION

CORE REGION

MINERAL RESOURCE REGION

DEPRESSED AREA

AGRICULTURAL COLONIZATION AREA

SCALE
0   500   1000 KM

2.6 TWO THEORIES OF REGIONAL ECONOMIC DEVELOPMENT

Because data on regional economic development are so scarce attempts
have often been made to draw conclusions from cross-section data to
time series data and *vice versa*, though this of course is extremely danger-
ous. In so far as such a mixing of cross-section data and time series
data is permissible, we might conclude that the regions in each of the
regional groupings characterized above correspond to the same phase in
the process of economic development. For the 53 regions for which we
have analysed data for two points in time we shall in this and the next
section try to test the extent to which the regional groups actually make
a sequence such that regions in the first group in time tend to move into
the second group and regions in the second group tend to move into the
third group, and so on.

Both North (1955) and Perloff *et al.* (1960), in describing the development of regions from subsistence economy to the more complex economy of modern society, have distinguished between two theories of
regional economic growth.

The first theory, which has been called the sector theory, is based on
European experience. Starting with fairly densely settled regions based
on subsistence farming (phase 1), development is supposed to take place
through improvements in transportation, improvements which open up
possibilities for higher and higher degrees of specialization by making
trade possible over longer and longer distances. First, village industries
are created (phase 2); then a specialization of agricultural production
takes place to guarantee the food supply to the slowly developing urban
centres (phase 3); then, as diminishing returns in agriculture set in,
industrialization must start if economic growth is to continue (phase 4);
and finally, as productivity in manufacturing goes up a decreasing part
of the labour force is required to keep production going, but an
increasing part is then required for organizing production and for the
production of services both for regional consumption and for export
(phase 5).

The second theory is based on North American experience. The point
of departure for this theory is a very thinly settled area based on a subsistence economy (phase 1). Growth in the region starts when some valuable
natural resource in agriculture or mining is found, and some outside
source invests in the exploitation and export of the resource. If the initial
investment is profitable money and migrants will continue to flow into
the region, and with them local services will be established (phase 2).
As the resources become scarcer their exploitation will become more

intensive, and semi-processing of the resource before export may be initiated (phase 3). As population and income in the region increase the regional market becomes larger and larger, and if it becomes large enough manufacturing industries may settle in the region and produce both for the regional market and for export. This, however, will not necessarily take place. The region might well develop service industries without ever having any large manufacturing industries (phase 4). Finally, the last stage is, as in the first theory, the mature region exporting capital, skills and specialized services (phase 5).

In brief, we could describe the first development process as an internally generated process, while the second is generated by the export of a natural resource (the export-base) demanded outside the region.

2.7 CHANGE AND STABILITY OF REGIONS IN SOUTH AMERICA

Relating the groups of the regional typology with the above phases of development it is clear that the agricultural settlement areas correspond to the subsistence economy while the core regions correspond to the last phase, the mature region, of each of the theories. The depressed areas and the resource regions represent the intermediate phases of the first and second theory, respectively (see Figure 2.11).

Export-base theory   *Sector theory*

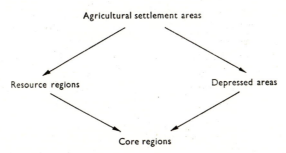

Fig. 2.11. *The four types of economic regions arranged in sequence according to the two stage theories*

To see first, if a development sequence of regions exists at all and secondly, if this sequence corresponds to the sequences postulated by the sector and export-base theories, in Figures 2.4–2.6, for the 53 areas where data exist for two points in time, we have shown an arrow going from the 1950 to the 1960 point.

The diagrams show that generally the static characteristics of the regions correspond to the way they change over time so that areas in the same group of regions all tend to move in the same direction. In the right part of Table 2.3, we have tried to summarize these relations between the static and the dynamic characteristics.

It appears from Figure 2.4 that the first dimension – urbanization – is increasing in all areas except three, and thus for all regional types.

In the demographic dimension, most of the export-base dependent regions are increasing their proportion of dependent population. This is partly at least because the effect of immigration on the population structure decreases when the population grows. Consequently, the economically more diversified regions, which tend to have higher population densities, either remain constant in the demographic dimension or have a slowly increasing proportion of dependent population. This indicates that the large influx of population in the active age group is more than offset by the increasing birth rates or the higher survival rates for children.

Finally, in the third dimension – export-base dependency – the core regions are developing more diversified economies. The same is true of the mineral resource regions which have a large proportion of their population in the active age group. All other regional types tend to become more export-base dependent. In evaluating the terms 'more or less export-base dependent' it should be kept in mind that the dimension is dichotomous (manufacturing v. mining employment) in the sense that the two ends of the dimension have different meanings. When core regions become less export-base dependent they tend to become more industrialized. When the mineral resource regions with a large proportion of active population become less export-base dependent this means that the importance of mining employment decreases, but it need not mean that manufacturing employment increases, although this tends to be the case. When the depressed areas become more export-base dependent, this means that the importance of their manufacturing employment goes down (because employment in handicrafts decreases when cheap manufactured products are imported to the region), but it is generally not employment in mining which takes over, but rather employment in services. Finally, when the agricultural settlement areas and the mineral resource regions with a large proportion of dependent population become more export-base dependent this means that employment in natural resource extraction increases in importance, but it does not say anything about manufacturing employment.

The above discussion leads to the conclusion that although the level of urbanization is growing in all regional types, it is only in the core regions and in those mineral resource regions which have a large proportion of active population that this growth takes place through growth in secondary and tertiary employment. In all other areas, the growth of the economy appears to take place rather through increased resource exploitation, either in mining or in agriculture.

These findings are partly contrary to the development sequences of regions postulated in Figure 2.11 on the basis of the two theories of economic development. In Figure 2.12 we have shown the development sequence corresponding to the 1950–1960 South American data. Starting with the agricultural settlement areas, we can see that these have moved in the direction of the mineral resource regions while the mineral resource regions either stay in the same group or move in the direction of the group of core regions. This is basically in accord with the left side of Figure 2.11, except that the move from resource region to core region does not necessarily take place.

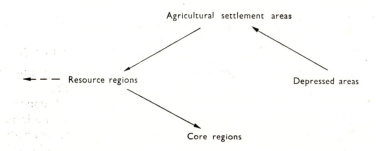

Fig. 2.12. *The dynamic behaviour of the regions in South America, 1950–1960*

On the right side of Figure 2.12 the deviations between the theories and the empirical findings are larger. First, there is little indication that agricultural settlement areas move in the direction of the depressed areas. This only occurred in two of our regions. Secondly, there is little indication that the depressed areas develop into core regions, this only took place in one case. Rather the main trend is that depressed areas as a result of backwash effects (Myrdal, 1957) are pushed out in the periphery and thus only have a chance to reach higher levels of development if they have natural resources to exploit, or if they are subsidized.

In conclusion, it is illuminating to see how the regions have changed position along the three oblique axes: urbanization, modernization, and industrialization (Figures 2.4–2.6).

As people have moved from rural areas to the towns, urbanization in a physical sense has by definition gone up. Only in Argentina and a few other areas, however, did the creation of new high productivity manufacturing jobs keep pace with migration and only here did industrialization, therefore, take place. Finally modernization was extraordinarily stable in all regions. This, of course, does not mean that the average level of modernization in South America as a whole has not risen; it only means that the creation of new schools and social services has nowhere more than just kept up with migration.

2.8 SUMMARY

In this chapter it has been shown that a typology of regions on the South American continent should take into account at least three orthogonal dimensions, which have been interpreted as:

Urbanization (urban – rural regions);
Demographic structure (active – dependent population);
Export-base dependency (manufacturing – mining development).

The first of these orthogonal dimensions corresponds to the physical aspects of urbanization, urban places as types of settlements.

The second dimension corresponds partly to the sociologists concept of urbanization as 'a way of life', or modernization; but while modernization is highly correlated (though not identical) with physical urbanization, the second dimension by definition is orthogonal to the first dimension, urbanization. Thus the second dimension, demographic structure, represents only those aspects of modernization which have not already been accounted for by physical urbanization.

In the same way the third dimension corresponds to those aspects of the economic centre-periphery concept which have not already been accounted for by the two first dimensions.

The three dimensions have formed the basis for the construction of an eight-group typology of regions (Table 2.3 and Figure 2.10). It has been shown that the eight groups are meaningful not only in terms of the static characteristics of the regions, but that all areas in each of the eight groups tend to change in the course of time (between 1950 and 1960) in the same direction. This correspondence between the static and the dynamic aspects of regional differentiation is very fortunate, since it greatly increases the relevance for planning and development purposes of the typology enunciated.

That the regions in each of the groups of the typology all tend to develop in the same direction supports the idea that the regional types are stages or rather phases of development. The sequence of the regional types resulting from the dynamic characteristics of the South American regions between 1950 and 1960, however, does not correspond to the sequences postulated by the export-base and sector theories of development.

The South American data indicate that the depressed regions dominated by agriculture, but with a sizeable handicraft industry, tend through backwash effects to lose their handicrafts and develop very one-sided economies based only on agriculture. The agricultural settlement areas on the other hand, develop through increased resource exploitation or through direct or indirect subsidies from the national government, if they develop at all. Finally, the resource regions grow either through increased resource exploitation or through industrialization. It is characteristic that only the already urbanized resource regions move in the direction of the core regions.

We can conclude that development in South America is at present a process generated by the export of natural resources rather than an internally generated process.

The relations between the variables, which have been revealed by the factor analysis, will be explored in more detail in parts III and IV.

CHAPTER 3

South America, a system of regions

3.1 THE REGIONAL SYSTEM

The eight types of regions identified in chapter 2, are not isolated entities. By flows of persons, goods, information and capital they are linked to other regions in or outside the countries of which they are a part. We can consider South America as a hierarchical system consisting of national subsystems each of which is a system of regions.

The hierarchy, however, is far from perfect. In a perfect hierarchy the regions would be oriented completely towards the national core regions and the national core regions would be oriented towards some continental core region. In reality, many of the regions have as large contacts outside their country as with the national core region, and the existence of a continental core region might well be doubted.

Also, the flows among the regions at the three levels of the regional hierarchy, the intercontinental, the international within South America, and the interregional within the nations, are of greatly varying importance. Of the total tonnage of goods transported around 1960 within South America and to and from other continents only 2–3% were shipped among the South American countries, while transportation in and out of the continent amounted to a little less than 40%, and transportation within nations amounted to about 60% (Pedersen and Stöhr, 1969).

In order to be able to say something about the structure of the continental system of regions – does it function as a system of regions or is it a set of isolated regions? – this chapter has been devoted to an analysis of some of the existing flow channels in South America.

3.2 THE INTERCONTINENTAL FLOWS

It can be safely assumed that the intercontinental flows of goods use maritime shipping, while the intercontinental flows of passengers use mainly air transportation. We shall, therefore, study the intercontinental

46

flows by analysing the structure of the networks of regular international maritime shipping and air routes; and we shall try to answer the two questions: Which of the South American regions interact with the other continents and with which continents do they interact?

We shall use information on the frequency of scheduled departures rather than the size of the flows. This is partly because more detailed information has not been available, but it is not considered a great disadvantage because the route frequencies are a measure of the quality of the service, and thus for development purposes they are probably more relevant than information on the actual flows.

The two maps in Figures 3.1 and 3.2 show the number of monthly shipping route departures and weekly air route departures from South America towards the United States and Europe. The data given on these maps have been summarized in Table 3.1 which shows from which type of region the departures take place. One might well have expected that the departures took place especially from the large cities. This, however, is only partly true, because while the largest cities are concentrated in the

Table 3.1 *Distribution according to regional types of cities with frequent scheduled departures of maritime shipping and airline routes out of Latin America, 1967*

Regional types	Towns with more than 250,000 inhabitants in 1960*	Towns with 10 or more monthly departures of regular shipping lines mostly to			Towns with scheduled airline departures out of the continent. Relatively most departures to		
		North America	Europe	Total	North America	Europe	Total
Core regions	13 (15)	2	8	10	1	7	8
Depressed areas	5 (7)	1	2	3	3	2	5
Natural resource regions	2 (2)	7	4	11	6	0	6
Agricultural settlement areas	1 (7)	2	3	5	3	2	5
No data	10 (0)	1	0	1	1	0	1
Total	31	13	17	30	14	11	25

*The numbers in the parentheses show the distribution of towns obtained when the 10 towns, for which no 1960 data are available, are distributed according to the 1950 data.

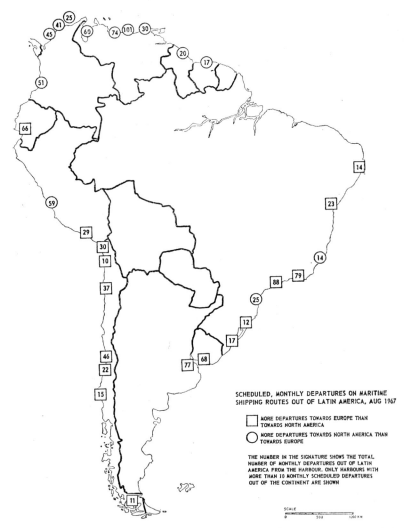

Fig. 3.1. *Scheduled, monthly departures on martitime shipping routes out of Latin America, Aug. 1967*

Fig. 3.2. *Scheduled weekly airline frequencies out of Latin America, Nov. 1967*

core regions and the depressed areas, the route departures take place from the core regions and the natural resource regions. This is clearly related to the composition of the trade. More than 95% of the total tonnage exported from South America consists of unprocessed or semi-processed natural resources, and this necessarily influences the structure of the transport network.

To get an impression of the direction of the trade, we have on the maps divided the route frequencies into two groups, namely, departures for North America and departures for Europe. Figure 3.1 shows that with regard to maritime shipping we can distinguish an area of North American predominance, located to the north of a line running from Lima to Belém, and an area of European predominance, located to the south of this line.

With regard to airline traffic, North America dominated all but a few airports. The degree of predominance, however, decreases the further south one comes, and at the same time the European influence increases. This is demonstrated in Figure 3.2, where predominance has been defined on the basis of relative frequencies of departure towards Europe and North America, rather than on absolute frequencies. The relative frequency of departure from an airport, for instance, towards Europe, is defined as the absolute frequency of departure towards Europe divided by the sum of departures from all airports towards Europe. Figure 3.2 shows very much the same picture as Figure 3.1, and we must conclude that for air traffic also, the influence fields decrease with the distance from the main world economic centres in North America and Europe; only the hinterland limit between the two predominance fields is pushed out somewhere in the Atlantic.

In Table 3.1 the towns with intercontinental flows have been cross-classified according to both regional type and North American-European predominance. It appears from the table that North American predominance is concentrated in the natural resource regions, while European predominance tends to be strongest in the core regions. This is in part simply a result of the greater concentration of core regions in the southern part of the continent lying within the field of European predominance (see Cole, 1965, p. 106); but it is probably also significant that North American influence has been based almost exclusively on capital investment and other economic interests, while European influence in addition to economic interests has also been culturally oriented, based on the migrants and their ties with their countries of origin, and these migrants are mostly Europeans who have settled in the present core regions (see Figure 3.6).

3.3 INTER-METROPOLITAN FLOWS. FLOWS AMONG NATIONS[1]

For the international flows among the Latin American countries it is also to a large extent true that freight goes by sea and passengers by air. Brown (1966) says that less than 5% of the total trade between the Latin American countries goes by inland transport. This is in part a result of the large proportion of the trade constituted by unprocessed resources. However, a rough estimate indicates that even of the trade in manufactured products only about 15% is transported by inland transport.[2]

In the absence of more detailed data, the foreign trade statistics have been used to give a picture of the freight flow pattern and the airline frequencies to give a picture of the passenger flows. *The freight flow* pattern among the metropolitan centres will thus be illustrated by international trade flows in South America, assuming that all the trade takes place exclusively between the national capitals.

Figure 3.3 shows the most important South American export flows for each of the countries (*i.e.* all flows which represent more than 20% of the country's exports to other South American countries).

The flows are shown separately for trade in unprocessed raw materials and in manufactured goods. At present trade in raw materials is much more important than trade in manufactured goods (by value, unprocessed goods make up 54%, semi-processed 34%, and manufactured goods 12% of the international trade within South America in 1959–61 – Baerresen, Carnoy and Grunwald, 1965), but in the future the role of trade in manufactured goods will probably increase. The differences in trade

---

[1] The information in this section was first presented in Pedersen and Stöhr (1968)

[2] How big a part of the international trade in manufactured goods is actually transported by inland transportation is difficult to estimate from the available statistics) Brown (1966, p. 44) writes that probably less than 5 per cent of the total trade between the South American countries goes by road and rail transportation. For manufactured goods alone, however, the percentage must be bigger. If we leave petroleum, minerals, and grain in bulk out of the goods transported by sea, and make some additions to United Nations data on the road transport on account of unregistered trade (which the Interamerican Development Bank in *Posibilidades de Integracion de las Zonas Fronterizas Colombo–Venezolanas* (Washington D. C., 1964) estimates at 12 times the size of the registered trade between Colombia and Venezuela), we get the following distribution by transport mode of the international trade in manufactured goods within South America around 1960:

	10^3 tons	%
Road	200	7
Rail	250	9
Ship	2360	84
Total	2810	100

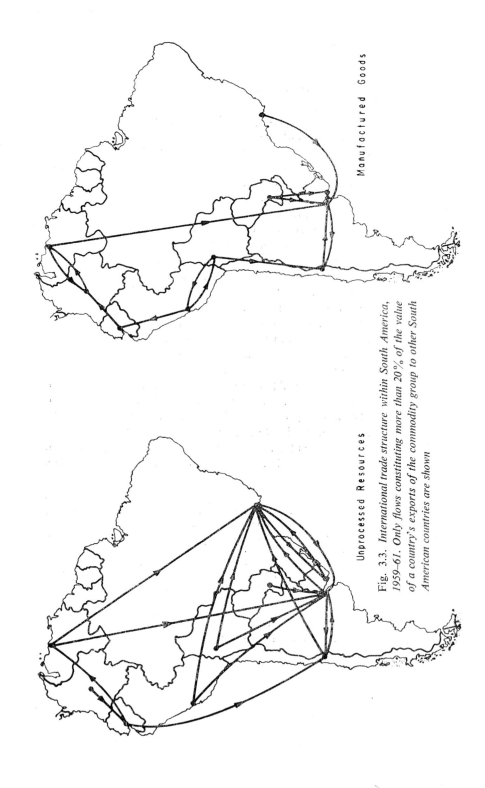

Manufactured Goods

Unprocessed Resources

Fig. 3.3. International trade structure within South America, 1959–61. Only flows constituting more than 20% of the value of a country's exports of the commodity group to other South American countries are shown

structure for raw materials and manufactured goods, therefore, will give us an idea of the direction of future changes in the general trade pattern. The two maps in Figure 3.3 show that:

– Raw materials from all the South American continent flow to the main core regions of Buenos Aires and southern Brazil, and that distance decay in the trade pattern is quite limited;
– Manufactured goods primarily flow over short distances between neighbouring countries.

This is paradoxical in as much as traditional location theory would lead one to expect a greater distance decay for heavy bulky goods than for high value manufactured goods.

The explanation for this must be that:

– Raw materials are dependent chiefly on sea transport, where cost is influenced only slightly by the distance moved, while manufactured goods rely much more on inland transport, where cost depends much more on distance;
– Raw materials are consumed by a relatively small number of large firms which have ready access to information about market possibilities, while the diffusion of information about market possibilities for manufactured goods is much more difficult and insufficient, and this diffusion of information probably has a strong distance decay (see, *e.g.* Olsson, 1965).

To get a complete picture of the relative importance of the different modes of transportation for the inter-urban *passenger movements* is not possible. However, there is no doubt that air transportation is very important. The data available for passenger traffic across the Chilean border indicate that 58% of the passengers in 1965 went by air (see Table 3.2), while about 40% went by rail or road. For the Santiago – Valparaíso region the proportion of international travellers going by air was even higher, namely 78%, while only 19% used land transport. For the rest of the country, on the other hand, 75% of the international travellers used land transport, while only 24% went by air.

Here passenger flows will be represented by data on airline frequencies among 58 cities in South America, *i.e.* the main centres of those of the 74 regions used in chapter 2, which were served by the air network in November 1967. This is the only type of data for which detailed geographic disaggregation has been possible.

Although the airline frequencies do not say anything about the transport or about the actual passenger flows, they probably give a much better picture of the quality of the service than passenger flow information would do.

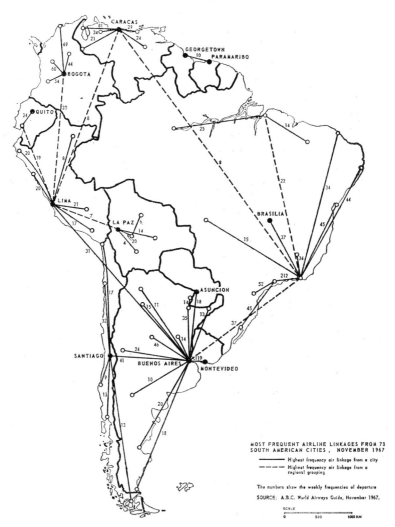

Fig. 3.4. *Most frequent airline linkages from each of 73 South American cities, November 1967. Only airlines between South American cities are included*

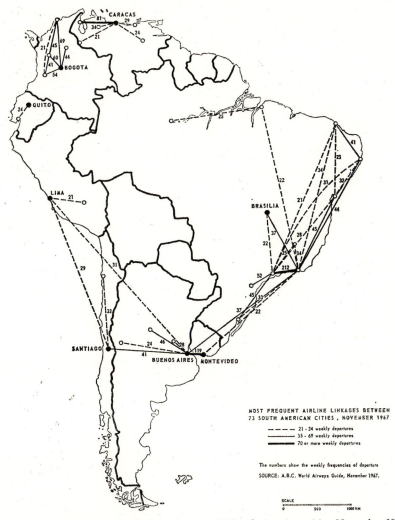

Fig. 3.5. *Most frequent airline linkages between 73 South American cities, November 1957*

Figures 3.4 and 3.5 are based on these data. Figure 3.5 shows the airline routes with the largest weekly frequencies, *i.e.* those routes on which
there were more than three daily flights in 1967. The figure shows that a
very dense network exists along the Atlantic coast of South America
from Recife down to Buenos Aires and continuing across the continent
to Santiago. In the northern part of the continent Colombia has a very
dense national airline network, but the international network is less dense.
The high density of the airline network in Colombia is probably due to
the relative underdevelopment and insecurity of land connexions.

The other figure, Figure 3.4, indicates the way the urban centres dominate each other. It shows for each city the airline route which has the
highest frequency of scheduled flights.

The figure indicates the existence of eight relatively isolated regions
in the route network, which have more highly developed relations internally than with the seven other regions.

The eight regions are:

1. Argentina, Uruguay, Paraguay, Chile, and Peru centred around
   Buenos Aires;
2. Brazil, except the Amazon area, centred on Rio de Janeiro;
3. The Amazon area, centred on Belém;
4. The Guianas;
5. Venezuela, centred on Caracas;
6. Colombia, centred on Bogotá;
7. Ecuador;
8. Bolivia, centred on La Paz.

That Colombia, Venezuela, and Bolivia appear as independent national
systems in the network may result from the high frequencies found on
the national airline routes in these countries. This explanation, however,
is only partly valid, because the frequency of international routes from
these countries is also much smaller than it is from the other countries.
This can be seen from the dotted lines in Figure 3.4, which show the air-
routes between the 'isolated' regions which have the highest frequency
of traffic. Taking these international routes into account we can identify
the following main centres in the network:

   – Buenos Aires, with Santiago and Lima as 'satellites';
   – The axis Rio de Janeiro – São Paulo, with the loosely associated
     satellite of Belém;
   – Lima, with La Paz, Guayaquil and Bogotá as loosely associated
     satellites;
   – Caracas, with equally loose connexions to Rio de Janeiro and Lima.

Table 3.2 *Passenger movements to and from Chile by mode of transportation,*
1965

	Percentage of total traffic for each mode of transportation					Percentage of total traffic
	Railroad	Ship	Road	Air	Total	
To and from Santiago region*	8.3	2.9	10.6	78.2	100	70.0
To and from the rest of the country	21.9	1.3	53.3	23.5	100	30.0
To and from Chile – total	13.3	2.3	26.3	58.1	100	100

*This includes land connexions via Trasandino and Portillo, ship connexion via
Valparaíso and air connexion via Los Cerillos.
Source: *Estadística de Turismo* (1965), Dirección de Estadística y Censos, Santiago
de Chile.

3.4 THE METROPOLITAN HINTERLANDS. INTERNATIONAL PERIPHERAL FLOWS

The picture we have thus far painted of the flows between the South
American countries is based largely on the assumption that the international flows are flows between the main cities. Although this assumption was formerly more or less true it is probably becoming less so.
Information about the flows between the peripheries of the countries,
however, is very difficult to get, partly because the flows to a large extent
consist of contraband, *e.g.* between Colombia and Venezuela (see footnote 3.1), or of illegal labour migrants, *e.g.* from Chile, Bolivia, and
Paraguay into Argentina.

The only two types of flows for which information has been available
are migration and airline frequencies, neither of which in all probability
are very good indicators of the actual flows.

The available migration data are census data on the proportion of the
population born in other South American countries. These data are
shown in Figure 3.6.

They indicate that Argentina and Venezuela in particular, the two highest income countries on the continent, receive migrants from their neighbours. Of the four largest groups of migrants, namely Colombians in

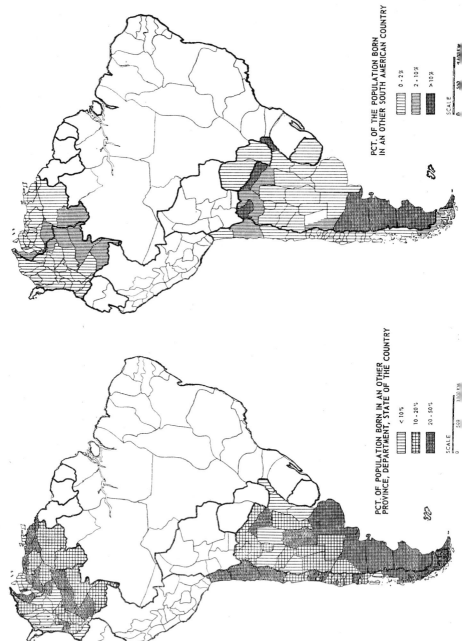

TOTAL MIGRATION

INTERCONTINENTAL MIGRATION

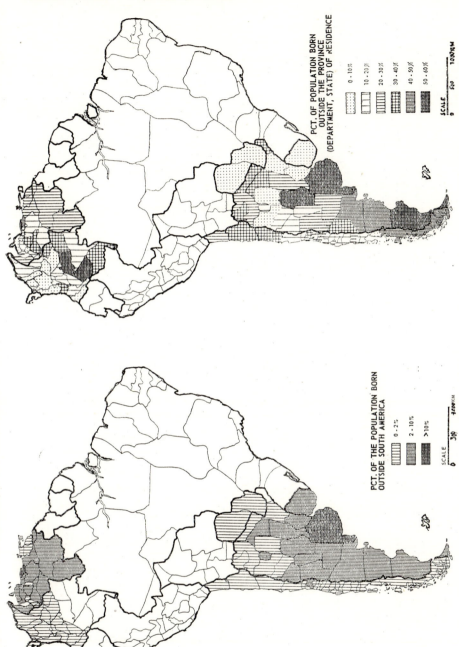

PCT. OF POPULATION BORN
OUTSIDE THE PROVINCE
(DEPARTMENT, STATE) OF RESIDENCE

0 - 10%
10 - 20%
20 - 30%
30 - 40%
40 - 50%
50 - 60%

SCALE
0   500   1200 KM

PCT. OF THE POPULATION BORN
OUTSIDE SOUTH AMERICA

0 - 2%
2 - 10%
>10%

SCALE
0   500   1200 KM

Fig. 3.6. *Interregional, international and intercontinental migration in some South American countries.*
Sources: population censuses Argentina 1960, Chile 1960, Colombia 1964, Paraguay 1962, Venezuela 1961 and Uruguay 1963

Fig. 3.7. *Scheduled border-crossing air routes from provincial towns, November 1967*

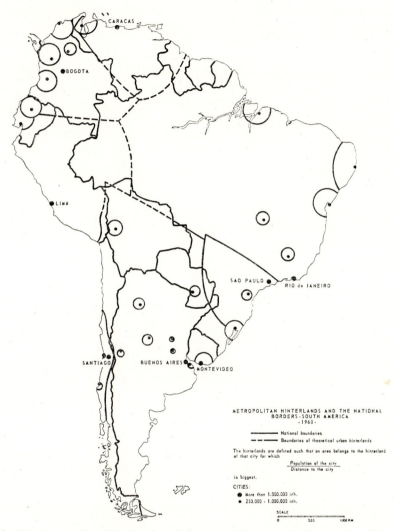

Fig. 3.8. *Metropolitan hinterlands and the national borders, South America, 1960*

Venezuela and Paraguayans, Bolivians, and Chileans in Argentina, the Bolivians and Chileans include a very large proportion of males, indicating the seasonal character of these two migration flows.

The existing peripheral airline routes are shown in Figure 3.7. We can distinguish between two types of peripheral flows: those which connect two peripheral towns, and those which connect a peripheral town in one country with a main city in another country. The first type is in part a result of the migration streams and the local traffic created by the migrants. The other type might be regarded as an indicator of the metropolitan hinterlands extending across the national boundaries into the neighbouring countries.

That such attempts at hinterland expansion actually go on is indicated by the development programmes for peripheral areas which many of the governments have initiated and by the tension existing along many of the international borders. For instance Chile has made Arica and Punta Arenas free ports to support their peripheral position, and Colombia has made its Amazon harbour, Leticia, a free port; Peru has established a ring of military colonization villages along its border in the Amazon area (Eidt, 1962), and Brazil has an extensive road construction programme in the Amazon area (Miller and Gakenheimer, 1971, p. 66); Colombia and Venezuela are constructing systems of parallel roads on each side of their common border (Crist, 1965); and Argentina has been attempting commercial expansion into the lowlands of Bolivia (Valerie, 1967).

To be able to evaluate the extent of these attempts at hinterland expansion, we have shown in Figure 3.8 the national boundaries and some theoretical hinterlands of all cities with more than 250,000 inhabitants in 1960.

In drawing the hinterland borders, it has been assumed that the centrality of each urban centre is proportional to its population, and that the decay of the urban field is reciprocally proportional to the travel time from the centre. (For a definition of travel time, see chapter 7.3). These assumptions are admittedly crude, but they are the best which can be made at this time without extensive research.

The map reveals surprisingly good correspondence between the theoretical hinterland limits and the national boundaries. The only important difference between the borders of the nations and of the hinterlands is that the hinterland of Buenos Aires extends into the extreme ends of Chile and into most areas of the small nations, Bolivia, Paraguay, and Uruguay. This extension of the theoretical hinterland of Buenos Aires into neighbouring countries might well be due to the use of too simple computational procedure. The concentration of peripheral border-crossing air routes along the Argentine border, however, indicates that the hinterland extension is real enough. If the extension of the Buenos Aires hinterland is a reality, this indicates that the insistence of the smaller nations on preferential treatment in the common market may not be unwarranted.

The hinterland borders in the Amazon area are largely meaningless because there is no transportation network in the area, except the river. The borders are therefore shown by a dotted line in Figure 3.8. The influence of the large metropolitan centres is minimal in the area, and (see Figure 3.4) tends to constitute an independent region though it does not have a large dominating centre. The existence of an international air route along the river is consistent with this independent status of the area.

The generally close correspondence between the metropolitan hinterlands and the national boundaries might be explained in two ways: the national boundaries might originally have been established so as to fit the urban influence fields, or the urban areas might have grown in response to the once established boundaries. As only relatively small changes have taken place in the national boundaries, while the urban population has grown tremendously in this century, it seems that the latter explanation – that urban size is a result of hinterland size – is the more probable. This is an important conclusion, for it indicates that the size of the urban places can be expected to change as a result of the creation of a Latin American common market.

3.5 INTERREGIONAL FLOWS

For the interregional flows within each country rail and road transportation play an important role. Unfortunately our knowledge about these modes of transportation is very poor so it is impossible to give a detailed quantitative picture of the interregional flow pattern. Instead we shall attempt to paint a picture of each of the regional types and their flows with the rest of the world, both nationally and internationally.

The core region: the metropolitan region and its direct hinterland

The economy of the core region is more diversified than that of other regions. The manufacturing industry is the most important in terms of output, but the core region might still contain an important part of the national production in both agriculture and mining. Agriculture will be more modern than in the depressed areas but still little mechanized. Population density, urbanization, and *per capita* income are all relatively high. The region will probably contain some middle-sized cities in addition to the national capital.

The metropolitan region is characterized by large population growth due both to immigration from the depressed areas and to natural growth. It will import heavy industrial products from abroad, some raw materials from the resource areas, and some agricultural products from the depressed and agricultural settlement areas. It will export manufactured consumer goods to all parts of the country. Capital is likely to flow in, both from the depressed areas and from foreign areas, in the form of payment for exports from the resource areas.

The depressed area

The area's economic life is dominated by traditional agriculture, either organized into *mini-* or *latifundios* and possibly also plantations. The degree of urbanization is usually low, but because of the rather dense population, large cities might well exist in the area. *Per capita* income is low and the income distribution very unequal.

The area is characterized by a large outflow of people to the national core region, although not large enough to make up for the rapid natural increase in population. The area will export agricultural products and import manufactured products. The trade, which is probably small, takes place principally with the national core region. The net capital flow is probably outwards from the region.

The mineral resource area

The economic life of the area is dominated by the extraction of one or more minerals for export. The population density is low, but the degree of urbanization is high. *Per capita* income is high, often more than twice the national average.

The area is characterized by high immigration, mostly of skilled workers from the national centre and others from nearby depressed areas. The area exports nearly all the extracted minerals not only out of the country, but out of South America as well; only a small part will go to the national centre. Payments for these exports will go partly to the region itself, but mainly to the core region. The region will import manufactured products from the centre and in some cases from abroad.

The agricultural settlement area

The economic life of the area is dominated by agriculture, partly subsistence farming and partly crops for export out of the region. Population density, urbanization, and *per capita* incomes are low.

The area is characterized by some inflow of people from depressed areas, mostly unskilled agricultural workers. If there is any net capital flow at all, it is likely to be a small inflow from the core region. There will be a small exchange of agricultural products for manufactured products between the area and the core region.

PART II

Development of the urban system
A process of innovation diffusion

CHAPTER 4

The innovation processes

Figures 4.1 and 4.2 show the rank-size curves and a growth chart for the largest Latin American cities. The figures reveal a surprisingly regular structure of the urban system and pattern of urban growth. Though far from perfect the rank-size curve for the Latin American cities is relatively straight-lined, a feature most writers on urban systems claim to be characteristic of integrated urban systems (Berry, 1970); and the growth chart on Figure 4.2 shows that the long-term urban growth of the large cities in Latin America throughout this century has been almost independent of city size and country, a feature which is necessary for the linear rank-size curve to develop and be sustained.

This picture of the South American urban system as an integrated system is supported by Pedersen (1970), who has shown that the large cities in Latin America throughout the last century were linked into a system of cities by surprisingly regular processes of innovation diffusion. Apparently, however, it conflicts with the relatively small physical flows found between the South American countries.

This apparent conflict might be solved if urban-regional development is hypothesized to be a result of information and innovation diffusion rather than a result of the physical flows.

Such an hypothesis would be in accordance with the finding in Figure 3.3, that trade in manufactured products, requiring more market information, is more distance-dependent than trade in unprocessed resources, even though transport costs are more important for resources than for manufactured products.

The failure to take innovation and flows of information into account explicitly also seems to be the main deficiency of traditional theories of urban-regional development.

The classic economic growth theory, stating that the product of a region is a function of the input of capital, labour, land, and an undetermined residual called innovation, fails because studies indicate that the

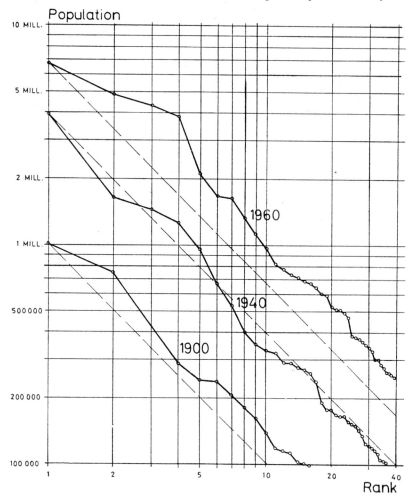

Fig. 4.1. *Rank-size curves for the Latin American urban system, 1900, 1940 and 1960*

residual in the developed countries accounts for 50–80% of the total growth (see, for example, Solow (1957), Dennison (1964), and Hagen (1968)); and even though innovation is probably less important in the developing world, Bruton (1967) has estimated that innovation in the period 1960–1964 in five Latin American countries accounted for 20–50% of the economic growth.

The location theories tell us where a given activity with given inputs and markets will locate. This might be helpful in the short run where we shall predict the location of known activities, but not in the long run

POPULATION 1960 o
POPULATION 1900 +

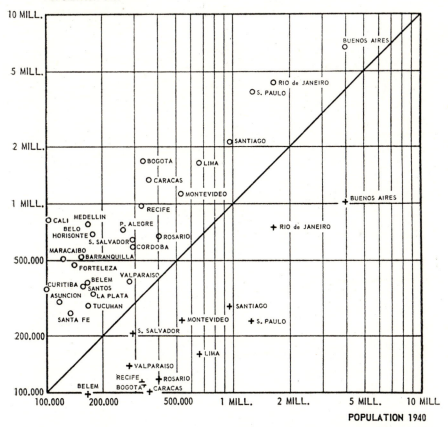

Fig. 4.2. *Growth chart for the large cities in South America, 1900–1940 and 1940–1960*

where we shall predict the location of activities not yet invented. Even in the short run the validity of the assumption about given activities is doubtful, because many firms now change the products they manufacture very rapidly (see, for instance, Mueller *et. al.*, 1961).

Finally, the trade theories state that the production of a given product will be concentrated in that region which has the largest relative locational advantage. However, except in the relatively few cases where locational advantage is based on natural resources, the trade theories do not specify which regions have locational advantages.

Thus the deficiency of all the theories is that none of them takes the process of innovation specifically into account. A theory of urban-regional development must be able to take into consideration changes in technological and organizational structure both in time and space. To be able to elaborate such a theory some relevant empirical findings about the innovation process will be reviewed below.

In chapter 5 these findings will be used to explore the relations between the innovation processes and the development of the urban system.

4.2 THE INNOVATION

By an innovation we shall understand any new product, technique, organization, or idea which is introduced into a social system. This is a somewhat broader definition than is sometimes used in economic litera- ture where emphasis is put on technical innovations. From the point of view of economic development, however, such a narrow definition is unreasonable, because improved allocation of resources due to organiza- tional innovation seems to be at least as important for productivity increases as changes in technology.

On the other hand, it is clear that not all changes will have a favourable effect on the regional development process; some might even have a nega- tive effect. To use the term innovation with an implicit positive evaluation as is often done, therefore, would not be unreasonable. However, to specify which innovations will have a positive and which a negative effect would be extremely difficult, if not impossible. A positive evalua- tion, therefore, will be avoided here, except in so far as someone will need to evaluate an innovation positively if it really is to spread; *e.g.* some planners might find the spread of the private automobile a negative inno- vation, but the people who buy the cars will evaluate the innovation positively; on the other hand, a government which initiates an agrarian reform, as well as those who are to benefit from it, will evaluate the reform positively, while those whose land will be expropriated might object to it.

4.3 HOUSEHOLD VERSUS ENTREPRENEURIAL INNOVATIONS

We shall distinguish between two levels of innovations: household inno- vations and entrepreneurial innovations. Household innovations are innovations which spread among private households or individuals and which might be accepted by all the population or by groups of the popula- tion with particular characteristics. Examples of such household innova- tions are the use of durable consumer goods (refrigerators, television, automobiles, etc.), installation of running water in dwellings, or membership of associations or co-operatives.

An entrepreneurial innovation is an innovation which has direct consequences for people other than the adopter and his family; therefore, it most often involves a higher risk to the innovator, economically, socially, or politically, than the equivalent household innovation. Depending on the type of innovation, the entrepreneur could, for instance, be the local government, a committee of citizens, or a private businessman.

Many household innovations have a corresponding entrepreneurial innovation. Membership in a local association, for instance, requires that the association exist; installation of running water in a dwelling requires that a water supply system has been established in the community; and, although the spread of consumer goods in a community is not conditioned by the establishment of a shop for dealing with the particular good, the speed of adoption of the innovation by households will be increased if a shop is established.

In the same way that many household innovations can only spread in a town when the corresponding entrepreneurial innovation has been adopted, an entrepreneurial innovation can in many cases only be adopted when a sufficient number of households are ready to adopt the corresponding household innovation. This, however, is not always the case; new production techniques in an already existing firm, or changes in local government administration procedure need no direct household response in order to be adopted.

Much of the literature on innovation diffusion has been concerned with diffusion of household or agricultural innovations[1] within local societies (see, for example, Rogers, 1962).

However, it appears that entrepreneurial innovations in general will have a more direct effect on regional productivity than household innovations, and although it is clear from the above that the diffusion of an entrepreneurial innovation cannot be viewed completely independently of the diffusion of the corresponding household innovation, we shall here concentrate on the diffusion of entrepreneurial innovations.

---

[1] Although agricultural innovations are in a sense entrepreneurial innovations, the adopting unit is the rural household (except where the innovation involves co-operative action); they must therefore, according to the definition used here, be classified as household innovations.

4.4 THE INNOVATION PROCESS

The literature on innovation distinguishes between four stages in the process of innovation (Organization for Economic Co-operation and Development (OECD), 1968):

1. *The scientific discovery*, when the theoretical principle behind an innovation is discovered. This results from basic research;
2. *The invention*, when it is for the first time made clear that the production of a given product or process is possible. This results from applied research;
3. *The innovation*, when the product or process is for the first time applied successfully in practice. The innovation is the result of product development;
4. *The innovation diffusion process*, by which an innovation spreads from the first innovator to other potential innovators.

As the following pages will be concerned mostly with innovation diffusion, we shall depart from OECD's definition of 'innovation', and define it as the adoption of some product, process, idea or organization by a group of people which have not used it before; *i.e.* innovation does not refer to something which is new in the world, but to something which is new to the adopter.

The first introduction of an innovation in a town or region can come about either by local invention or by imitation from outside innovation centres. Historically, however, most scientific discoveries and inventions have taken place in a few large urban centres in North America and Europe, and in the developing countries innovation by imitation is likely to be by far the most frequent. Even in North America and Europe the active interest in research and development only goes back to the turn of the century. Therefore, there is good reason for starting this review of the innovation processes with an account of the last of the above points – the innovation diffusion process – and then returning later to the first points – scientific discovery and invention.

4.5 THE INNOVATION DIFFUSION PROCESSES

In the literature on this subject a large number of factors has been put forward as influencing the innovation diffusion process. Here we shall summarize these factors under five heads, which cover most if not all of the factors proposed in other studies, namely:

1. Exposure to the innovation;
2. General willingness to adopt innovations;
3. Economic and technical feasibility of the innovation in the town or region;
4. Presence of a potential entrepreneur in the town or region;
5. Control of decisions.

4.6 EXPOSURE TO THE INNOVATION

The authors of all studies of innovation diffusion agree that the process of information diffusion is central to the innovation diffusion process; clearly a first and necessary condition for people to adopt an innovation must be that they have heard or read enough about it to be familiar with it. (For reviews of the literature see Rogers, 1962 and Brown, 1968). Thus everything else being equal, the person who has first received a sufficient amount of information about an innovation will also be the first to adopt it. Therefore, the innovation diffusion process will be a function of the communication channels. In the case of the diffusion of household innovations within a local community, as studied for instance by the the sociologists Coleman, Katz, and Menzel (1957), the communication network has been treated as identical with the social structure. In our case, where we are rather concerned with interregional or inter-urban diffusion, the physical communication structure, for instance road and telephone networks, becomes more important, and we shall in the following concentrate on these communication channels.

The most accessible points on the interregional transport and communication networks are generally the large urban centres. According to the above, the adoption of an innovation in a country is likely to occur first in that city which has the fullest exchange of ideas, people, and products with other cities in the country and with cities in other countries. This city will most often be the national capital, but in some instances where large harbour cities or centres of massive immigration are distinct from the capital city, such harbour cities or immigration centres may rank as high as the capital in communication flows with foreign cities. This is clearly illustrated by the Chilean case studied by Pedersen (1970). He found that five out of seven innovations studied were adopted first in Santiago, while the two others were adopted first in the largest harbour town, Valparaíso. For Venezuela, this is confirmed by Lasuén (1969).

When the first city has adopted the innovation, information about it will flow through the communication networks to other cities in the country. When they have received sufficient information about the innovation, entrepreneurs in the cities will adopt it and also these cities will start sending information about the innovation to the towns which have not yet adopted it, until all centres have adopted the innovation.

In general, the exposure to an innovation will be a function of the information about the innovation flowing into the town from towns which have already adopted it. At a time prior to the introduction of mass media such information flows could only occur through personal contacts, which throughout the world tend to decrease more or less rapidly with distance. The introduction of mass information media has opened up a possibility of information diffusion which, at least in later stages of the development process, is virtually unrestricted by distance.

There are, however, many studies which show that, although the first information about an innovation may be obtained from the mass media, the final decision to adopt it is most often a result of personal contacts. It would seem probable that the dependence on personal contacts would be greater the greater the risk involved, and this is confirmed by the findings of Coleman, Katz and Menzel (1957) and Bowers (1937), *i.e.* that personal contacts tend to be most important at the beginning of the diffusion process. As entrepreneurial innovations generally are characterized by relatively high risks, we should expect personal contacts to be of special importance for the diffusion of such innovations.

But even if personal contacts are decisive for the diffusion of entrepreneurial innovations over a wide range of socio-economic development levels, the distance decay of the information flows is likely to decrease with time, partly because the distance decay of personal contacts has been found empirically to decrease as the means of transportation and communication improve, and partly because the influence of the mass media increases through time.

Many empirical studies show that in general both information flows and person flows per time unit, I_{ij}, between two urban centres, i and j, can be approximated to the gravity model[2]

$$I_{ij} = K \frac{P_i P_j}{r_{ij}^x}$$

where P_i and P_j are the populations of the two centres, r_{ij} is the distance between the centres, K is a constant, and the exponent x is a parameter, which has been found to vary with the level of economic development

---

[2] Many different formulations of the gravity model exist. For reviews of the literature on gravity models see, e.g., Isard (1960) chapter 11 or Olsson (1965). It makes no difference which alternative is used here. The model presented is the simplest and the most commonly used.

so that large values (2 to 3 or larger) are found in developing countries with little developed transportation and communication networks, while low values (0 to 1) are found in developed countries where the networks are more dense.

This expression indicates that the amount of information about an innovation which flows into a town from the towns which have already adopted the innovation is a function of the size of the town, and of its distance from the towns adopting the innovation earlier. Which of the non-adopters will be the next to have received sufficient information for the adoption of the innovation will therefore depend in part on the size of the towns and in part on their distance from the earlier adopters, especially the large earlier adopters.

Which of the two factors, town size or distance, will be the most important depends on the size of the distance exponent. In the least developed areas where the distance exponent is very large, the distance factor will clearly become dominant. In the highly developed areas where the exponent is close to zero, the distance element becomes insignificant, and the diffusion process is determined completely by urban size.

The first case corresponds to the spatial diffusion process described in many archaeological and anthropological studies of diffusion in primitive cultures. In this case, the innovation spreads from town to town along the physical transport network in the form of a wave-like moving frontier (Morrill, 1968).

The second case corresponds to the diffusion down the urban hierarchy which has been described in more recent studies of the innovation diffusion process in the developed countries (Berry and Neils, 1969). In this case the innovation diffuses from the largest to the next largest town and so on down to smaller and smaller towns.[3] Using empirical data for the diffusion of epidemics during the nineteenth century in North America, Pyle (1969) has shown how the character of the diffusion process shifted from spatial to hierarchical diffusion as the development of the urban system proceeded, and Pedersen (1970) has by simulation shown how this shift can be explained by the simple gravity model of information diffusion outlined above.

Most diffusion processes, of course are mixed processes containing elements of both spatial and hierarchical diffusion. As an example Table 4.1 and Figure 4.3 show the effect of distance and urban size on the

---

[3] Even in cases where the innovation is invented or adopted first in a small town or a rural area, the large cities will be likely to receive information about it at a very early stage of the diffusion process, so that the majority of the country anyway will receive the innovation from the large cities through the urban hierarchy (Pred, 1972).

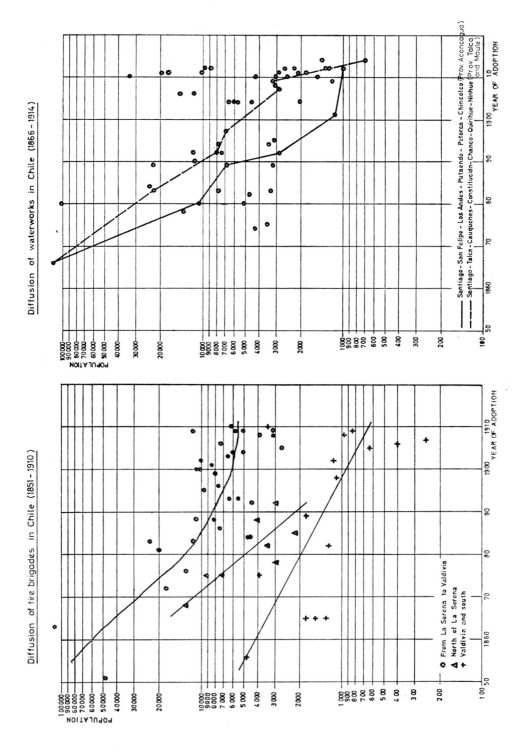

Diffusion of waterworks in Chile (1866-1914)

Diffusion of fire brigades in Chile (1851-1910)

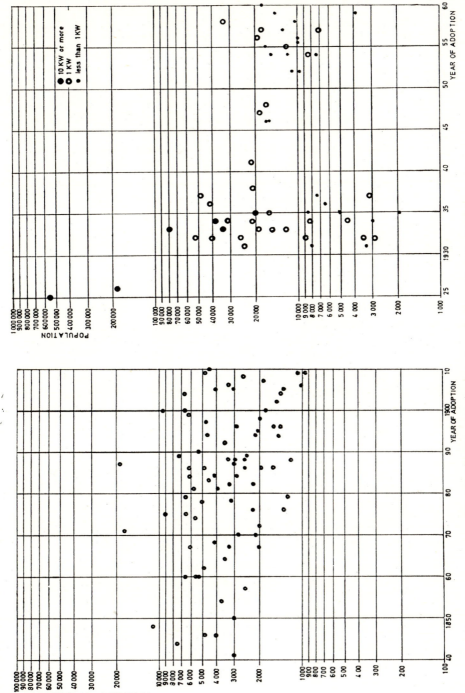

Fig. 4.3. *Diffusion of innovations down the urban hierarchy in Chile*

diffusion of some Chilean innovations. The figure shows a weak tendency for hierarchical diffusion and the table indicates that *there is a strong tendency for a town not to adopt an innovation before one of its nearest, larger neighbours has adopted it, but when two towns have the same nearest neighbour it might not necessarily be the largest which adopts the innovation first; often it will be the nearest.*

Table 4.1   *Town size and distance as determinants of innovation diffusion in Chile*

Innovation	Percentage of cases in which a town adopted the innovation:		
	after its nearest larger neighbour	before its nearest larger neighbour, but after the second-nearest	before its two nearest larger neighbours
Hospitals	79.7	13.1	7.2
Newspapers	77.4	14.3	8.4
Fire brigades	84.9	13.2	1.9
Waterworks	71.7	17.0	11.4

Changes in the distance exponent in the gravity expression not only influence the structure of the diffusion but also its speed.

When x decreases, the distance decay decreases, and the flow of information increases. Therefore, we should expect the diffusion time to decrease. The data shown in Figure 4.4 for a number of Chilean innovations indicate that this holds good. The figure, however, is based on a very few innovations which are in no way representative of all innovations.

4.7 GENERAL WILLINGNESS TO ADOPT INNOVATIONS

While the diffusion of information constitutes an important necessary condition for the diffusion of innovations, it clearly is not by itself sufficient for their diffusion.

In the simple formulation of the gravity model presented above, in which the masses are measured as total population, it is implicitly assumed that the population is homogeneous in its willingness and ability to participate in the innovation diffusion process. Clearly, this assumption need not be true, first, because the *per capita* participation in the communication flows might vary from town to town; and secondly, because the amount of information necessary for the adoption of an innovation may vary from town to town.

One reason for the variation from town to town in *per capita* participation in communication flows is that the town populations have different

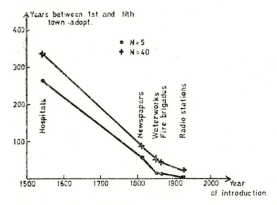

Fig. 4.4. *Changes in the innovation diffusion time*

compositions in terms of income and education. This will lead to inter-urban differences in participation rates, because inhabitants with different characteristics participate to different degrees in the communication process, *e.g.* people with a university education are likely to participate more frequently than most other groups, and the illiterate population might not participate at all; also high income households are likely to participate more than low income households.

Different participation rates also result, because many innovations in an industrialized society will only be of interest for certain groups in the society and only these groups, therefore, will participate in the process of information diffusion, *e.g.* a new device for an automobile will only spread among automobile owners, and a new hearing-aid will only spread among those hard of hearing.

The information level at which an innovation is adopted might differ from town to town depending on the social structure of the town and the characteristics of the innovation. In general, the necessary information level is likely to be larger in towns with a rigid traditional social structure than in towns which have recently experienced heavy immigration.

7

In all cases where the entrepreneurial innovation depends on the diffusion of an equivalent household innovation, such differences in the participation rates will clearly delay the innovation process, because the development of a sufficient market for the innovation will be delayed.

4.8 ECONOMIC AND TECHNICAL FEASIBILITY OF THE INNOVATION

The spread of some innovations is limited to certain regions either because, as is the case with mining technology, they are tied to a specific natural resource, or because, as is the case with irrigation techniques, they are tied to a specific problem which only appears in specific regions. Such resource-oriented innovations relevant only in specific regions will not be discussed here.

There is, however, another more general type of economic-technical limitation to innovation diffusion, namely, limitations related to scale and agglomeration economies. Many products can only be produced economically on a certain scale; many technical innovations can only be adopted by production units of a certain size; and many forms of organization require a certain minimum of support to exist. This means that such innovations can only be adopted in cities or regions above a certain size, because only there will the potential market for the product or the potential number of supporters of the organization be large enough, and only there will a large-scale production unit find a large enough specialized labour force. For other types of innovations there will simply not be any demand in small towns, because the demand for the innovation first arises at a certain city size; examples of this could be a sewage disposal system or traffic lights.

Thus, for many innovations a threshold level will exist at a certain city size, below which the innovation cannot be adopted (or if adopted, cannot be sustained).

This threshold level has throughout the industrialization period tended to rise, partly because technical innovations, especially in the field of transportation, have increased the optimal scale of production for many products, and partly because many of the new products developed along with industrialization have been specialized products oriented towards smaller and smaller segments of the population in a town.

The effect of the threshold level is to stop the diffusion down the urban hierarchy when the threshold is reached. Further adoptions only take place as more towns, through growth, reach a size above the threshold level. As the threshold level for innovations tends to rise, fewer and fewer towns will be able to adopt the innovations.

4.9 PRESENCE OF A POTENTIAL ENTREPRENEUR IN THE TOWN

Persons with entrepreneurial abilities are scarce, especially in the early stages of the economic development process. This means that, even if the households in a town are ready to adopt an innovation, this may be impossible because no entrepreneur is present.

The first three factors in the diffusion process have been treated in a deterministic way. Though a stochastic element at the present level of investigation is clearly inherent in the information flows, in the social structure and in the threshold level, these are concerned with such large groups of the population that the stochastic variation in most cases will be averaged out when averages are made over entire towns. However, as the frequency of entrepreneurs is very small, the stochastic element is likely to be so important that it must be taken into account explicitly.

If we assume that potential entrepreneurs are distributed stochastically throughout the population at a small frequency, q, then we can, by means of a Poisson distribution, find the probability $1 - p_0$ that at least one entrepreneur is found in a town of a certain population P, to

$$1 - p_0 = 1 - \frac{\lambda^0}{0!} e^{-\lambda} = 1 - e^{-\lambda} = 1 - e^{-Pq}$$

where λ is the mean number of entrepreneurs in towns of size P. This model indicates that the probability for innovation adoption will vary with town size, so that large towns have probabilities for innovation adoption close to 1.00, while small towns have probabilities close to zero. In Figure 4.5 we have shown this relation between town size and the probability of finding at least one potential entrepreneur in the town for two different frequencies of potential entrepreneurs, namely 1 and 2 per 10,000 inhabitants.

If the hypothesis that the potential entrepreneurs are randomly distributed in the population is valid, we should, at the moment when the innovation has been adopted by towns of all sizes down to the threshold level and in all regions of the country, expect the proportion of towns which have adopted the innovation to vary with town size in the same way as the probabilities in Figure 4.5.

To test this we have in Figure 4.5 also shown the empirical relation between the percentage of adopters and town size for two old innovations, namely fire brigades in 1910 and newspapers in 1930. It appears that the empirical data roughly correspond to entrepreneur frequencies at about 1–2 potential entrepreneurs per 10,000 inhabitants.

The fit is not perfect, and the curves indicate that the frequency of entrepreneurs is higher in the larger towns (about 2 per 10,000 inhabitants) than in the smaller towns (about 1 per 10,000 inhabitants), which seems reasonable.

According to the definition of an entrepreneurial innovation given above, we can define the potential entrepreneur as an individual or a group of individuals, who have access to sufficient capital and human

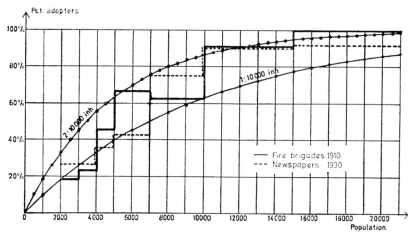

Fig. 4.5. *Per cent adopters among towns of different sizes. (The thin curves show the theoretical percentage of adopters, if adoption depends on the presence of an innovator in the town, and innovators are randomly distributed in the population at a frequency of 1:10,000 inh. or 2:10,000 inh. respectively)*

resources to introduce the innovation, and who are willing to take the risk involved, economically, politically and socially.

According to this definition the frequency of potential entrepreneurs in the population depends on the perception of the risk involved in introducing the innovation. This risk can be caused by:

– The characteristics of the *innovation*, its capital requirement, the rate of capital recuperation, the cost-benefit ratio, its degree of deviation from current practice, and its feasibility under local conditions;
– The characteristics of the *community*, its socio-economic structure, and the size of the potential local market, which determines the chances for obtaining support for the innovation;

– The psychological characteristics of the *innovator*, his degree of conservatism, which determines the degree of risk he perceives in a given situation.

All of these factors do at least partly vary with town size; small towns tend to have the most rigid social structure and the lowest *per capita* income; in the larger towns the necessary capital is more easily obtained and the probability of getting a market above the minimum size is greatest.

In short, we may say that a town will adopt an innovation at the time when it has received a sufficient amount of information about it from earlier adopters, if it has a size which is larger than the threshold level for the innovation and if there happens to be an entrepreneur in the town who is willing to take the risk of adopting the innovation.

4.10 CONTROL OF DECISIONS

In the above, the process of innovation was assumed to be a local process in which the only external influence was the flow of information. Friedmann (1970) stresses very strongly that where the power to control decisions is in the hands of people or organizations outside the local region this might influence the innovation process in both positive and negative directions. Where the control of decisions for instance is in the hands of the national government, this might impose innovations on local regions without local consent, and where the control of decisions lay with a colonial power, the colonial power might be able to delay the diffusion of competitive activities.

The relation between the control of decisions and regional development has only been very little investigated, so no detailed account of this relation can be given. It is, however, evident that any external control over an area must rest on continuous flows of information. It is no coincidence that the economic colonization of Latin America and the concentration of power in the capital cities coincided in time with the construction of railroad and telegraph networks. Neither is it a coincidence that Pedersen (1970) found that the diffusion of innovations in the colonial period followed the Spanish administrative hierarchy centered on Lima, while the diffusion after the liberation from the Spaniards shifted to two flows, one northwestward starting at the Atlantic coast (English influence) and one southward starting in Mexico (U.S. influence).

4.11 RESEARCH AND DEVELOPMENT

As the development process proceeds the model of innovation diffusion outlined above collapses. There are several reasons for this:

First, the diffusion time tends to decrease with the growth of the population, the increasing rate of participation and the improvement of the transport and communication networks (see Figure 4.4). This decrease in diffusion time leads rapidly to a situation where the spatial information diffusion becomes nearly instantaneous and therefore no longer represents a bottleneck in the innovation process. Instead, the other factors in the diffusion process – participation rate, threshold level, and presence of an entrepreneur – become the main determinants of the diffusion process.

Secondly, for many products the threshold level has increased so that fewer and fewer production units are necessary to satisfy the demand. Fewer and fewer towns, therefore, will be able to adopt the innovation, and at the limit only the first adopter will be able to adopt the high-order innovations. The emphasis, therefore, will shift from the innovation diffusion process to the process of invention.

Thirdly, production becomes more and more specialized. As this specialization proceeds, the senders and receivers of information can no longer be considered proportional to the population of the towns but will vary with the content of the information. Therefore, it becomes increasingly necessary to disaggregate the flows, and this tends to invalidate the gravity model (Isard, 1956, p. 72). At the same time, fewer and fewer become interested in any specific information and the chance that a message sent by one specialist will also be received by another interested specialist becomes smaller and smaller, if the information flows are not reorganized in one way or another.

Fourthly, increased specialization makes it more and more difficult to adopt innovations from outside sources without modification. The sharp distinction between innovation and invention therefore tends to disappear.

Finally, improved transportation and increased specialization lead to rapid increase in the flows of information, and increased scale of operation results in concentration of the flows to a small part of the flow networks. The result is that the maximum capacity of some of the links in the communication networks is reached and there is created what Meier (1962) calls stress in the system.

This collapse of the traditional innovation diffusion process has resulted in a gradual transformation and reorganization of the innovation process.

At the beginning of the industrialization process, most inventions were made by individuals, and the inventions were in most cases given practical application by an individual entrepreneur, who might be the inventor but often was somebody else. The entrepreneur would set up a new firm or organization for the sole purpose of utilizing the invention, and, if successful, his firm would continue working until some new and better invention made the first one obsolete. Then he would have either to adopt the new innovation, to continue the old production at a reduced level, or to go out of business. As the speed of innovation and the scale of operation have increased, the consequences of closing down have become more serious, and direct investment in research and development, have therefore, become a necessity for business firms if they are to survive. At the same time, increased specialization and scale of production lead to increased costs in product development and marketing, and therefore the integration of research, product development and marketing becomes desirable. The result has been the establishment of large research laboratories by private firms.

In the United States, this process started at the end of the last century (Mansfield, 1968), and investigations based on United States patent statistics show that the proportion of patents issued to firms rather than to individuals steadily increased from about 20% around 1900 to 60% around 1960 (*e.g.* Schmookler, 1957, and Pred, 1966).

The concentration of research investment in large-scale research laboratories has had two advantages. First, such large-scale laboratories are better able to provide the necessary facilities for modern research, libraries, computers, and instruments. Secondly, by gathering teams of specialists under one roof they facilitate communication and co-operation between them; this is done by substituting external flows of information by internal flows which are more easy to handle. Finally, the large research laboratory can take advantage of the scale economies obtained by co-ordinating the external and often long distance information flows which are still left. These external information flows are facilitated partly by the introduction of new types of telecommunication, such as closed television and data transmission networks, and partly by the development of national and international organizations and conferences (Alkjær and Eriksen, 1967).

Large-scale research laboratories, however, require large and risky investments which only large firms are able to finance. It is therefore no coincidence that their development was initiated at the time when the organizational structure of industry changed from single-product, single-plant firms to multi-product, multi-plant firms in the form of holding corporations (Lasuén, 1969). The two changes are clearly related to each other. Only the large corporation is able to finance investment in research. And once established, research laboratories often come up with inventions other than those actually sought; to get the full benefit of investments in research, the corporation must therefore be willing to embark on other than their traditional lines of production. Such a broadening of the field of interests in turn reduces the risks of both business and research, because the chances that all lines of production will be outmoded and all lines of research will fail at the same time are small.

The result of this development is that in the United States more than 80% of the total investment in research and development by private business is financed by companies with more than 5,000 employees (OECD, 1968). However, there is a limit to the scale economies of research, and as a percentage of sales, there is no indication that the largest firms in an industry spend more than the somewhat smaller firms in research and development.

There are at least two possible reasons for this:

First, the risks involved in investment in research and development are probably smaller than they are often assumed to be. In an analysis of the research at very large laboratories, Mansfield (1967) showed that few research projects last more than four years, that the estimated probability of technical success averages 0.80, that the results are expected to be applied only a few months later and that, if successful, the rate of return from investment in research and development is expected to be very high.

Secondly, the cost of research is only a minor part of the total cost of introducing a new product on the market. OECD (1968) writes that of the total cost of an innovation 10–20% only are used for research and advanced development, while 40–60% are used for tooling, 10–15% for starting up manufacturing, and 10–25% for launching the product on the market.

However, when we look at the 'smaller' firms, *i.e.* those with less than 500 or 1,000 employees, the amount spent on research will probably increase with their size, and as few firms in the developing countries have more than 500 employees, the size of firms becomes a very important determinant of the process of innovation.

In this most recent development of the innovation process, the inter-urban innovation diffusion process is replaced by processes of invention and inter-firm, inter-sector, and inter-disciplinary innovation diffusion. This development has also meant that the external control over decisions has come to play an increasingly important role in the spatial diffusion of innovations, while the autonomous diffusion process has become less important.

4.12 SUMMARY

Innovation is an important factor of urban-regional development. The innovation process, however, undergoes transformation along with the development process.

In the early stages of the development process, when communication networks are poorly developed and the urban system consists only of small towns and villages, innovations diffuse slowly from village to village.

Later when communication networks are developed and some of the towns have started to grow, the diffusion process becomes more rapid and the innovations tend increasingly to spread from the largest to the smallest towns, rather than from the nearest to the furthest towns.

Finally, in the last phase, when geographical diffusion becomes almost instantaneous and therefore uninteresting, intersectorial innovation diffusion and active research for invention become the critical elements of the innovation process.

These three phases: *spatial diffusion, hierarchical diffusion,* and *active research for invention,* are not discontinuous steps in development but rather *points in a continuous process of transformation.* The transitional periods between the phases are therefore more interesting than the stages themselves.

CHAPTER 5

Development of the urban system as a process of diffusion

5.1 INNOVATION AND URBAN DEVELOPMENT

Few regions in the world have developed economically in isolation. Economic growth and development are usually transmitted in time and space, from town to town and from region to region. To understand the process of regional economic development regions must be viewed as parts of systems of regions, a system which is linked together by flows of persons, goods and capital, but first of all by the diffusion of innovations.

A regional economy can, of course, grow without any innovation in the region itself. It might grow in response to innovations in other regions. Innovations in the capital region or in another country might increase the demand for some traditional product or natural resource produced in the region. Many regions in South America have grown in this way by increased resource exploitation rather than by innovation. Growth through such a one-sided multiplier effect, however, is not very reliable in the long run. Natural resources constitute a decreasing proportion of the total input for most forms of production. The prices of natural resources, therefore, have tended to decrease relatively to the prices of manufactured products. In some cases natural resources have even been forced almost completely out of the market by artificially produced substitutes. In South America this has happened, for instance, for nitrates in Chile and Peru and for rubber in Brazil (Aymans, 1966).

North (1955) in his staple theory has suggested that the money earned through increased resource exploitation in some parts of the world has created the capital necessary to start the process of economic development. This, however, supposes that the capital is actually invested in the region, and often this is not the case. One reason for this is that manufactured products in the short run are often bought more cheaply in the developed regions or countries than they can be produced in the developing regions.

Thus the income created by increased resource exploitation might lead to backwash effects rather than to economic development.

It appears that, while regional development might for a time take place through resource exploitation alone, long-term development in a region must be based on innovation in organizations, techniques, or products.

5.2 DEVELOPMENT OF THE CENTRAL PLACE SYSTEM

By transport and communication networks, towns and cities in a country or a continent are linked more or less tightly into a system of cities. For South America in 1960, the structure of this system of cities was described in chapter 3. It is through this system of cities that innovations spread.

In the first stage of the development process, society consists of small isolated villages all with approximately the same population structure. The transport system is rudimentary, and interchange among the villages is very small. This society can grow either by simple input expansion, or it can develop economically by the introduction of innovations, partly in the form of improved transportation, and partly in the form of higher order goods which require more than one village as hinterland. The introduction of higher order goods will slowly lead to the creation of higher order centres and the establishment of a hierarchy of towns; and the improved transportation will take the form of a structured network of roads or tracks leading from the centre to the nearest higher order centre. This network will be approximately a topological tree.

The hierarchy of cities represents an equilibrium situation. Introduction of an innovation into the hierarchy of centres will disrupt the equilibrium a little. If little or no growth takes place the equilibrium will be re-established as the innovation diffuses outwards through the urban system. At this stage of development the diffusion process is very slow, but as long as the rate of introduction of new innovations is even slower, the hierarchy of towns will remain in equilibrium, except that the centres will gradually rise to higher orders. This is the equilibrium described by Christaller's central place theory (see, *e.g.*, Berry, 1967).

In 1865, at the time of the first complete national Chilean census, the Chilean urban system had developed into such a step-wise hierarchy. Santiago and Valparaíso were at the top of the hierarchy with 115,000 and 70,000 inhabitants respectively. Talca, Chillán, Concepción, La Serena, and Copiapó were second order towns with populations ranging from 13,500 to 17,900, and then there was a step down to third order towns ranging from 7,100 to about 5,000 inhabitants. In the interval between the second and third order towns, only two towns were located,

namely San Felipe (8,700 inhabitants) and Quillota (10,000 inhabitants),
which were both located very favourably on the road from Santiago to
Valparaíso. The existence of a step-wise hierarchy is also evident from the
statistics of business taxes from 1871. According to these statistics,
Valparaíso and Santiago had, respectively, 100 and 97 different types of
business establishments (not different firms). Six towns had from 41 to 53
different types of activities, and then there was a group of towns with
about 27 to 30 types of activities and another group with from 13 to 18
different types of activities. The population data and the tax statistics do
not fully correspond. Chillán, which according to its population was a
second order town, had too few activities; and San Felipe with a size
between the third and second order towns and Valdivia, which was only
a bridge-head in the undeveloped southern frontier, both had a sufficient
number of different business activities to rank as second order towns.

5.3 FROM THE CENTRAL PLACE HIERARCHY TO AN INTEGRATED SYSTEM OF CITIES

Along with development both the rate of invention and the speed of innovation diffusion tend to increase. As long as population growth is slow
and the rate of invention is slower than the speed of innovation diffusion,
the disruption introduced by an innovation will have disappeared before
the next innovation is introduced, and equilibrium will be preserved.
But if the rate of invention (or central innovation) becomes faster than
the speed of diffusion, equilibrium will not be re-established between two
innovations, and slowly the disequilibrium will reinforce itself. This disequilibrium will give those towns which are generally early adopters of
innovations an advantage over slower adopters. The above summary of
the innovation diffusion process indicates that these early adopter towns
are in part the larger, higher order centres and in part the towns located
close to the first adopter town. Exactly which towns will benefit and by
how much will depend both on the specific geographical conditions and on
the way the transport and communication networks are developed.
    Pedersen (1970) attempted to simulate this joint process of innovation
diffusion and urban development in an idealized closed urban hierarchy.
He assumed that as soon as an innovation was introduced in the largest
town in the system, it would start to spread to other towns. The innovation diffusion process would be a function of the spread of information
from those towns which had already adopted the innovation to those which
had not. This spread would be determined by a simple gravity model,
subject to constraints with regard to the amount of information necessary

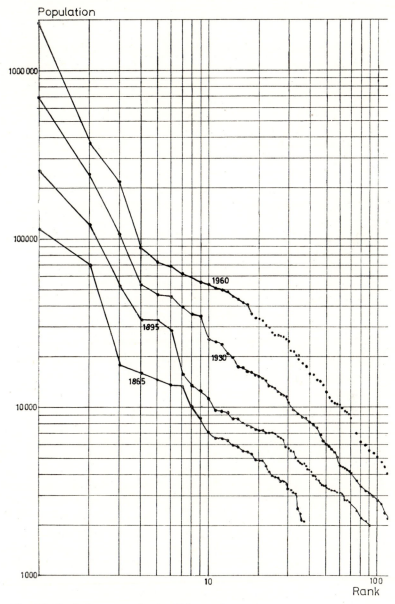

Fig. 5.1. *Rank-size curves for the Chilean urban system*

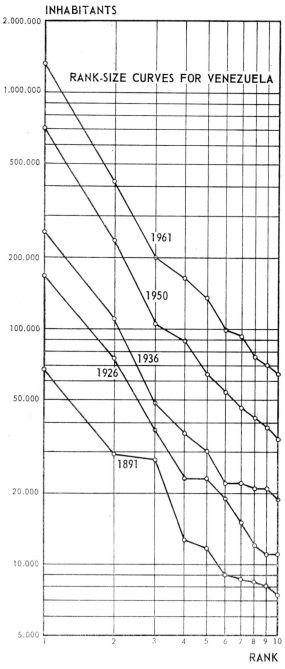

Fig. 5.2. *Rank-size curves for the Venezuelan urban system*

for a town to adopt the innovation, and with regard to a threshold size of the adopting towns. Secondly, he assumed that the growth rate of a town would increase relatively to that of other towns when an innovation was introduced.

The resulting joint process of innovation diffusion and urban growth did not generally lead to changes in the rank order of the towns at the upper end of the hierarchy. The simulations showed changes in the rank order of the towns only where the total growth rate was very high and the diffusion process very slow.

This is in accord with the findings of Lasuén (1969) that the rank order of the largest Spanish towns was very stable throughout the entire century from 1860 to 1960, with those of Friedmann (1966) that the same held for Venezuelan towns from 1926 to 1961, and with those of Gould and Törnqvist (1969) that the pattern of innovation diffusion in Sweden has been extraordinarily stable since the end of 19th century.

For the national urban systems in South America, the ranks held by the towns are in general also stable, except that towns in the land-settlement frontiers, when the frontier has been developed, have sometimes made large leaps in the rank order. In Chile, for instance, this was the case with Valdivia which jumped from the twenty-fifth rank in 1885 to the ninth rank in 1920, and Antofagasta which jumped from the fifteenth rank in 1885 to the fourth rank in 1920.

However, even though the ranking of the towns in general has been stable, the absolute differences between them have changed. Pedersen's (1970) simulations show that the discrete steps in the urban rank-size distribution for a Christaller hierarchy tend to level out during the joint processes of innovation diffusion and urban growth. Empirically this is illustrated very neatly in the case of Chile. Figure 5.1 shows how the discrete steps in the rank-size curve for Chilean cities in 1865 have been slowly levelling out, reflecting a transformation from the Christaller hierarchy towards an integrated urban system characterized by a linear rank-size distribution. Figure 5.2 shows a similar development in the Venezuelan rank-size curve.

This hypothesized relation between the development of the urban system and the process of innovation and information diffusion is also in line with the extremely rapid increase in communications which took place in Chile after 1865.

The mail service, which in this period was the most important means of communication, was expanded rapidly. From 1863 to 1871 the mail flow went up by 12.4% a year from 2.2 million to 5.5 million pieces of mail a year. This rapid increase was due both to a large decrease in postage rates and to the extension of the service (see Table 5.1), and it continued throughout the rest of the century although at a slightly slower rate.

At the same time, the telegraph network was developed, starting with the entry into service of the cable from Valparaíso to Santiago in 1852. By 1867 the network of cables extended from Copiapó in the north to Concepción in the south, and in 1872 the first international cable from Santiago to Buenos Aires came into service, bringing Chile with regard to information two weeks closer to Europe (Johnson, 1948).

Finally, the development of the central Chilean railroad network followed the opening of the railroad from Valparaíso to Santiago in 1863 (Marin Vicuña, 1900).

Table 5.1   *Development of the mail service in Chile, 1795–1895*

Year	Million pieces of mail	Average annual growth rate (%)	Pieces of mail *per capita*	No. of towns served by mail	Average annual growth rate (%)
1795	—			22	
					1.4
1817	—			30	
					4.2
1861	2.2		1.2	182	
		12.4			7.8
1873	5.5		2.8	332	
		10.6			
1894	57.4		20.1	—	
		10.9			
1895	63.7		22.8	—	

— = No data available.

Sources: *Annuario Estadístico de Chile 1871–72* (1873) and Espinoza (1897)

How this transition from a step-wise central place hierarchy to an integrated urban system takes place depends on the extent and quality of the transport and communication networks. In the first phases of economic development, when transport and communication networks are little developed, the innovation diffusion process will be to a large extent spatially determined. Third order towns located close to the first order centre are likely to adopt innovations before second order towns located farther away, and they will therefore grow more rapidly. The result is that the step between second and third order towns will be levelled out before the step between the first and the second order towns. This leads to the creation of a primate city distribution, characterized by a predominant first order town and decreasing difference between the third and the second order towns. This differential growth will be stronger where the national growth rate is high, and it will last longer where the diffusion time is low. The primacy will therefore tend to be especially strong where the national growth rate is large and diffusion time slow.

The third order towns which grow especially fast are those located close to the primate city. Therefore, around the primate city what Friedmann (1966) calls a core region consisting of the primate city and a number of medium-sized towns will tend to develop and will reinforce the dichotomous centre-periphery structure. This reinforcement of the centre-periphery structure has taken place in most of the Latin American countries.

In chapter 4 a distinction was made between household and entrepreneurial innovations. So far, we have assumed that the diffusion of these two types of innovations occurs simultaneously. However, where there are no potential local entrepreneurs, the entrepreneurial innovation might not be adopted, even though the households were ready to accept it. In this situation the households' demand for the innovation might well be satisfied by importation from outside sources, if the transport network is sufficiently developed; and the chance for local adoption of the entrepreneurial innovation might be forfeited. These are what Myrdal (1958) calls backwash effects, and this of course will further reinforce the centre-periphery structure.

When the transport and communication networks are developed, the original links are improved and new links are added, so that the topological tree characteristic for the central place hierarchy is transformed into a complete network.[1] As this happens, the distance becomes a less important and town size a more important determinant of the innovation diffusion process (see section 4.6). The old second order towns, which have still maintained their high ranking (though they have got close competitors in the core regions) will again improve their position and increase both their speed of innovation and their rate of growth. The kink in the rank-size curve between the first and second order towns will start to level out, the primacy will diminish, and the centre-periphery structure will be weakened. Therefore, we should expect primacy to increase during the first stages of economic development, but decrease again during the later stages (Figure 5.3).

[1] For references on changes in transport networks see Haggett (1969).

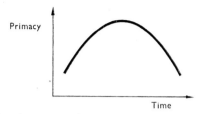

Fig. 5.3. *The change in primacy over time*

The picture which we have painted here of the development of the urban network from a step-wise central place hierarchy to a fully integrated urban system is based on only one factor, namely, that of information and innovation diffusion in the urban system. This is clearly an over-simplification. Even though innovation and information diffusion might be very important, there are of course many reasons why in real life this picture would not be true in detail. First of all, the traditionally considered factors, capital and labour, still play a role. Another reason is that the original central place hierarchy will vary from country to country, either because of specific features of the natural geography, or because of imposed national borders. A third reason is that the timing of the development of transport and communication networks will differ from country to country; in some cases they may be developed in advance of urban development, but in most cases they will probably lag behind it. A fourth reason is that not only the national transport and communication flows but also the international flows should be considered. This will be especially important in export-oriented countries and in countries with heavy immigration, and where this foreign traffic passes through it, the largest city will have its primacy reinforced.

Empirical studies, however, indicate that this transformation of the urban system from the step-wise hierarchy via the primate city distribution to the linear rank-size distribution actually takes place, even though it is not difficult to find exceptions. In an interesting study Linsky (1965) has shown that high primacy was found in ex-colonial export-oriented countries with a large growth rate and low income. The distribution, however, was not symmetrical, and low primacy was associated neither with a small growth rate, low income or ex-colonial status nor with export-orientation, but with the size of the country. The relations between primacy and developmental variables thus seem to be non-linear, and this is supported by both Metha (1964) and by El Shaks (1965), who have found that an index of population concentration tends to increase with economic development in the developing countries but decreases in the developed countries.

5.4 THE URBAN FIELD

As development takes place the speed of innovation diffusion increases. At the same time, however, the threshold level of many activities rises so that in most countries they can be adopted in only one or a few places. Also the degree of specialization increases so that innovations made in one region often have to be modified before they can be adopted in another. As seen in chapter 4 large organizations are created to carry out the necessary research, development and marketing, and these organizations, which are very sensitive to information accessibility, are sure to be attracted to the large cities and their environs.

When many new products and services have to be supplied to the whole country from the capital city and at the same time a growing number of research organizations want to locate there, the demand for land and labour will increase. Wages and land rents are therefore driven up.

The increasing level of specialization also means that the traditional single-plant firm becomes more and more dependent on inputs and services from other firms and organizations. The demand for transportation and communication therefore increases drastically to the point where a reorganization of the production structure becomes necessary if overloading, or what Meier (1962) calls stress in the communication system, is to be avoided.

New activities with growing demands will not be hurt by the rising costs of land and labour, and the increasing difficulties of transportation and communication, but older activities with stagnating markets and keen competition from other towns will not be able to stand up to these rising costs. They will see an advantage in leaving the capital city. This could also be true for many research organizations which as they become larger and larger also become more self-contained. This process of spreading consequent on rising costs has been called the spill-over effect.

The key to understanding this process of spreading is the communication structure of large firms and the development of modern telecommunication networks. This communication structure has been analysed in a number of recent Swedish investigations. Among them Bertil Thorngren (1970) has analysed the external and internal communication flows of 100 large Swedish firms. He found that 70% of all the 15,000 contacts which he registered were short, routine, one-way messages, which generally did not require an answer. For these contacts face-to-face contact is not needed, and where this is not already done they can easily be transferred to the telecommunication networks: telephone, telex, data-transmission channels, or closed television networks. 25% of the contacts

8*

consisted of more complex two-way exchanges of information between persons with previously established relations. These are contacts in which the persons know with whom they want to talk and what they want to talk about; at present, they are carried out in part by telephone and in part by face-to-face contacts, but with improved telecommunication most of them can probably be transferred to such media. The last 5% of the contacts consists of complex, time-consuming negotiations, often between more than three participants. This 5% contains 80% of firms' new contacts with other firms and organizations, and it is through these contacts that firms expand and develop. They represent the search for innovations, for new markets and new sources of inputs. At present they are all carried out by face-to-face contacts, and though some of them can be transferred to new improved telecommunication networks, it is unlikely that this will be possible to any large extent. Most of these complex contacts are carried out by a small number of senior officials who spend practically all their time on them. In an investigation of three large Swedish firms, Seebass (1969) found that the highest officials in these firms spend more than 40 hours a week on external communications. For these officials time is clearly very scarce, and easy access to the people they have to contact is an imperative.

In the traditional single-product, single-plant firm innovation was not of crucial importance, and both the market and the sources of inputs were therefore relatively stable. Competition was in price rather than in quality, and to secure low costs close contact between management and production was more important than complex external contacts. At a time when telecommunication was little developed, close contact between management and production could only be secured by joint location of management and production.

This need for joint location of management and production has determined the traditional pattern of manufacturing location, in which growing innovative industries competing both in price and quality had to buy a metropolitan location to secure easy external access for their management, while less innovative, stagnating industries, competing mainly in price, would be forced out to peripheral locations where land rent and labour costs were lower.

However, as telecommunication systems have been developed to such an extent that the relatively simple type of contacts, which are the most frequent between management and production units, can be carried out over these networks, geographical separation of management and production has become possible.

Development of the telecommunication network has for some time past been a reality in the United States, and in Europe the networks are developing rapidly. The possibility of separating the management and production functions thereby created has solved one problem, namely, that of the rising costs of labour, land rent and transportation in the large urban areas; but it has not solved the most pressing problem of communication overload on the management units. To solve this problem a reorganization of production structure by the creation of large multi-plant, multi-firm corporations is necessary. By joining several production units under the same management unit, many of the formerly external contacts which are difficult to handle and time-consuming are replaced by internal contacts, which can be more easily institutionalized and handled by lower ranking officials. At the same time only such large organizations have sufficient capacity to bring subcontractors and service organizations, such as marketing and research institutes, into direct association with the corporation.

The effect this development will have on the urban-regional structure can be seen from some of the first attempts which have been made in Sweden to disaggregate employment statistics for the period 1960–65 according to a functional classification rather than to the traditional sectorial classification (Törnqvist and Gould, 1969, and Engström 1970). The resulting pattern shows that in general the employment opportunities in the manufacturing industries have increased outside the largest cities and decreased within the largest cities. However, when only the administrative job-opportunities in the manufacturing sectors are considered, this picture is reversed, and finally if only the high ranking administrative jobs are considered, by far the largest growth has taken place in the large urban centres.

Thus, improved communication networks seem to give manufacturing plants more freedom of location, because they are no longer geographically tied to management. The question, however, is how free have they become. What are the limits to freedom of location?

The first limit is set by the size of the business organization. It appears that the possibility of separating production and management is often dependent on the creation of large multi-plant corporations. Thus the extent to which manufacturing functions can be moved away from the core regions will depend on the speed of reorganization of the organizational structure of the firms.

The second limit is set by the cost of communication over long distances. Wright (1967), who analysed this problem for Great Britain, concluded that the growth in private long-distance telecommunication lines was very moderate, probably because of high costs; and for the United States, Zeidler *et al.* (1969, p. 27) reports that communication costs do not at present enable remote computation on a competitive basis beyond a range of 100 miles but that, on the other hand, transmission costs can be expected to decrease in the future. (As an example of the distance dependency on data transmission costs, Zeidler *et al.* (1969, p. A12) gives the following data for line charges for the first three minutes: 20 miles, intrastate: US $ 0.28; 100 miles: US $ 0.60; 500 miles: US $ 1.20; 1000 miles: US $ 1.40; 3000 miles: US $ 1.70).

The third limit is set by the requirement for production inputs: labour, subcontractors and natural resources. Improved transportation and increased value-added, however, has reduced the importance of this limitation. The large transport and communication flows, stressed in the traditional location theories, can be handled cheaply and effectively by specially designed transport and communication systems, and they are not likely to influence the location decisions as long as they remain within certain limits. It is rather the small, infrequent and unpredictable flows that will influence the location decisions in the future and they are likely to favour location in or in the neighbourhood of the large urban agglomerations (Karaska, 1969). In this connexion the neighbourhood might be estimated to cover the area within 100–150 km. This is approximately the distance a truck-driver can make as a round trip including loading and unloading in a normal working day. Above this limit costs rise sharply on account of overnight subsistence allowance and overtime payment, or because more vehicles are required to move a given volume of freight (Chisholm, 1966).

This indicates that although the freedom of location increases rapidly, it is not likely to extend beyond what Friedmann and Miller (1965) have termed *the urban field*. Empirically they let this urban field extend about 150 km outwards from each of the metropolitan areas with more than 250,000 inhabitants, which is the size limit which Berry and Neils (1969) consider to be necessary to secure self-sustained growth. This urban field also has similarities to Melvin Webber's (1964) non-place urban realm, though Webber appears to visualize a situation without any distance constraint at all.

In large parts of the United States and Europe the fields of individual metropolitan areas have merged into large continuous conurbations, and in South America as well such a development is likely to take place. Figure 5.4 indicates the extent of such future South American urban fields. In this figure, circles of 150 km radius are shown round cities which in 1960 had more than 250,000 inhabitants.[2]

---

[2] One might argue that if 250,000 inhabitants are necessary to secure self-sustained growth in the United States, larger populations will be necessary in South America where incomes are lower.

Fig. 5.4. *The urban fields of South America*

The figure shows that a nearly continuous belt is likely to develop along the Atlantic coast from Rio de Janeiro to Buenos Aires and continuing across the continent to Santiago. In the northern part of the continent a continuous belt is likely to develop from Caracas down through Colombia and Ecuador to Guayaquil. Finally a minor development axis might in time develop along the coast of north-eastern Brazil, centered on Recife and Salvador.

Outside these belts of urban fields, development is not likely to take place on a large scale except where specific natural resources are available. Among these potential resources, attractive surroundings and a good climate are likely to be the most important. Mineral resources, which at earlier stages of development were an important agent of peripheral economic development, are not likely to be so to the same extent in the future. Few, if indeed any, of the production processes, which used to be resource-oriented are so any more, in part because the cost of transporting the resources has decreased, and in part because the increased value-added has made other factors, such as access to qualified labour, more important. Good climate and beautiful natural surroundings, however, are still immobile, and rising income regions which have these resources are likely to attract people, first for vacations, but later also for permanent settlement. In the United States such a movement of people towards the attractive climate areas of Florida and Arizona has been going on for some time (see, for instance, Chisholm, 1963), and in Europe migration from the northern countries to Spain has recently begun.

What impact such a development will have in South America we can only guess; but the impact might not be very large, because the areas which are developed today, already include some of the areas with the most pleasant climate in South America.

5.5 THE URBAN FIELDS IN DEVELOPING COUNTRIES

Continuous belts of urban fields are developed as a result of the spill-over effect, which has played an important role in many developed countries. In the developing countries, however, the spill-over effect seems to be much less important. There are several reasons for this. First, the rapid migration to the large cities combined with limited growth in production has put the labour force in a very poor bargaining position, and the effective wage therefore has not increased very much. However, even the cost increases which have taken place, for instance, owing to congestion in the large cities, have not resulted in spill-over, because high inter-urban transport costs and tariff walls exclude competition from

Table 5.2   *Offices and conferences of international organizations in Latin America*

	Headquaters			Subsidiary offices			All offices			No. of conferences		
	1954	1959	1964	1954	1959	1964	1954	1959	1964	1954	1959	1964
Bogotá	–	3	3	2	4	4	2	7	7	–	11	14
Buenos Aires	7	6	6	2	13	15	9	19	21	6	15	10
Caracas	–	–	2	1	7	7	1	7	9	8	1	13
Lima	–	1	1	3	9	12	3	10	13	1	5	15
Mexico City	6	15	13	3	10	10	9	25	23	5	13	33
Rio de Janeiro	1	4	5	7	17	14	8	21	19	8	14	14
Santiago de Chile	3	2	7	2	11	6	5	13	13	8	10	11
Latin America	37	56	77	30	110	106	67	166	183	115	119	203
Percentage of the world	3.1	3.9	3.8	13.1	14.6	13.5	4.7	7.5	6.5	10.9	6.8	9.2

Source: Ejler Alkjær and Jørn L. Eriksen (1967).

other than local firms, which all face the same cost increases. Finally, the infrastructure outside the largest cities is often so poor that it might be virtually impossible for an activity to move out.

The development of urban fields, therefore, is contingent upon a number of assumptions which at present are not fulfilled in South America:

- Incomes must be distributed more equally among social groups;
- Infrastructure in the metropolitan hinterlands and access to them must be improved;
- Competition between the large urban regions must be increased both within and between countries.

At present, it seems that the largest advances are being made with regard to the third point while little or nothing seems to happen with regard to the first two points. While international conferences flourish (see Table 5.2), intellectual activities outside the largest cities are negligible. The Panamerican highway network is rapidly being developed, but few local roads outside the metropolitan areas are paved and the road networks in the metropolitan areas are congested. Long distance telecommunication *via* satellites is highly developed, while many villages are still not connected to the network and the networks of the cities are overloaded.

5.6 SUMMARY

Growth of peripheral regions, and thereby the creation of more balanced urban-regional systems, can take place by

- Increasing output in the traditional lines of production, *i.e.* through the multiplier effect;
- Adopting new lines of production or new techniques of production, *i.e.* by innovation;
- Moving of old activities into the region, *i.e.* through the spill-over effect.[3]

The first of these processes dominates the first phases of economic development, while the last is most important in the last phases.

---

[3] These three types of growth are similar to the classification made in many industrial location studies (see, *e.g.*, C. M. Law, 1970) of growth due to
- Growth of old firms;
- Creation of new firms locally;
- Moving old firms or branches of old firms into the region.
The two classifications, however, are not identical as old firms might take up new lines of production and new firms might produce old products.

The extent of the interregional differences in a country depends partly on which of the three processes is the most important and partly on how they function.

In the very first phases of development, where the urban system does not yet exist and where communication is very slow, regional income differences must have been of minor significance. Interregional trade may well exist, but no single region will consistantly benefit more from the trade than others, as long as no dominant centre has developed.

However, as soon as a high accessibility innovation centre has developed, this centre is likely to benefit more from the trade than other regions, because it will be in a monopoly position.

The slow process of innovation diffusion from the centre to the periphery found in the early stages of economic development will support the growing regional income differences. In this period the step-wise central place hierarchy is developed possibly with a strong primacy.

Later, however, when the role of innovation in the economy increases, when the speed of innovation diffusion goes up and when the diffusion process changes character from spatial towards hierarchical diffusion, the regional differences might start to decrease again. The primacy in the urban system might be reduced and the step-wise central place hierarchy will develop into an urban system characterized by a linear rank-size town distribution. This transformation is shown for Chile and Venezuela in Figures 5.1 and 5.2.

The extent to which this holds true, however, depends on the extent to which the threshold levels have been rising. If the threshold level rises very rapidly, it may offset the effect of more rapid innovation diffusion. In many developing countries this seems to have been the case. Here the threshold levels are probably in general higher than they were in the developed countries at an equivalent level of development, first, because the income distributions are very skew, and secondly, because the developing countries take over techniques from the developed countries.

Finally the spill-over effect might lead to decreasing regional differences. Recent investigations from the developed countries, however, indicate that this is far from certain. The spill-over effect no longer consists in the movement of complete industrial organizations. Development of improved communication networks has made it possible to send much of the most routine-type information, which formerly needed face-to-face contact, over the telecommunication networks. This has made it possible to separate the production and management units of large manufacturing organizations, so that only the production units are moved out, while the high-income management units are retained in the high accessibility

Table 5.3   The phases of urban-regional development

The innovation process	No innovation or spatial innovation diffusion	Mixed innovation diffusion	Hierarchical innovation diffusion	Conscious research and development
The importance of the spread effects	Multiplier effect	Innovation diffusion		Spill-over effect
The urban system	Independent villages	A step-wise central place hierarchy	An urban system. Rank-size distribution of towns	A system of urban fields
Degree of specialization	None	Sectorial specialization between cities of different size	Also specialization between cities of the same size	High level of specialization both according to functions and sectors
Transport and communication network	No network. Equally bad access in all directions	Multi-purpose network in form of a topologial tree	Complete inter-urban network	Specialized transport and communication networks

centre (Thorngren, 1970). In these circumstances the income effect of the spill-over is rather uncertain.

In any case, many non-agricultural activities will spread to the areas surrounding the large cities, and what Friedmann and Miller (1965) have characterized as urban fields are likely to develop. Friedmann and Miller estimate for the United States that the urban fields cover the areas within 150 km from cities with more than 250,000 inhabitants.

In Figure 5.4 these areas have been shown for South America, 1960. At present, these areas cannot, of course, be characterized as urban fields, but the figure may indicate the area of future urban fields of South America.

The changing structure of the innovation process is thus discernible as a changing structure in the urban-regional system. While the innovation process passes through the phases: no innovation at all or slow spatial innovation diffusion, more rapid mixed innovation diffusion, rapid hierarchical innovation diffusion, and conscious research and development, the urban-regional system passes through the following phases (see Table 5.3):

1. *Independent villages* with no specialization and only a rudimentary transport network;
2. *A step-wise central place hierarchy* with specialization among cities of different size according to the 'order of the goods' and connected by a network in the form of a topological tree;
3. *An integrated urban network* with rank-size distribution of the town sizes and connected by a complete inter-urban network. Here also inter-sectorial specialization between towns of the same size may take place;
4. *A system of urban fields* linked by specialized transport and communication networks and specialization both according to functions and sectors.

This, of course, should not be understood as a rigid system of stages. The three spread effects, the multiplier effect, the innovation diffusion process and the spill-over effect, are at work during all the phases, only their relative importance changes.

PART III

Integration and regional economic
development in South America

CHAPTER 6

Economic development as a process of integration

6.1 ECONOMIC DEVELOPMENT IN SOUTH AMERICA: AN HISTORICAL ACCOUNT

The spatial pattern of the South American continent is at present dominated by a number of coastal regions surrounded by narrow strips of integrated periphery, while the interior of the continent constitutes a largely non-integrated periphery.

This structure has come about through a development process in which three broad phases can be distinguished, the resource export phase, the import substitution phase, and the national integration phase. In the natural resource export phase most of the national income originated from the extraction of natural resources for European and North American markets, and practically all manufactured goods were imported. In this period most large South American cities were either terminals or transhipment points for foreign trade or administrative centres. Trade between South American countries was minimal. The cities that grew rapidly were, with few exceptions, seaports with good access to overseas markets.

With the onset of the economic crisis between the World Wars, the demand for natural resources decreased suddenly and drastically, and the dependence on natural resources as a source of income proved clearly unsatisfactory. Therefore, an attempt was made to strengthen the already slowly developing manufacturing industry through import restrictions and protective tariff walls. These policies favoured the largest of the shipping and administrative centres, which contained most of the national buying power for manufactured goods, and had the necessary infrastructure as well as access to decision-makers, bureaucracies and sources of information; they therefore led to further concentration in the few existing centres.[1]

---

[1] These first paragraphs as well as the theoretical framework for the empirical analysis in this chapter were presented for the first time in Pedersen and Stöhr (1969).

As the possibilities for industrial expansion within the limited markets of the capital cities became exhausted, new policies for economic development were sought through market expansion. The first of these policies to be applied were policies for national integration, *i.e.* for the incorporation of the national territories into the national market. These *national integration* policies have since the 1930s and especially after the Second World War been realized through industrial development programmes for provincial towns, regional development programmes, national development banks, and national transportation plans in many of the South American countries.

National integration policies, however, were soon seen to be insufficient. The buying power in most South American countries is simply too small to support specialized manufacturing production. The solution for this problem has been sought in policies for *international economic integration*, and during the 1960s such policies have been a prominent item on the agenda of discussions about economic development in Latin America. The purpose of international integration has first of all been to unite the core regions of Latin America in a common market; furthermore, national integration policies, especially in border areas and river valleys, would be greatly facilitated by multi-national co-operation.

A second reason for the insufficiency of national integration policies is that large proportions of the population even in the large cities are socially and economically marginal to the rest of the community; they do not participate in the market economy, or in political life. Therefore, only part of the possible effect of national integration effort has been achieved. The solution for this problem is the *social integration* of the marginal groups in the rest of society, and this played an increasingly important role in the discussion of economic development in the last part of the 1960s. This is especially true of the large cities, where the size of the marginal groups has increased rapidly, and where the ability of the national and international integration policies to solve the problems is least obvious.[2]

6.2 ECONOMIC DEVELOPMENT AS A PROCESS OF INTEGRATION

The problem of economic development in South America can therefore be considered a problem of social, national, and international integration. Integration is a process by which interaction among some units,

[2] For extensive and partly conflicting reviews of these policy issues see for instance Furtado (1970) and Frank (1967) and (1968).

groups, regions, or countries, is increased. A necessary condition for integration is easy access among the units, so that information about the possibilities for interaction can flow freely. But this alone is not sufficient.

There must also be structural relations between the units, such that each unit has something to offer which is demanded by one or more of the other units, and there must be somebody who is willing and able to organize the exchange. Finally, if the integration process is to continue, the units must be technically, economically and socially adaptable to changes in their environment: both to changes forced on them from outside and to those which result from the integration process itself, *i.e.* they must be able to innovate.

In the case of the social integration of marginal population a necessary condition is that the marginal families know about the possibilities open to them, such as health services, education, and work. Often the usual channels of information diffusion are not open to the marginal man, who may, for instance, be illiterate. But even if full information is available the marginal family might not be helped, either because it does not have the means of utilizing the services, or because the services supplied differ from those demanded or are offered on inappropriate terms. It will then be necessary to subsidize the services if social integration is to take place.

In the developed countries local markets were originally expanded through innovations which reduced unit costs, but required an increased scale of production. Introduction of such new large-scale technology became possible, because the increased demand created by price reductions was sufficient to absorb the increased production. Where the income distribution, as in South America, is very skewed this mechanism does not necessarily function because the price reduction made possible by an innovation may not increase demand sufficiently to offset the increased scale of production.

Also, in the case of national integration accessibility is a necessity, though not by itself a sufficient, prerequisite for integration between the core and the peripheral regions. An adequate interregional network of information flows is indispensable if knowledge about new technology, new organizations and new markets is to spread from the core regions to the periphery. However, even if the communication and transport networks are highly developed, integration will only take place (1) if the peripheral regions have something which is demanded by the core region to offer in exchange for the services and manufactures provided by the core region, and (2) if there is an entrepreneur who is willing and able to organize the exchange. If these conditions are not fulfilled, integration and development of the periphery can only take place if the core region is willing and able to subsidize the development effort.

In the developed countries the products and services which the periphery has generally been able to offer to the core region are natural resources and labour. Natural resources were demanded by the large cities in part as inputs to the manufacturing industry and in part as foodstuffs for the urban population. The increasing demand for labour was to begin with satisfied through migration to the cities, but as the cost of land and labour in the cities grew, the cheap labour available in the periphery became attractive to the most cost sensitive manufacturing sectors, and investments in these sectors started to spread to the periphery.

In South America these processes of diffusion through trade and investment are impeded by three factors. First, the demand of the large cities for foodstuff is often supplied more cheaply from abroad than from the national periphery. Secondly, the manufacturing industry is not sufficiently developed to utilize the mineral resources which can be supplied by the periphery; the mineral resources, therefore, must be exported to the more developed countries and the result is disintegration rather than integration. Thirdly, where economic development in the United States and Western Europe led to labour shortage and rising wages in the cities, the trend in South America has rather been for the labour supply in the cities to increase much more rapidly than the demand; in general therefore wages have not increased sufficiently to offset the disadvantages of moving to the periphery.

Finally, in the case of international integration Figure 3.3 indicates that as production shifts from primary to secondary production, the easy flow of market information between the trading countries becomes increasingly significant. Accessibility, however, is not a sufficient, only a necessary, condition for integration. The other key concept in the discussion about international integration in Latin America has been complementarity. The argument is that as long as all countries in Latin America produce almost the same products, namely, primary products and consumer goods, none of the countries will have anything to offer which the other countries do not have already. The national economies, therefore, must be planned so that they will in time become complementary to each other. The Latin American Common Market made provisions for such complementarity agreements, but in reality only a few have been carried out (Dell, 1966, p. 129). One of the reasons for this might be that much of the complementarity discussion has been carried out on the basis of an industrial classification that is too crude; for instance, which country should produce aluminium and which steel. A decision of this kind, to renounce producing aluminium for the right to produce steel, could in time of crisis have far-reaching consequences, both economic and political, and no government in South America has been willing to take any such decision.

Complementarity at this level of industrial classification is also contrary to the complementarity dominating the European Common Market. Here, the complementarity is found among much more specialized sectors; it is complementarity among 5–6 digit sectors rather than among 2–3 digit sectors. Such highly specialized complementarity has far fewer political consequences, because production in a moment of crisis can be reorganized with relative ease to produce products which can no longer be imported. It is also likely to lead to much more trade. This can be illustrated by the input-output matrices for Chile, 1962 (ODEPLAN) and Brazil, 1959 (Rijckeghem, 1967). These matrices contain 54 and 32 sectors, respectively, of which in both cases 20 are manufacturing sectors. Of the total trade between and within these 20 two-digit manufacturing sectors, 42% and 54% respectively, took place within the 20 sectors (*i.e.* they appeared in the diagonal elements of the matrix) while 58% and 46% took place between the sectors; and 44% of the imports into the 20 sectors in Chile came from the same two-digit sectors in the exporting country.

If highly specialized complementarity is necessary for integration rather than a more broad-sectored complementarity, complementarity can only be achieved through specialization, which in turn can only be achieved through innovation. Accessibility, therefore, will be a necessary condition not only for integration, but also for complementarity.

6.3 INTEGRATION AND THE ROLE OF ACCESSIBILITY

The three aspects of integration:[3] accessibility, structural relations, and adaptability or ability to innovate are not independent of each other.

No matter how good the accessibility of a region may be, interaction with other regions will only be meaningful and rewarding if structural relations exist between them. These structural relations might be based on complementarity, such as specialization in different economic sectors, or on similarity, as is the case in Latin America with the common language and the common anti-North-American feeling.

Structural relations can only be exploited where interaction takes place, and where structural relations do not exist, they might be developed

[3] For a similar exposition see Deutsch (1970).

by planned innovation, of the kind indicated in the goals of the Latin American Common Market.

Finally, the adaptability of a region or its ability to innovate is, as we saw in chapter 4, highly dependent on both interaction and structural relations with other regions. For instance, technological innovations in most cases require larger hinterlands than were needed by the technology existing before, either because of the scale economies in production, or because the demand is so specialized that only a small fraction of the population belongs to the potential market. Innovation, therefore, often requires increased accessibility, and increased accessibility is of little consequence if it is not followed by innovation.

The purpose of chapters 7 and 8 is to explore the effect of integration on regional economic development. In this exploration integration will be measured in terms of accessibility or potential interaction. It is here assumed that interaction between the regions of the continent will initiate an innovation process that will create and maintain a set of structural relations between the regions.

This, of course, will not necessarily be the case. Although the empirical analysis to be carried out in chapter 7 does indicate that a measure of accessibility can explain a large part of the regional differences in urbanization and regional economic development, concentration on the accessibility aspect of integration is clearly a weakness of the investigation. Accessibility has been shown to be an important factor in the innovation process but it is not the only one, and the analysis, therefore, is only a partial analysis of the role of accessibility in regional economic development.

CHAPTER 7

An accessibility model of regional economic development

7.1 OUTLINE OF A MODEL

The purpose of this chapter is to investigate empirically the role of information accessibility in determining the spatial distribution of urbanization and economic development in South America.

The initial hypothesis, which we will have to modify later, is that the spatial distribution of urbanization and economic development is determined basically by the level of information accessibility. Information accessibility functions through the joint processes of innovation and integration. Innovation in a society can occur either through the rationalization of old activities or through the introduction of new activities. In both cases innovations are likely to lead either to higher *per capita* incomes or more jobs, or to both, and thus to attract a stream of migrants. Although both urbanization and economic development are determined by the level of information accessibility, they are not necessarily simultaneously determined; rationalization might well lead to increased income without creating new jobs, and the creation of new jobs need not result in increased *per capita* income.

On the other hand, urbanization and economic development will tend to reinforce each other partly through multiplier effects and agglomeration economies and partly through the changes in population structure resulting from selective migration. Higher incomes and increased urban population both result in increased demand or urban products and services; both will therefore tend to generate more income and attract more labour.

The predominance of young adults among the migrants leads to higher activity rates in the urban areas than in the rural and therefore to higher *per capita* incomes. This effect will be treated in part IV.

Finally urbanization and economic development will influence accessibility and thus the future process of innovation diffusion. This feedback effect is the topic of chapter 8.

119

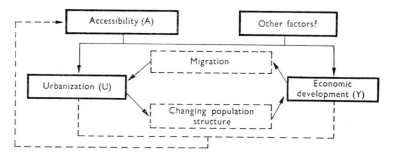

Fig. 7.1. *Accessibility as a determinant of urbanization and economic development. A model*

These hypotheses are summarized in the flow chart shown in Figure 7.1. In the following sections the three relationships between information accessibility, urbanization, and economic development taken two at a time will be investigated on the basis of the data for the same regions which were analysed in chapter 2. However, before empirical tests of these relations can be carried out, measurements of the three concepts involved must be obtained. None of the concepts is easy to capture in single indices, as will be attempted here, and clearly with the available South American statistics only crude and approximate measurement can be made.

By *urbanization* we shall understand the percentage of the population living in urban places. The concept of urbanization thus corresponds to factor 1 in the factor analysis in chapter 2, and emphasizes the physical aspects of urbanization. For a discussion of the data, see appendix A.

As a measure of *economic development*, regional *per capita* income will be used. A discussion of the data base and estimation procedure for the income figures is given in appendix B.

The most difficult of the three concepts to measure is that of information accessibility. This will therefore be discussed at some length in the following section.

7.2 MEASURING INFORMATION ACCESSIBILITY

The shape of an index of information accessibility depends on the structure of the communication network. In a village economy, where all information from the outside world is received from the neighbouring villages, only the connexions to these villages need to be included in the index; and in a central place hierarchy, where all information is received from the nearest higher-order town, only the connexion to this town needs to be included. In an integrated system of cities information can be received from everywhere, and we need, therefore, a more complex index of the communication flows between all the cities. Finally in the urban fields we shall need specialized indices for different activities.

Most of the regions of South America are in the period of transition from a step-wise central place hierarchy to a fully integrated urban system. We need, therefore, an index which can describe the information flows from every point to all centres of population. Such an index can be based on the gravity model.

Application of the gravity model to information flows was discussed in section 4.5. There it was concluded that the flow of information I_{ij}, between two regions i and j with the populations P_i and P_j, can be described approximately by a gravity model saying that,

$$I_{ij} = k(u_i P_i)(u_j P_j) f(r_{ij}) \tag{7.1}$$

where u_i and u_j are weights introduced because not all the inhabitants participate equally in the interaction, $f(r_{ij})$ is a decreasing function of the distance (or interaction cost) between i and j, and k is a constant. Based on this gravity model we can construct an index A_i of the accessibility from a population unit in point i to the population in all regions j ($j = 1, 2, \ldots, n$) by setting $u_i P_i = 1$ and summing over all j,

$$A_i = k \sum_{j=1}^{n} u_j P_j f(r_{ij}) \tag{7.2}$$

The value of this index can be computed in a large number of points i, and the variation over space of A_i will give an idea of the variation in accessibility. As we are only interested in the relative differences in accessibility, we can set $k = 1$ to simplify expression (7.2).

We shall assume the distance decay function in (7.2) to be

$$f(r_{ij}) = \frac{1}{r_{ij}}$$

Although empirical investigations from other parts of the world show that more complicated functions often fit reality better, such a complication does not seem justified here because we have no empirical investigations from South America to base it on. The error introduced by using a too simple distance decay function is also likely to be smaller in expression (7.2) than in expression (7.1), because many of the errors in (7.1) will tend to disappear in the summation.

The resulting accessibility index[1]

$$A_i = \sum_{j=1}^{n} \frac{u_j P_j}{r_{ij}} \tag{7.3}$$

reflects the structure of the transport and communication network. Changes in the communicating masses of population $u_j P_j$, or in the links between them, r_{ij}, will lead to changes in the accessibility index. We can, therefore, use the index to study the effects on the accessibility structure of network improvements and population growth if the masses and distances are measured in relevant units.

In the expression (7.3) the mass ($u_j P_j$) should be a measure of the information generated in region *j*. It is clear that not all people participate equally in the communication process; populations with a central location and a high level of education and with a high income are likely to participate more frequently than others. We might consider u_j as a measure of participation or social integration. As a substitute for information generation we shall use the urban population (= total population × urbanization). From a theoretical point of view this is not a very satisfactory substitute, especially in South America where the immediate impression is that the participation of large groups of the urban population is rather low. In practice, however, level of urbanization, level of literacy, and income *per capita* all are highly correlated. Any of the three measures could therefore be used empirically without much difference. For the sake of policy conclusions, however, it is extremely important to remember that u_j should refer to participation and not to urbanization, even though the distinction is less important at the present level of generalization.

The distance, r_{ij}, will be interpreted as a measure of the resistance to spatial information flows. The important aspect of access is considered to be that of communication rather than that of transportation. Transportation costs have seldom been prohibitive to trade. Long distances to European and North American markets, for instance, were never a serious hindrance to Japanese exports. However, every flow of goods is preceded by a flow of information in the form of letters, cables, calls, and personal trips, and it is important that these flows should be carried out with ease.

How the spatial resistance is to be measured depends, of course, on the

[1] In much of the literature this index is known as the 'potential'. For bibliographies and detailed descriptions of the gravity and potential concepts, see Olsson (1965), and Isard (1960).

communication network. Where telecommunication networks are highly developed, part of the information flow clearly uses these networks; but, as we discussed at length in chapter 4.6, a large part of the most important information flow is likely to continue to be face-to-face contacts, and the transportation network, therefore, is likely to be at least as important as the communication networks.

In South America this is even more true because, although long distance telecommunication connexions have in recent years been established by means of satellites, the spread of telephones outside the largest cities has still not proceeded very far, and many of the smallest towns either do not have a telephone at all or only have one (Lipinsky, 1969).

Finally, widespread use of telecommunications in a community develops in most cases in response to demand rather than in advance of demand, and demand for telecommunications does not generally exist where no physical interaction takes place. From a development viewpoint, therefore, the transportation networks appear to be much more important than communication networks, even though we are basically interested in the information flows.

Among the transport networks road transportation is most important, especially over short distances. But even over long distances bus transportation plays an important role; for instance, there was in 1967 a regular bus service on the route Santiago–Lima–Quito (5,600 km), and between Asunción and Buenos Aires (1,500 km) there is a daily bus service, except after heavy rain when the road is impassable.

Over long distances the air route network is important for passenger traffic; and although shipping routes are generally of little importance for passenger transportation, they predominate in goods transportation, and since new products in themselves have an important information content, the spread of new products is an important means of information diffusion. Both airline and shipping routes, therefore, should be taken into account.

On the other hand, there are only a few places on the continent where the railroads play an important role, except in bulk transportation, which has a very small information content; and even where railroads are important in passenger transportation, bus services are often both cheaper and faster, though they may not be as comfortable. Railroads are, therefore, not likely to add much to accessibility.

The complete accessibility of the South American regions should be computed as a weighted sum of accessibility indices for the road, airline, and maritime shipping networks. Unfortunately we have no way of determining the weights which should be used. Rather than introduce arbitrary weights it was, therefore, decided not to take into account the airline and maritime transportation accessbilities, but simply use the road accessibility (see appendix F).

7.3 DISTANCES IN THE ROAD NETWORK

In the road network distances are computed as actual road distances weighted by an index for travel costs per km.

Information on the distances has been obtained from the gasoline companies' road maps; editions from the first half of the 1960s were used.

The travel cost index assumes that the kilometre cost for travel on gravel roads is twice the cost of travel on paved roads, while travel costs on dirt roads are four times the cost of travel on paved roads. Unfortunately there are few investigations against which to check these assumptions. One of the few is made by Soberman (1966) for Venezuela, and some of his results are shown in Table 7.1.

Table 7.1   *Total truck operating costs on paved, gravel, and earth roads (in Venezuelan bolivars per vehicle-kilometre)*

	Truck capacity in metric tons:					
	7.8		15.9		23.5	
	Bolivars	Index	Bolivars	Index	Bolivars	Index
Paved roads	0.685	1.00	0.902	1.00	1.113	1.00
Gravel roads	1.311	1.91	1.743	1.93	2.181	1.96
Earth roads	1.491	2.18	2.060	2.29	2.581	2.32

Source: Soberman (1966), p. 68.

Soberman's results show that the cost factor 2 between paved and gravel roads is realistic, while a cost factor 4 between paved and earth roads is too large. The reason for nevertheless choosing the cost factor 4 is that the earth roads are generally impassable for part of the year. This is a serious hindrance to development and should in one way or another be taken into account. As we have no investigations on which to base an evaluation of this interruption of traffic, the factor 4 is simply an arbitrary choice.

In measuring distances two difficult problems need to be solved. The first is the determination of the accessibility within the region itself. As the internal distances are small the accessibility due to the region itself will be large; it is, therefore, unfortunate that the internal distances are so poorly determined. When the regions are, as here, rather large and the population is unevenly distributed, the average internal distances will tend to be too large, resulting in too small accessibilities. To avoid this the accessibilities due to the regions themselves have been computed as the largest of the following two measures:

1. Total urban population in the region divided by an estimated average internal distance;
2. Population of the largest metropolitan area in the region divided by a distance equivalent to 100 km of paved road.

The defect of this simplified proceedure is that it does not allow changes in the local road networks to be taken into account specifically, and the development of these are sure to be very important. However, to the extent to which local road improvements follow the degree of urbanization, they are accounted for.

The second problem in measuring distances is to evaluate the influence of international borders. Where such borders are crossed, customs and the cost of delays should be added to the transport costs. We have no way of constructing a general index of border crossing costs and shall therefore work with two extreme alternatives, one in which border crossing costs are assumed to be infinity and where transport and communication across the borders therefore cannot take place at all, and one in which border crossing costs are assumed to be zero and where borders therefore represent no hindrance to transport and communication. The first assumption seems reasonable for the situation before 1950, and the second assumption represents the future date at which the process of international integration has been completed.

In 1960 we are likely to find an intermediate situation in which the cost of crossing international borders was still very high though not completely prohibitive. Customs duties at 50–100% are still not unusual, and the delays at the border are often long (Dell, 1966, p. 223); border crossing with an automobile requires a guaranty deposit of U.S. $ 2,000 in most countries, and telephone calls between the South American countries in many cases had until recently to pass through New York.

Ideally, these border crossing costs should be added to the transport and communication costs. Unfortunately, we have no direct way of evaluating these costs; therefore in the empirical study we shall attempt to evaluate the effect of integration indirectly by assuming that total accessibility is the sum of accessibility to the regions within the nation and a fraction, h, of the accessibility to the regions in other countries, *i.e.*

$$A_{\text{Total}} = A_{\text{National}} - h A_{\text{Integration}}$$

where h varies from 0 to 1; representing the average level of integration h might be considered a measure of international integration. Clearly h is only a very crude average; first, because the border crossing costs are not the same at all borders, and secondly, because the effect of a given border crossing cost depends on the transport and communication cost to which it should be added, and thus will be relatively more important for regions close to the border than for regions far from the border.

In the empirical analysis in this chapter we shall assume that the value of h in 1960 was $\frac{1}{4}$. This value has been selected on the basis of an empirical analysis in which the correlation coefficients between accessibility and urbanization and between accessibility and *per capita* income were computed for different values of h ($h = 0$, $\frac{1}{4}$, $\frac{1}{2}$, $\frac{3}{4}$ and 1). The result of this analysis was very inconclusive as the correlation coefficients only varied by a few per cent when h varied from 0 to 1. However, in both sets of correlations the maximum value of the correlation coefficient was obtained for $h = \frac{1}{4}$ (see appendix E). As this value of h seems reasonable it was chosen even though the empirical analysis is far from conclusive. Fortunately the qualitative conclusions of the analysis in this chapter are not very sensitive to changes in h.

7.4 THE INTERRELATION BETWEEN URBANIZATION AND ECONOMIC DEVELOPMENT

In this section we shall analyse the relationship between urbanization and economic development defined as, respectively, per cent urban population and income *per capita* in the different regions around 1960.

According to the model outlined in section 7.1, the relation between urbanization and economic development is one of interdependency rather than one of dependency, a two-way relation rather than a one-way cause and effect relation. The main axis of the two-dimensional distribution of urbanization and economic development will therefore be computed instead of the ordinary regression equation.

As the shape of the relationship between the two variables is not known, both a linear, an exponential, and a power function have been tried. The results are shown in Table 7.2 and in Figures 7.2 and 7.3. The correlation coefficients show that the linear relation is definitely poorer than the two others, while the exponential and power functions are approximately equally good.

To evaluate the three equations we shall try to extrapolate the relationship to zero and 100% urbanization respectively to see what consequences this has for the level of *per capita* income.

Extrapolation of the linear relation to zero urbanization leads to large negative incomes, which is not very realistic. This relation, therefore, must be rejected.

The exponential function for zero urbanization leads to a *per capita* income of about US $ 100 *per capita* per year. This income corresponds to the income found in South American regions with 15–20% urban population, and it is about twice as high as the income found in the least urbanized countries of the world, such as Malawi, which in 1960 had a *per capita* income below US $ 50 and less than 10% of its population living in urban places. The exponential function, therefore, must also be rejected.

Finally, the power function leads to zero income for zero urbanization. When it is remembered that the income measured by our data is money income only, this seems reasonable, because where there is no urban population there is no market for rural products and consequently no rural money income. For 10–20% urbanization, it results in incomes of US $ 20 to US $ 65 per year, which corresponds to the incomes found in the least urbanized countries in the world.

For 100% urbanization the linear relation leads to a *per capita* income of US $ 2,040, the exponential relation leads to 1,330 US $ *per capita*, and the potential relation to US $ 1,530 *per capita*. If we leave out of account the linear relation, which we had to reject above, the power function comes closest to the incomes found in the most urbanized countries in the world, although it is still far below them.

For several reasons we shall therefore, in the following prefer the power function between urbanization and *per capita* income:[2]

$$\log Y = -0.585 + 1.8847 \log U$$

or

$$Y = 0.26 U^{1.88} \qquad\qquad (R = 0.79; \ R^2 = 0.63)$$

This equation has two interesting consequences. First, it shows that *per capita* income inreases more rapidly than the level of urbanization, *i.e.*

[2] National differences, both those that are real and those that are due to variations in definitions of urbanization are one of the reasons why the correlation coefficient is no higher than $R = 0.79$. To test the importance of such national differences we included for each country a dummy variable having the value 1 for regions within the country and the value zero in other regions. Of these dummy variables only the one corresponding to Argentina proved to be significant. When this variable was included the correlation rose from 0.79 to 0.86.

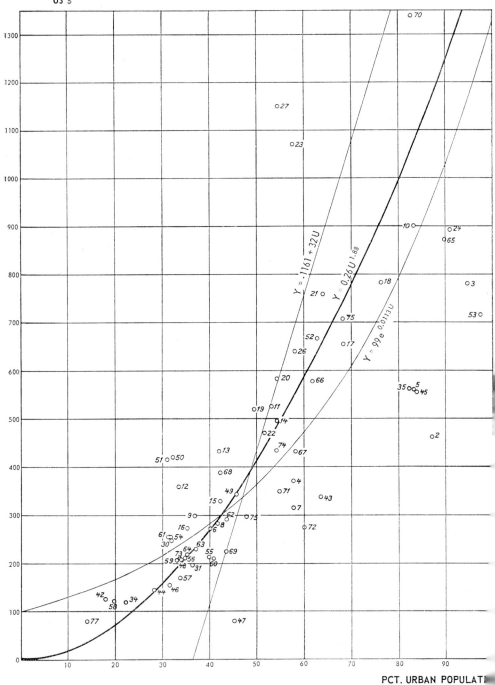

Fig. 7.2. *The relation between per capita income, Y, and urbanization, U, estimated by linear, exponential, and power functions, 1960*

the income increase corresponding to a 10% increase in the level of urbanization from 70 to 80% is larger than that corresponding to a 10% increase in urbanization from 20 to 30%.

Secondly, it shows that the income, US $ 1,530 *per capita* per year, corresponding to 100% urbanization in Latin America is much smaller than the equivalent income found in the world generally. This could be a

Table 7.2 *Regression between urbanization (U) and per capita income (Y), 1960 (67 regions*)*

	Coefficients in expressions of the form			Value of Y in US $ *per capita*, per year for U equal to		
	Linear relation ($R = 0.62$; $R^2 = 0.39$)					
	$Y = a+bU$					
	a	b	δ_b	0%	100%	
Regression equation: $Y = f(U)$	-158	12.94	1.94	-158	1091	
Regression equation: $U = f(Y)$	-1170	32.09		-1170	2039	
Main axis: $f(Y) = f(U)$	-1161	32.01		-1161	2040	
	Exponential relation ($R = 0.75$; $R^2 = 0.57$)					
	$\log Y = a+bU$					
	a	b	δ_b	0%	10%	100%
Regression equation: $\log Y = f(U)$	2.007	0.0110	0.0012	102	130	1261
Regression equation: $U = f(\log Y)$	1.576	0.0193		38	59	3164
Main axis: $f(\log Y) = f(U)$	1.994	0.0113		99	128	1331
	Potential relation ($R = 0.79$; $R^2 = 0.63$)					
	$\log Y = a+b \log U$					
	a	b	δ_b	1%	10%	100%
Regression equation: $\log Y = f(\log U)$	0.3435	1.3315	0.1261	2.21	47	1014
Regression equation: $\log U = f(\log Y)$	-0.958	2.1079		0.11	13	1820
Main axis: $f(\log Y) = f(\log U)$	-0.585	1.8847		0.26	20	1528

*Data for Bolivia and the Guianas are not available.

All regression coefficients are significant at far above 99% level.

10

result of the over-urbanization which has often been claimed to exist in Latin America (see, for instance, Friedmann and Lackington, 1967, and Sovani, 1964). Over-urbanization means that urbanization has proceeded more rapidly than industrialization, resulting in the creation of a large group of workers who are unemployed, semi-employed, or employed in very low productivity occupations, service and handicraft jobs. Although living in urban areas, part of the urban population does not in reality participate in the urban economy, and ought not be counted as urban population. The line in Figure 7.3 should therefore be shifted to the left. If we assume that a 100% urbanized country without over-urbanization will have a *per capita* income corresponding to the incomes of the most urbanized countries around 1960, that is US $ 2,000 to US $ 2,500 per year, we shall reduce the level of urbanization with a factor at between 0.77 and 0.87 corresponding to a marginal urban population at 13–23%. This estimation of marginal population is of the same order of magnitude as that found by people who have tackled this problem more directly (Friedmann and Lackington, 1967).

The lower incomes for a given level of urbanization found in South America can also be due to under-utilization of the available productive capacity. There are many indications that this is actually the case, for instance Dell (1966, p. 19) wrote that the production of the Brazilian automobile factories corresponds to only 20–50% of one workshift, and in Argentina insufficiency of electricity has created a bottleneck for manufacturing production. In a paper on gross productivity growth in five Latin American countries, Bruton (1967) found that in fact the productivity gain during the 1950s was about zero because the innovations which had been introduced had not been fully utilized.

7.5 THE INCOME-ACCESSIBILITY RELATION

Areas with high accessibility will tend, according to the theory outlined in part II and in the beginning of this chapter, to adopt innovations more rapidly than areas with low accessibility. Innovation means either new activities or productivity increases in old activities. We should therefore expect high accessibility areas to be high income areas and to find a high correlation between accessibility and *per capita* income.

To test this hypothesis we plotted the regions of South America on the accessibility – income diagram in Figure 7.4, and computed the correlation coefficient between accessibility (as defined in sections 7.2 and 7.3)

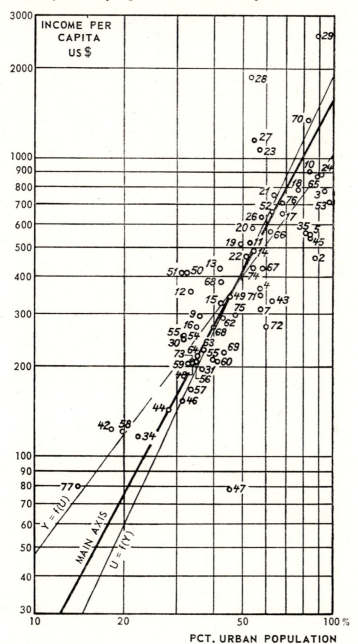

Fig. 7.3. *The relation between per capita income, Y, and urbanization, U, estimated as a power function, 1960*

and *per capita* income.[3] At first the result was very discouraging. The correlation coefficient only was $R = 0.32$, indicating that only 10% ($R^2 = 0.10$) of the total variance in *per capita* income can be explained by differences in accessibility.

Closer inspection of the diagram on Figure 7.4, however, showed that the deviant regions correspond closely to those which in chapter 2 were designated as peripheral regions, so that the mineral resource regions tend to have higher incomes than expected, while the agricultural settlement areas tend to have lower incomes than expected. When these peripheral regions were excluded from the correlation, the correlation coefficient rose to $R = 0.76$, indicating that 57% ($R^2 = 0.57$) of the income differences in the central regions can be explained by differences in accessibility. The relation between *per capita* income Y_{60} and accessibility A_{60} in the consolidated regions is given by the regression equation:

$$\log Y_{60} = 1.04 + 0.68 \log A_{60}$$
$$(0.09)$$

or

$$Y_{60} = 10.94 \, A_{60}^{0.68} \qquad\qquad (R = 0.76; \ R^2 = 0.57)$$

This finding, that *per capita* income in the consolidated regions is dependent on information accessibility while this is not the case in the peripheral regions, indicates that, while accessibility is the most important determinant of economic development in the consolidated regions, some other factors, such as capital and natural resources, are more important in the peripheral regions.[4]

Unfortunately we have no ideal measure of natural resource availability to enable us to test this hypothesis directly but, as poor substitutes, the two variables *per cent of total work force employed in mining* and *population density* may be used. The inclusion of these variables in the regression equation actually improves the correlation coefficient for all regions from $R = 0.36$ to $R = 0.65$ and thus supports the hypothesis that natural resources are an important determinant of income in the peripheral areas (see Table 7.3). When the improvement in correlation is not larger than from 0.36 to 0.65, this may be because the high *per capita* incomes found in the peripheral regions are not always due to natural

---

[3] A logarithmic transformation was used on both variables, first, because tests showed this to give the best result and secondly, because only then will the three equations between income, urbanization and accessibility be consistent.

[4] For an analogy with social physics see appendix G.

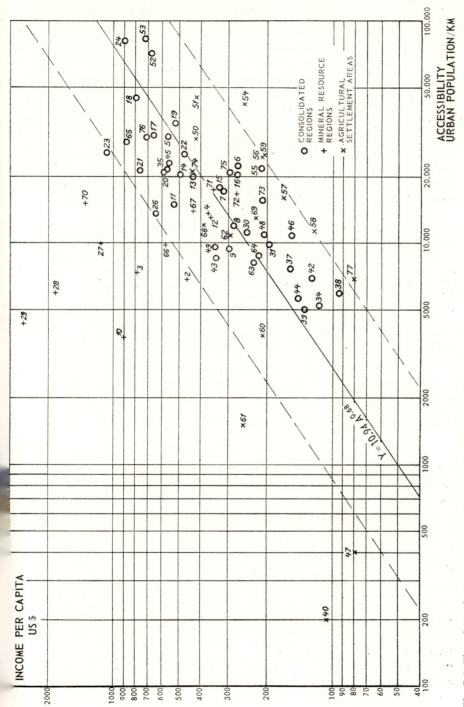

Fig. 7.4. *The relation between per capita income and accessibility, 1960*

resources; sometimes they are due rather to relatively high employment in services often subsidized by the national government, for instance, in the form of government service or military establishments. Although such subsidies also occur in consolidated regions, they are likely to be much more visible in peripheral regions with a small population, because even a large *per capita* subsidy here is unlikely to be a heavy burden on the total national budget.

The main finding of this section, that information accessibility is an important determinant of the income level in the consolidated, but not in the peripheral regions, is consistent with the results of investigations in the United States, Sweden, and Denmark.

In the United States, Warntz (1965) found that the *per capita* income was only correlated with the income potential (US \$/mile) when the southern and western states were excluded from the correlation. The

Table 7.3 *Multiple regression between per capita income (log Y), as dependent variable, and accessibility (log A), mining employment (log M), and population density (log D), as independent variables, 1960*

(54 regions*)

Independent variables	Regression coefficients b	Standard error of regression coefficients δ_b	Beta- coefficient β	Correlation coefficients		
				log M	log D	log Y
Constant	1.54	–	–	–	–	–
Accessibility, log A	0.56*	0.12	0.60	−0.16	0.52*	0.36*
Percentage mining employment, log M	0.20*	0.05	0.45	1.00	−0.14	0.40*
Population density, log D	−0.15*	0.06	−0.33	–	1.00	−0.06

Multiple correlation coefficient $R = 0.65^*$; $R^2 = 0.42$

*Data for Bolivia, Brazil, and Guianas are not available.
Regression and correlation coefficients marked with * are statistically significant at a 99% level.

southern states had consistently lower incomes than expected while in the western states incomes were consistently higher than expected. This seems to be fully consistent with our finding for South America, because mining and services tend to be more important in the western states than elsewhere, while agriculture is more important in the southern states than elsewhere (Perloff, Dunn, Lampard and Muth, 1960, p. 263).

When *per capita* income was replaced by income density (US $ per sq. mile) Warntz found the correlation to be valid for all states ($R = 0.92$). The reason for this becomes clear when it is remembered that income density can be written as

$$\frac{\text{Income}}{\text{Area}} = \frac{\text{Income}}{\text{Inhabitants}} \times \frac{\text{Inhabitants}}{\text{Area}} \tag{7.4}$$

or the product of *per capita* income and population density. If, as we did above, we consider population density as a crude (negatively related) measure of resource availability, equation (7.4) shows that the variance of the *per capita* income due to resource availability has been partly removed by multiplication with population density.

To test this hypothesis on the South American data, we have made the correlation between income density and accessibility for all regions. The correlation coefficient was found to be $R = 0.70$, which is much higher than the correlation found for all regions between *per capita* income and accessibility ($R = 0.32$), and is comparable to the correlation found for the consolidated regions between income *per capita* and accessibility ($R = 0.76$).

In Sweden Nordborg (1967) found a correlation coefficient $R = 0.72$ between *per capita* income and potential. This correlation coefficient, however, would be very much improved by eliminating the four northern districts, which are truly peripheral in the economic system, and have higher incomes than expected, just as was found for the mineral resource periphery in South America.

Finally, for Denmark Larsen (1970) found for all regions a correlation coefficient between *per capita* income and accessibility which varied from 0.74 in 1950 to 0.83 in 1960 and 0.89 in 1965. As there is no region in Denmark which can be characterized as peripheral these high correlation coefficients were to be expected. It is interesting to note that the importance of accessibility seems to be increasing (see section 7.8 below).

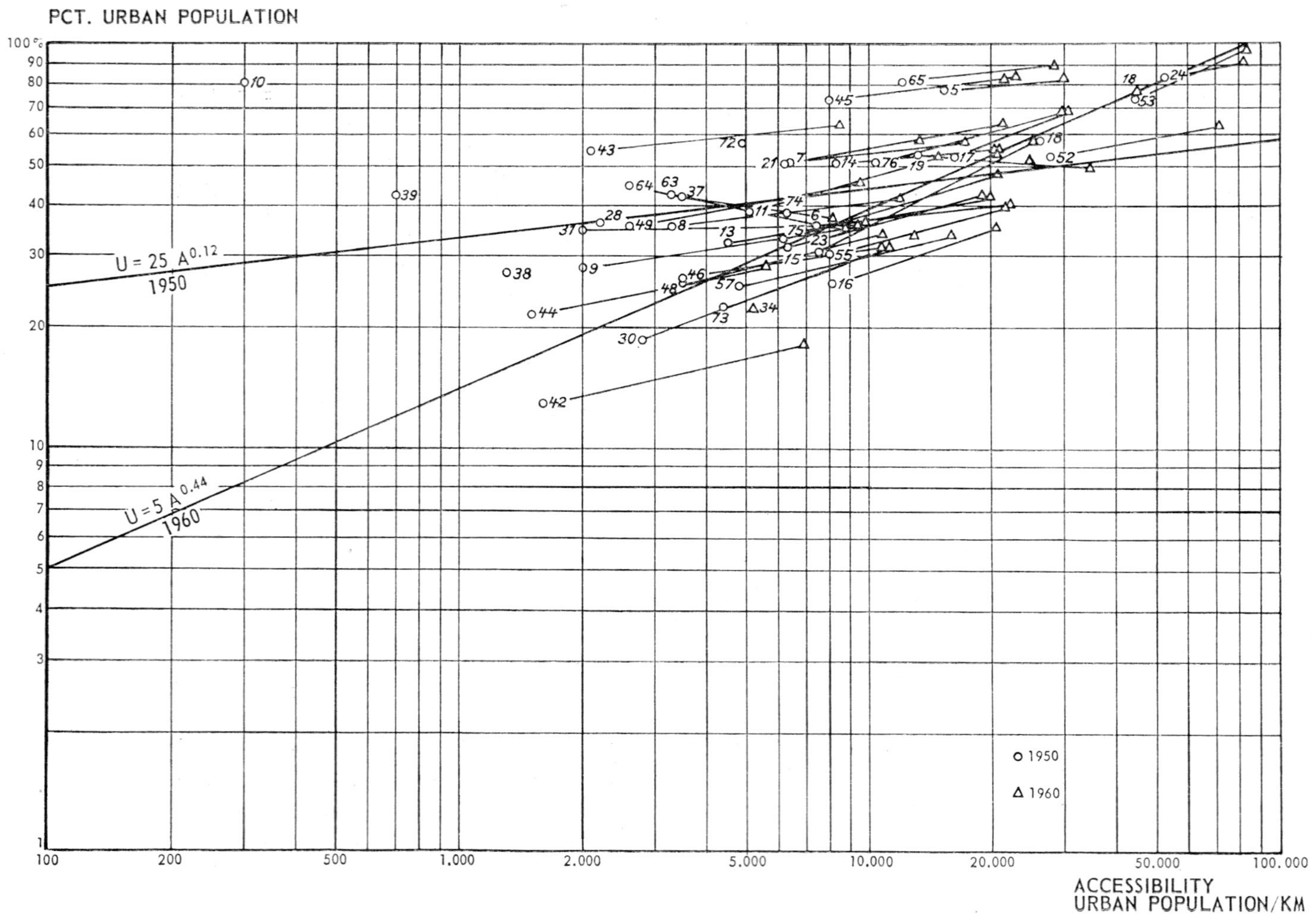

PCT. URBAN POPULATION
ACCESSIBILITY
URBAN POPULATION/KM
U = 25 A^0.12
1950
U = 5 A^0.44
1960
o 1950
Δ 1960

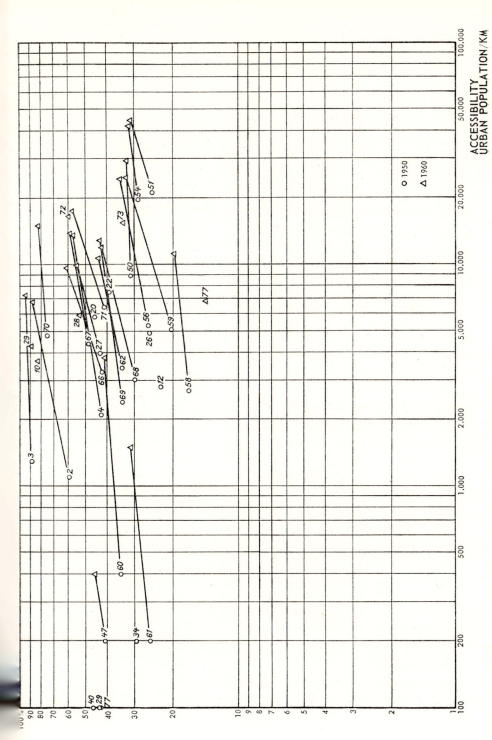

Fig. 7.5b *The relation between urbanization and accessibility. Peripheral regions*

7.6 THE URBANIZATION-ACCESSIBILITY RELATION

For the third relation, between urbanization and accessibility, the same
regressions and correlations were run as for the second. The results of
these regressions and correlations are shown in Table 7.4 and Figure 7.5
a and b. They are wholly analogous to those obtained for *per capita*
income. It can be seen that the relation is only significant for the consolidated regions and can be expressed by the regression equation:

$$(41 \text{ regions}) \quad U_{60} = 5.0 \, A_{60}^{0.44} \qquad (R = 0.73; \, R^2 = 0.54) \quad (7.5)$$

Because no income data are available for 1950, it has not been possible
to compute the first two regressions for that year. However, both accessibility and urbanization have been estimated for 1950, so we can
construct the accessibility-urbanization regression. The results of this
regression for all regions and for the consolidated regions alone are shown
in the lower part of Table 7.4. Neither of the equations are significant at a
99% level; but as expected, the regression for the consolidated regions is
a little better than that for all regions, though not much.

Table 7.4 *Regression equations between urbanization(U) and accessibility (A),
1950 and 1960. Consolidated regions (C.r.) and all regions (A.r.)**

Year	Regions included	Regression equations	Coefficients of correlation R	determination R^2
1960	C.r. (41)	$\log U = 0.70 + 0.44^* \log A$ (0.07)	0.73*	0.54
	A.r. (67)	$\log U = 1.41 + 0.12 \log A$ (0.06)	0.25	0.06
1950	C.r. (44)	$\log U = 1.40 + 0.12 \log A$ (0.05)	0.34	0.12
	A.r. (63)	$\log U = 1.46 + 0.07 \log A$ (0.04)	0.22	0.05

*Coefficients marked * are significant at a 99% level.

Two reasons may be advanced for the very low correlation and regression coefficients found for 1950: first, information accessibility might have been less important for development in 1950 than it was in 1960; secondly, the information accessibility index for 1950 might have been wrongly computed. Both reasons are probably true: the first, because the relative importance of natural resources is likely to decrease in time and should therefore have been more important in 1950 than in 1960; the second, because the urban system in 1950 was much less integrated than it was in 1960.

The rapid increase from 1950 to 1960 in the role of accessibility in the explanation of the level of urbanization indicates that the process of development in this period underwent an important change. The change which took place was the development of the urban system from a traditional urban hierarchy and isolated towns into an integrated urban system. This process is still going on, and we should therefore expect the correlation coefficient between accessibility and urbanization to continue to increase. This is also in line with the increasing correlation coefficient between income and accessibility which Larsen (1970) found for Denmark (see section 7.5 above).

In connexion with the structural change which seems to have taken place between 1950 and 1960, we might ask at which levels of urbanization and accessibility this shift took place. A tentative answer to this question might be afforded by the level of urbanization corresponding to the nearly horizontal regression line for 1950, or about 25% urban population.[5] On the regression line for 1960 this 25% urban population corresponds to an accessibility of 3,000 to 4,000 inh./km, which in turn corresponds to a *per capita* income of US $ 110 to US $ 135 per year.

At the upper end of the distribution, urbanization by definition cannot be larger than 100 per cent. According to the equation Figure 7.5a, 100% urbanization should be achieved with information accessibility at about 90,000 to 95,000 urban inhabitants per km. After this point economic development can no longer take place through urbanization in the physical sense of the word, and the structure of the development process will have to change again. The change which is likely to take place is the one described in chapter 5. The multi-purpose town centres and the multi-purpose communication networks will be replaced by large corporate organizations and specialized communication channels.

In the United States this change has already started; it might, therefore,

---

[5] This tentative conclusion depends, of course, on the hypothesis that it is possible to conclude from time series data to cross-section data, a hypothesis which need not hold true.

be interesting to see at what accessibility level this change took place there. Unfortunately, the only accessibility measures published for the United States are based on airline distances and either population or income, and they cannot be compared directly with our results for South America. However, a rough estimate of a North American potential comparable to the one computed for South America can be made on the basis of Warntz's (1965) income potential map for 1956.[6] This estimate indicates that in 1956 only the western third of the United States, except California, had accessibilities below the 90,000 to 95,000 inh./km. According to Berry and Neils (1969), practically all the rest of the country is within commuting range of a metropolitan area of more than 250,000 inhabitants, and thus in reality can be considered fully urbanized.

It seems therefore that the accessibility level at which full urbanization has been reached in the United States corresponds roughly to the accessibility at which equation (7.5) predicts that full urbanization will take place in South America. The *per capita* income corresponding to this accessibility is, however, smaller in South America than in the United States.

It seems that the urban system in South America around 1960, on an average, was in a period of transition between a step-wise central place hierarchy and an integrated urban system. If the above analysis is correct this period of transition starts with the level of urbanization at about 25 per cent and accessibility at 3,000 to 4,000 urban inh./km both as here defined. And it ends at a level of urbanization close to 100% corresponding to an accessibility at 90,000 to 95,000 urban inh./km. Beyond this point development no longer takes place by urbanization, in the restricted physical sense of the word used here, but by spatial specialization and corporate growth, as described in chapter 5.

---

[6] The potentials for United States computed by Warntz (1965) for 1956 vary from 254 million dollars per mile in the state of Oregon to 1496 million dollars per mile in New Jersey. To convert this to the unit used in the South American accessibility measure it is necessary to:

1. Convert the miles into km by dividing by 1.609;
2. Transform the airline distances into transport cost indices. Assuming that all roads in the Unites States are asphalted, this can be done by transforming airline distance into road distance. On the average this can be done by dividing by 1.1–1.2;
3. Transform income into urban population. As the level of urbanization in the states is close to 100 per cent we can do this by dividing by a *per capita* income somewhat higher than the average, *i.e.* US $ 1500 to US $ 2000 *per capita*.

This means that the United States potential corresponding to the 93,000 urban population per km in South America in 1956 was between $ 250 million and $ 360 million per mile.

7.7 SUMMARY AND REFORMULATION OF THE MODEL

The above empirical analysis shows that the model outlined in the introduction of this chapter must be revised, or rather that its area of validity must be limited to the consolidated regions. Within these regions the empirical tests support the hypothesis that accessibility is a very important cause of regional economic development. This, of course, does not mean that capital is unimportant for development in the consolidated regions, it only means that capital tends to be allocated among the consolidated regions in proportion to their accessibility.

Outside the consolidated regions, in the peripheral areas, accessibility seems to be unimportant. Here availability of capital and natural resources appear to be important in their own right.

The revised model has been outlined in Figure 7.6.

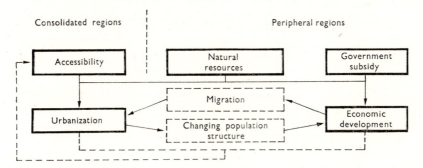

Fig. 7.6. *Accessibility, natural resources and capital inputs as determinants of urbanization and economic development. A revised model*

This two-dimensional nature of the economic development process is consistent with the two economic dimensions of regional structure found in the factor analysis in chapter 2.

Both the income-accessibility and urbanization-accessibility curves appear to be S-shaped. For the consolidated regions both curves were downward bending in 1960. For the low-accessibility, peripheral regions in 1960 and for all regions in 1950 the correlation coefficients were insignificant, indicating an almost horizontal relation. The shift between the horizontal line and the downward bending curves roughly corresponds to an accessibility level of 3,000 to 4,000 urban inh./km, to 25% urban population, and to a *per capita* income of US $ 110 to US $ 135 per year. When accessibility increases above this level it becomes a more and

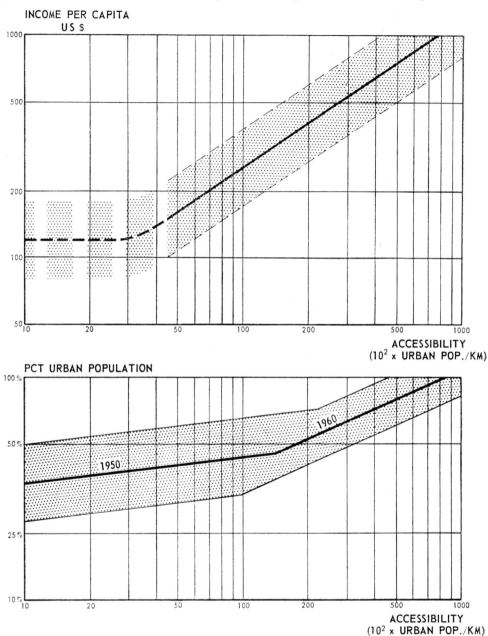

Fig. 7.7. *Accessibility-income and accessibility-urbanization curves. Shaded areas are within one standard deviation from the regression lines (68 per cent limit)*

more important cause of development, and the variation around the income-accessibility and urbanization-accessibility curves tends to decrease.

The urbanization-accessibility curve seems to correspond roughly to the equivalent curve for the United States, but the income-accessibility curve appears to be lower, so that the *per capita* income corresponding to 100% urbanization in South America is only about 3/4 of that in the United States.

The approximate shape of the S-shaped income-accessibility curve is sketched in Figure 7.7. (The upper turn of the S-shape has been levelled out by the logarithmic transformation). The turning point corresponds to accessibilities around 10,000 urban inh./km. In 1960 most of the regions in South America were located around this turning point.

The income differences between the South American countries thus seem to be due in part to the accessibility differences and in part to the different composition of regions. The factor analysis in chapter 2 showed that particularly in Venezuela (1960) and Brazil (1950) non-consolidated regions predominate and that income therefore in these two countries should be relatively little influenced by the accessibility levels. In the other countries the consolidated regions are more frequent.

CHAPTER 8

Accessibility and the trend of regional income differences

A simulation model

8.1 INTRODUCTION

The South American continent is characterized by very large *per capita* income differences. Among the 74 regions of South America used here, the *per capita* income in 1960 varied from less than US $ 100 to more than US $ 1000, or with more than a factor 10. In comparison the *per capita* incomes among the North America states in 1956 varied only with a factor 3 from US $ 960 in Missisippi to US $ 2820 in Connecticut. In this chapter we shall try to simulate the process by which these regional income differences change in time.

The basis for the simulation will be the income-accessibility curve developed in chapter 7. This income-accessibility curve indicates that, everything else being equal, the income will increase when the accessibility increases. The S-shape of the curve indicates that the increase in income for a given accessibility increase varies with the absolute size of the accessibility, so that the income effect will be smallest in regions with a very high and very low accessibility and largest in regions with intermediate accessibility. Finally, the relatively good empirical fit of the income-accessibility curve in the consolidated regions indicates that the *ceteris paribus* assumption on the average should not be too far wrong in these regions. In the non-consolidated regions, on the other hand, the *ceteris paribus* assumption is much less likely to hold true.

In the simulation, we shall assume that the income-accessibility curve shown in Figure 7.7 is valid and stable in time. Given this curve, changes in income differences between two regions will depend in part on the two regions' location on the curve and in part on the changes in accessibility in the two regions.

Of these factors, the last is especially interesting because it is at least in part subject to policy decisions. If our model holds true, it opens up some possibilities of influencing the income differences by changing the accessibility differences.

The accessibility in a region was in chapter 7 defined as

$$A_j = \sum_{\substack{\text{all } i \\ \text{within} \\ \text{nation}}} \frac{u_i P_i}{r_{ij}} + h \sum_{\substack{\text{all } i \\ \text{outside} \\ \text{nation}}} \frac{u_i P_i}{r_{ij}} \tag{8.1}$$

and we shall in the simulations assume that this expression is valid in the future as well.

This accessibility measure is sensitive to the growth of the urban population ($u_i P_i$), improvements of inter-regional transport and communication links (*i.e.* decreases of r_{ij}), and international integration (*i.e.* increase of h towards 1.0):

1. Of these three factors of accessibility increase it should be remembered that urban growth is used as a substitute for increased population participation (see section 7.2) and thus can be considered an index of social integration. Urban growth also increases the possibility of achieving urban and location economies, through interaction and co-operation among activities with common interests;
2. Transport and communication network improvements facilitate trade and interaction among regions and here especially between the core region and the periphery, and this is a precondition for efficient allocation of resources and for the start of the trickle-down process;
3. Finally, international integration results in a large increase in potential markets and thereby in the potential scale of production.

The spatial distribution of the accessibility increase resulting from each of these three causes is different. In the following sections we shall try to estimate the effect of the three causes of accessibility both in the period 1950–60 and in the future period from 1960 until full integration and improved transport and communication are realized.

The computations in this chapter are based on a number of assumptions, which will be specified as the computations are presented. These assumptions, of course, do not necessarily correspond to reality, though they are probably in general quite realistic. The computations should therefore be seen more as an attempt to simulate the general nature of the processes by which regional income differences are created and disappear than as an attempt to say anything specifically about South America. And to draw conclusions about any specific region is impossible on the basis of the present computations.

According to expression (8.1) the changes in accessibility result in part from changes in urbanization and economic development. Where the effect of accessibility on urbanization and economic development was

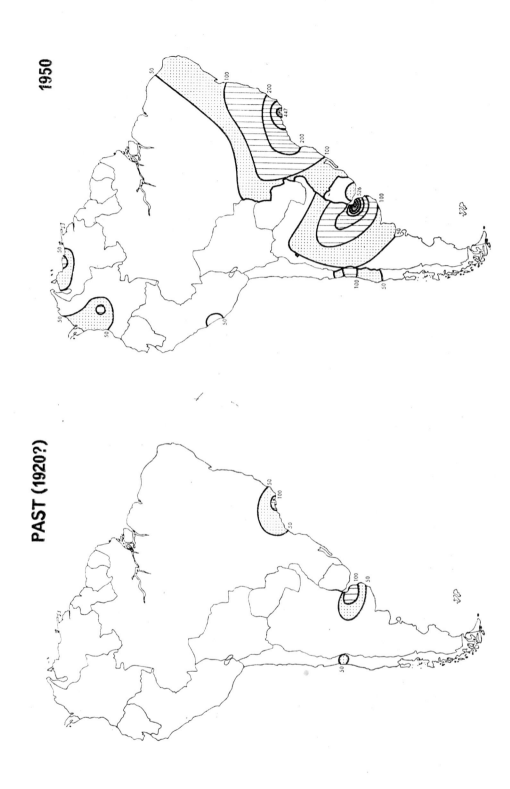

PAST (1920?)

1950

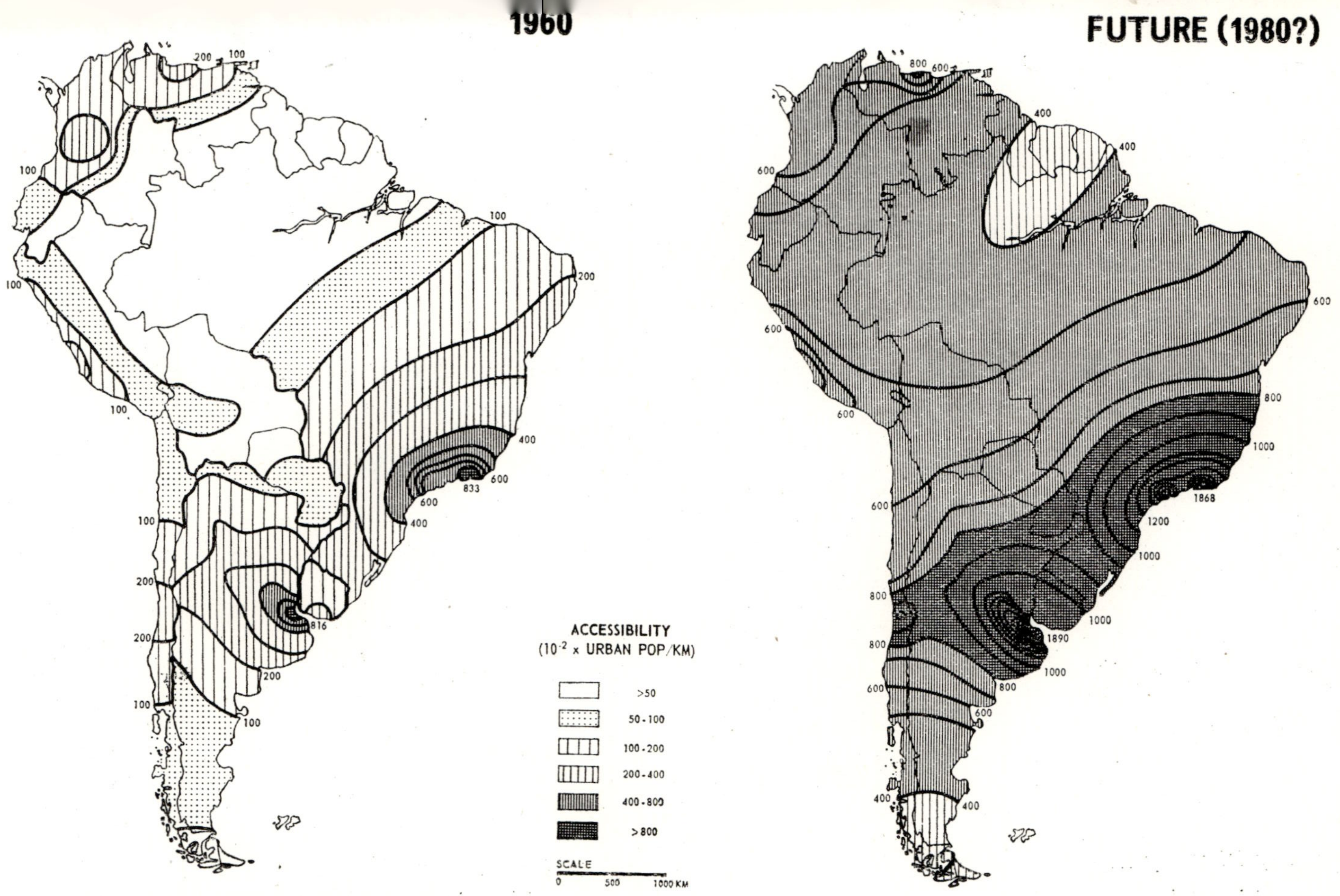

Fig. 8.1. *The development of accessibility*

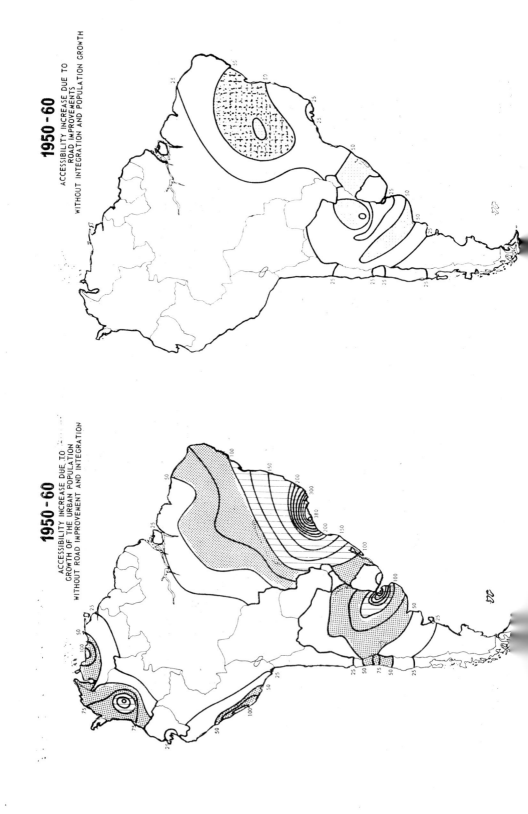

1950 - 60

ACCESSIBILITY INCREASE DUE TO
ROAD IMPROVEMENTS
WITHOUT INTEGRATION AND POPULATION GROWTH

1950 - 60

ACCESSIBILITY INCREASE DUE TO
GROWTH OF THE URBAN POPULATION
WITHOUT ROAD IMPROVEMENT AND INTEGRATION

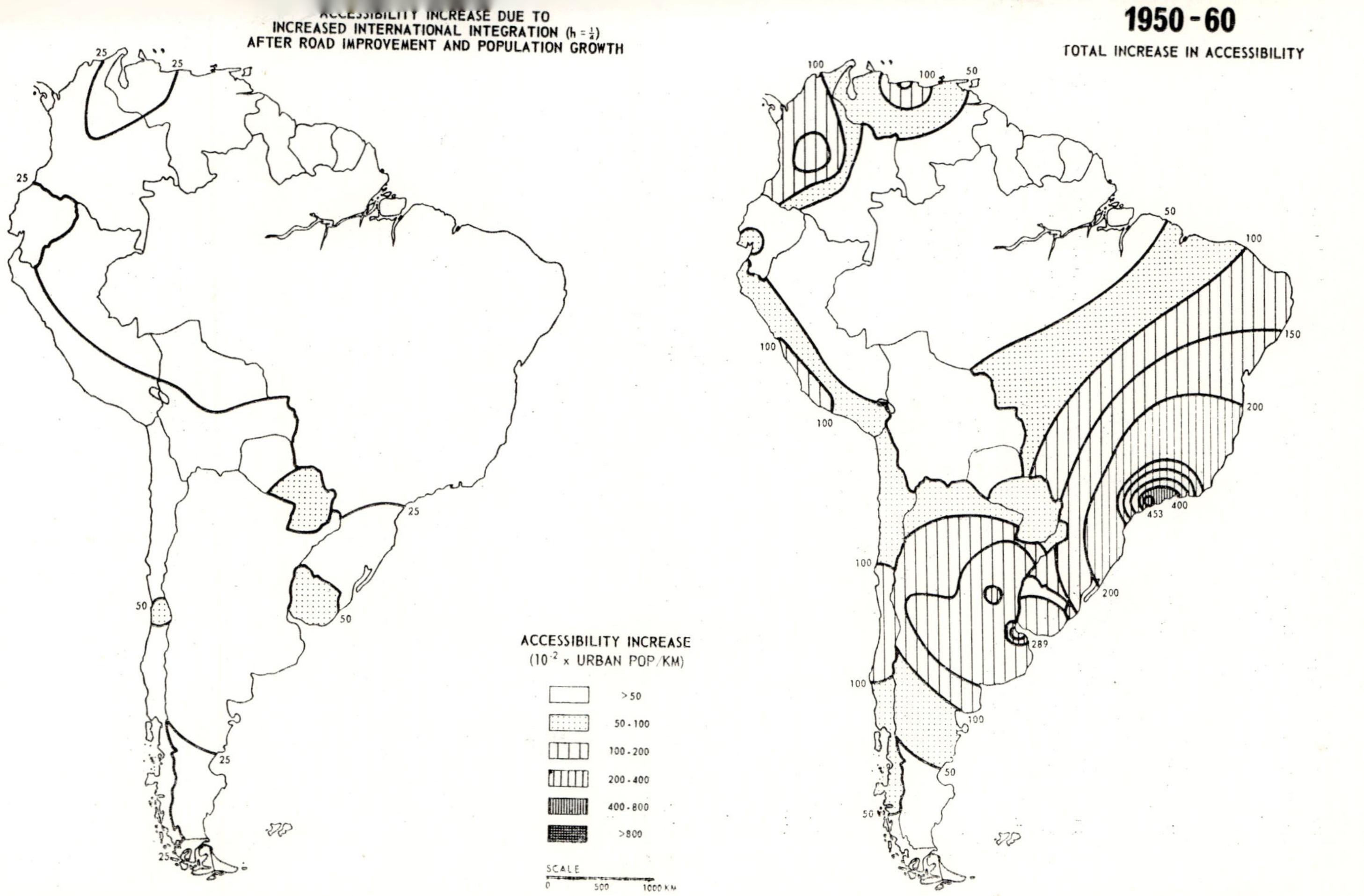

Fig. 8.2. *Accessibility increases, 1950–60*

analysed in chapter 7, this chapter can be regarded as an analysis of the feed-back by which urbanization and economic development influence the level of accessibility.

8.2 ACCESSIBILITY INCREASES 1950–60

In computing the accessibilities in 1950 and 1960, urban census populations and information about the road networks around 1950 and 1960 were used. In addition, it was assumed that the level of international integration increased from $h = 0$ in 1950 to $h = \frac{1}{4}$ in 1960. The resulting growth in accessibility can be divided into four parts. The first is the effect of transport and communication improvements, assuming fixed population and no international integration. The second is the effect of an increase in the urban population without integration and without transport and communication improvements. The third is the additional increase which results when both population increase and network improvements take place at the same time. Finally the fourth part is due to the partial integration from $h = 0$ to $h = \frac{1}{4}$.

The average size of these accessibility increases is shown in Table 8.1 *a* for regions at different accessibility intervals. Part *b* of Table 8.1 shows the size of the growth relative to the 1950-accessibility, and part *c* shows the percentage distribution of the four elements of growth. On the basis of this table we can draw the following conclusions about the growth of accessibility:

1. Taken as a whole for all regions included in the tables, the population effect represents 42% of the total accessibility increase, and it is thus much more important than the communication and integration effects (Table 8.1 *c*);
2. In absolute terms the *population effect* is most important in the high accessibility areas; in relative terms it is independent of the original accessibility level, except in the most peripheral areas where it is 3–4 times the average population effect. Thus on the average, the effect of increasing urban population is proportional to the original accessibility level, except in the areas with the lowest accessibility, where the effect has been larger than average;
3. The *network improvement effect* is in absolute terms largest in areas with intermediate accessibility, but in relative terms largest in the low accessibility areas. These accessibility increases are, of course, a function of the structure of the network improvements. In the period 1950–60 these improvements to a large extent linked the capital

Table 8.1   *The relation between accessibility and accessibility growth, 1950–60*

Accessibility 1950	No. of regions	Accessibility 1950 (1)	Transport network improvements (2)	Population increase (3)	Extra increase when both (2) and (3) take place (4)	1/4 international integration (5)	Total increase in accessibility (6) (=2+3+4+5)	Accessibility 1960 (7) (=1+6)
a. *Average increases of accessibility per region*								
0– 9	8	3	4	7	5	15	31	33
10– 19	6	14	5	9	2	32	47	61
20– 49	27	34	17	25	11	31	83	117
50– 99	19	69	39	49	22	36	146	215
100–199	6	145	30	98	18	34	180	324
200–499	4	300	25	240	17	29	310	610
500–	1	527	8	128	104	49	289	816
All regions	71	69	21	48	15	31	115	184
b. *Increases in accessibility relative to 1950-accessibility*								
0– 9	8	100	143	272	181	566	1,162	1,262
10– 19	6	100	34	62	17	225	338	438
20– 49	27	100	49	75	31	91	247	347
50– 99	19	100	55	71	32	52	210	310
100–199	6	100	20	68	12	24	124	224
200–499	4	100	8	80	6	10	104	204
500–	1	100	2	24	20	9	55	155
All regions	71	100	31	69	21	44	165	265
c. *Increases in accessibility as a proportion of the total increase*								
0– 9	8	—	12	23	16	49	100	—
10– 19	6	—	10	18	5	67	100	—
20– 49	27	—	20	29	13	37	99	—
50– 99	19	—	26	34	15	25	100	—
100–199	6	—	16	55	10	19	100	—
200–499	4	—	8	77	6	9	100	—
500–	1	—	3	44	36	17	100	—
All regions	71	—	19	42	13	27	99	—

cities with the biggest cities in the central regions of the countries. The regions surrounding the capitals thereby got access to the large metropolitan markets and thus experienced large accessibility increases. The capitals themselves, of course, improved their access to the hinterlands, but as the cities in the hinterlands are both poorer and smaller the resulting accessibility increase was smaller;

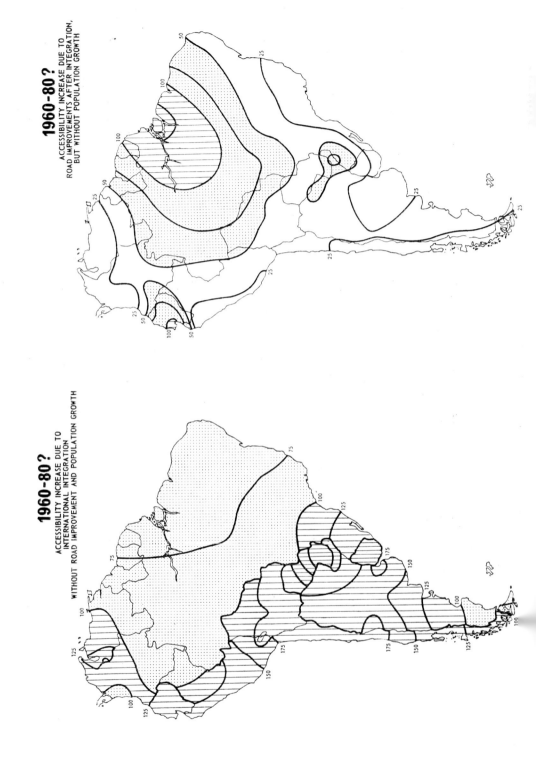

1960-80 ?

ACCESSIBILITY INCREASE DUE TO
ROAD IMPROVEMENTS AFTER INTEGRATION,
BUT WITHOUT POPULATION GROWTH

1960-80 ?

ACCESSIBILITY INCREASE DUE TO
INTERNATIONAL INTEGRATION
WITHOUT ROAD IMPROVEMENT AND POPULATION GROWTH

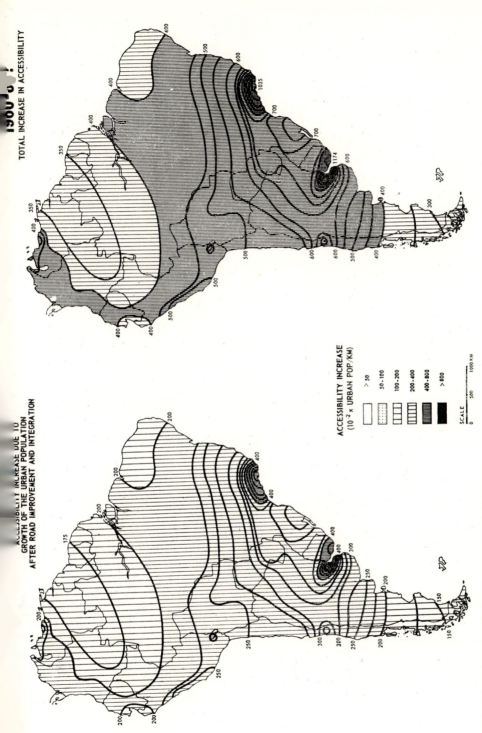

ACCESSIBILITY INCREASE DUE TO
GROWTH OF THE URBAN POPULATION
AFTER ROAD IMPROVEMENT AND INTEGRATION

ACCESSIBILITY INCREASE
(10^{-2} × URBAN POP/KM)

> 50

50-100

100-200

200-400

400-800

>800

SCALE
0   500   1000 KM

Fig. 8.3. *Future accessibility increases, 1960–1980 ?*

4. The effect of *integration* in absolute terms seems to be independent
of the original accessibility and, therefore, in relative terms largest
in the periphery. Instead of following the original accessibility, the
effect of integration will be large partly in the small countries located
close to the core regions of the large countries, *i.e.* Uruguay and
Paraguay, and partly in the peripheral regions close to the national
borders;

5. *The total increase in accessibility 1950–60* is in absolute terms largest
in the high accessibility areas but in relative terms largest in the low
accessibility areas.

8.3 ACCESSIBILITY INCREASES AFTER 1960

To get an impression of the accessibility changes which are likely to take
place after 1960, future regional accessibilities have been computed on
the following three assumptions:

An increase of 100 per cent in the urban population. This is likely to be
completed around 1975–80.[1] Corresponding to the proportional effect of
increases in the urban population between 1950 and 1960, it is crudely
assumed that the urban population growth rate is the same in all regions.

Improvement of the transport network so that all roads existing in 1960
will be asphalted in the forecast year and the following new roads will
be constructed, all with hard surface: Brasilia–Belém, Brasilia–Forteleza,
Brasilia–Asunción, São Paulo–Corumba–Santa Cruz (Bolivia), Santa
Cruz–Trinidad (Bolivia), Rio de Janeiro–Porto Velho–Lima, Porto
Velho–Manaus, Manaus–Caracas, Manaus–Bogotá.[2]

Full international integration, i.e. h = 1.0 in expression (8.1).

The last two assumptions correspond to the maximum accessibility
which can be achieved with non-specialized transport and communication channels. When these assumptions are realized South America
will pass into the post-urban era as described in chapter 5. At what future
date the assumptions will be realized we shall not attempt to prophesy.

How these assumptions will influence accessibility is shown in Table
8.2. The accessibility increases are divided into four parts: (1) the effect
of transport improvements at constant 1960 level of integration and
population; (2) the effect of full integration with 1960 network and

---

[1] Ducoff (1965) estimated that the urban population of Latin America will increase
from 95 millions in 1960 to 215 millions in 1980 or by 120–130%. This also corresponds with the results obtained by ILPES (1968).

[2] These connexions are suggested by Keating (1967).

population; (3) the additional effect of realizing both transport improvements and integration with constant 1960 population, and finally (4) the effect of a 100% increase in the urban population when transport improvements and full integration have been realized. On the basis of Table 8.2 the following conclusions can be drawn about the accessibility increases:

1. On the average, the *integration effect* is larger than the network improvement effect; but even together the integration and network improvement effects are only half the size of the population effect, and this even though the 100 per cent population increase must be considered very moderate compared with the improvements assumed for network and integration;

Table 8.2　*The relation between accessibility and accessibility growth after 1960*

Accessibility 1960	No. of regions	Accessibility 1960	Transport network improvements +1/4 international integration (1)	3/4 of the effect of international integration without network improvements (2)	Extra increases when both integration and network improvements take place (3)	Total increase in accessibility (4) (=2+3+4)	Future accessibility (1960 urban population) (5) (=1+5)	Future accessibility (100% increase in urban population) (6)	(7)

a.　*Average increases of accessibility per region*

Accessibility 1960	No. of regions	Accessibility 1960	(1)	(2)	(3)	(4)	(5)	(6)	(7)
0– 9	2	3	35	0	85	120	123	246	
10– 19	1	15	98	0	86	184	199	398	
20– 49	3	39	72	39	38	149	188	376	
50– 99	18	76	64	100	60	224	300	600	
100–199	21	140	67	91	44	202	342	684	
200–499	23	271	57	107	35	199	471	942	
500–	3	786	46	93	24	163	949	1,898	
All regions	71	184	62	92	46	200	384	768	

b.　*Increases in accessibility relative to 1960 accessibility*

Accessibility 1960	No. of regions	Accessibility 1960	(1)	(2)	(3)	(4)	(5)	(6)	(7)
0– 9	2	100	1,175	0	2,825	4,000	4,100	8,200	
10– 19	1	100	652	0	575	1,227	1,327	2,654	
20– 49	3	100	184	99	97	380	480	960	
50– 99	18	100	85	132	79	296	396	792	
100–199	21	100	48	65	32	145	245	490	
200–499	23	100	21	39	13	73	173	346	
500–	3	100	6	12	3	21	121	242	
All regions	71	100	34	50	25	109	209	418	

Changes in accessibility ($10^2 \times$ urban population per km) due to:

2. Only half of the effect of the investments in the transport network will be realized, if integration is not carried out;
3. The *effect of transport improvements* both in absolute terms and relative to the 1960 accessibility will be largest in the low accessibility areas. For the relative increase this corresponds to the findings for the period 1950–60, but for the absolute increase the maximum effect has moved from the medium to the low accessibility areas. The reason is clearly that the transport improvements after 1960 are extended into the distant peripheries;
4. The *effect of international integration* is largest in the high accessibility areas and not, as in the period 1950–60, independent of original accessibility. The reason for this is that the few regions which in 1960 were left in the group of low accessibility regions, had at that time no land connexions at all with the outside world. They will therefore first be able to realize the effect of integration when the transport network has been improved. In the four high accessibility groups there does not seem to be any trend;
5. As in the period 1950–60 we must conclude that the *total effect* of transport improvement and integration in relative terms is largest in the high accessibility areas, but relative to 1960 the increase in accessibility is largest in the low accessibility regions.

8.4 THE DEVELOPMENT OF REGIONAL ACCESSIBILITY DIFFERENCES

In Table 8.3 we have summarized some of the accessibility changes described above. The table shows for 1950, 1960, and 'the future' the average accessibility for the 35 regions with lowest accessibility and for the 36 regions with highest accessibility. It can be seen that the relative accessibility differences have been decreasing since 1950, while the absolute differences have been increasing.

It also shows that the same trend can be expected to continue in the future.

It is, however, unlikely that this trend can be extrapolated backwards in time. At some time in the past, the internal transport network of South America was almost uniform, uniformly bad, consisting only of mule tracks. In 'the future', as defined above, the transport network will also be almost uniform only of a much higher quality.

As a crude assumption therefore it might be assumed that 'the past' network of mule tracks and dirt roads was as extensive as 'the future' network of hard surface roads will be. According to our travel cost assumptions the past travel cost everywhere was four times as large

Table 8.3   *Development of accessibility differences in South America (100 urban inh./km)**

	Past[b]		1950		1960	Future
Average accessibility for the 36 *high* access regions[a]	26	(130)	117	(196)	302	1036 (518)
Average accessibility for the 35 *low* access regions[a]	12	·(60)	21	(36)	77	494 (247)
Absolute accessibility difference	14	(70)	96	(160)	225	542 (271)
Relative accessibility difference	2.10 (2.10)		5.68 (5.45)		3.91	2.10 (2.10)

[a]The areas included in the two groups of regions are not neccessarily the same in all years.
[b]See the text for estimation procedure.
*The numbers in parenthesis are computed on the assumption that the urban population is in all years equal to the 1960 urban population.

as the future travel cost. If we also assume that the proportional growth of the urban population effect which we observed from 1950–60 can be extrapolated backwards in time, then we can conclude that the relative accessibility differences at some early date must have been approximately the same as those we can expect to find in 'the future'.

The absolute differences of course must have been much smaller. If for the early date we use an urban population figure at 1/5 of the 1960 population, corresponding to around 1920, then the 'early date' accessibilities become 1/40 of 'the future' accessibilities or 2,600 urban inh./km in the high accessibility areas and 1,200 urban inh./km in the low accessibility areas.

The final conclusion, therefore, is that the absolute accessibility differences are steadily increasing as accessibility increases, while the relative differences follow an inverted U-shaped curve, so that the relative differences are small for very low and for very high levels of development and high for intermediate development levels. The point of maximum differences appears to have been reached either around 1950 or before (see Figure 8.4).

Integration and regional economic development

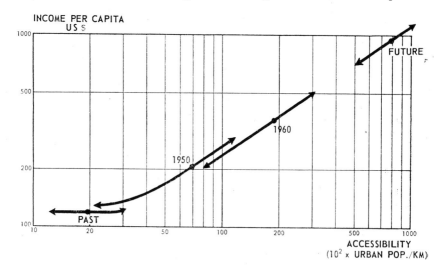

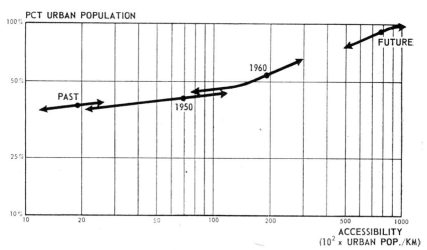

Fig. 8.4. *Accessibility-income and accessibility-urbanization curves. The changing regional differences in accessibility, per capita income and urbanization*

8.5 THE DEVELOPMENT OF REGIONAL INCOME DIFFERENCES

By combining the S-shaped accessibility curve and the inverted U-shaped curve of regional accessibility differences (Figure 8.5) we can estimate the regional income differences at different times.

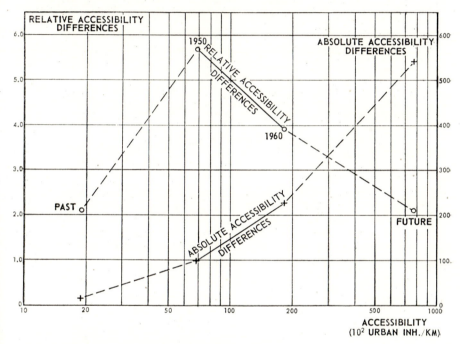

Fig. 8.5. *Development of regional accessibility differences*

These estimates are set out in Table 8.4. They show that we should expect the regional income differences to follow an inverted U-shaped curve when the development level increases. Contrary to what was found for the accessibility differences, which reached their maximum value in 1950, the income differences do not seem to reach their maximum value before about 1960, so that we should expect to find increasing income differences in the period 1950–60. However, as the data indicate that South America in the period 1950–60 was located on the flat part of the curve, close to the maximum, the trend of the income differences is not likely to be very pronounced.

Table 8.4   *Estimation of the development of regional income differences in South America**

	Past	1950	1960	Future
Average incomes *per capita* for the 36 high access regions	125 (100)	280 (280)	530	1230
Average income *per capita* for the 35 low access regions	110 (60)	120 (90)	210	740
Absolute income difference	15 (40)	160 (190)	320	490
Relative income difference	1.1 (1.7)	2.3 (3.2)	2.5	1.7

*The numbers in parentheses are estimated on the basis of a log linear accessibility-income curve.

8.6 THE DEVELOPMENT OF REGIONAL INCOME DIFFERENCES. SOME EMPIRICAL
    EVIDENCE

This pattern of regional income differences corresponds closely to the empirical findings of Williamson (1965). Williamson analysed the variation in regional *per capita* income differences both in time series and cross-section data and both in national and international data. In a cross-section analysis of regional income differences in countries at different levels of economic development around 1950–60 he found that the regional differences tend to increase with development in the least developed countries, but decrease in the developed countries. Unfortunately he was only able to obtain data for a few countries at low levels of development. It is therefore impossible from his analysis to say exactly at which development level the maximum regional difference is found; it does, however, appear to be at a rather low level, probably US $ 150 to US $ 250 *per capita* per year.[3]

[3] On the basis of Kuznets group classification Williamson has grouped the 24 countries included in his analysis into 7 groups. Of these the three lowest groups only contain 2 (Yugoslavia and Japan), 1 (Philippines), and 1 (India) countries, respectively. For the 7 groups he found average dispersion indices at respectively 0.139, 0.252, 0.335, 0.464, 0.292, 0.556, and 0.275. He seems to be of the opinion that the maximum dispersion is found in group 4 and treats the large dispersion found in group 6 (Philippines) as a deviation. However, on the basis of *per capita* incomes, the two countries which Kuznets placed in group 5 (Yugoslavia and Japan) would seem rather to belong to group 3 or 4 and group 6 to represent the maximum dispersion.

Time series analysis generally confirmed the inverted U-shaped relation between income and regional income differences. Time series analysis of a number of developed countries showed that the income differences here were decreasing. Only for two of these developed countries were the time series long enough to show maximum regional income differences, namely, for the United States, where the maximum appears to have been reached between 1840 and 1880, and for Germany where it was reached around 1907. Among less or medium-developed countries Williamson only analysed Italy (1928–60) and Brazil (1939–59). In both cases it was found that the regional income differences increased until 1952 and thereafter were stable or decreased. For Brazil this has since been confirmed in a more detailed analysis by Graham (1970).

To Williamson's and Graham's analyses of Brazil we can here add an investigation for Argentina, Brazil and Chile. In this investigation we shall be interested only in the consolidated areas, as defined in chapter 2 (see Figure 2.10), because only for these areas the accessibility-development relation is valid. The analysis thus covers 15 regions in Argentina, 3 regions in Brazil and 5 regions in Chile, or taken together 23 consolidated regions.

For each region and for the years 1950 and 1960 an index of *per capita* income was computed by dividing regional *per capita* income by national average. The change in this index represents the relative change in income (see Figure 8.7). The 23 regions were divided in two groups, high and low access regions, and for each of these groups the number of regions with increasing and that of those with decreasing relative incomes were counted. The result is shown in Table 8.5.

Table 8.5 *Test of the relationship between accessibility level, 1950, and change in relative per capita income, 1950–60. Argentina, Brazil, and Chile*

No. of regions in which the *per capita* income relative to the national average is:	Consolidated regions with accessibility in 1950		Total consolidate regions	Peripheral regions
	> 10,000 urb. inh./km	< 10,000 urb. inh./km		
Increasing	4	6	10	14
Unchanged	1	1	2	0
Decreasing	2	9	11	3
Total	7	16	23	17

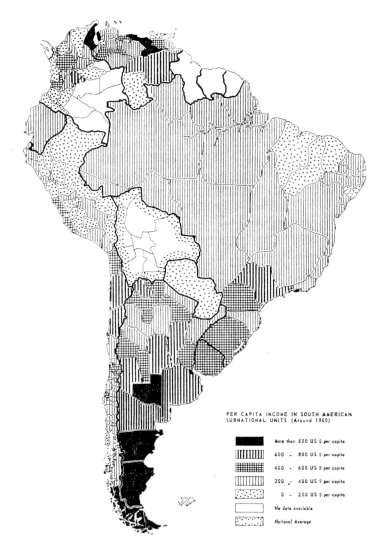

Fig. 8.6. *Per capita income in South American sub-national units around 1960*

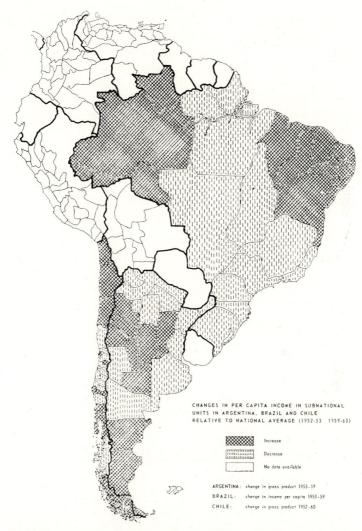

Fig. 8.7. *Changes in per capita income in sub-national units in Argentina, Brazil and Chile relative to national average (1952–53, 1959–60)*

12*

The table shows that there is a greater tendency for the consolidated regions to have increasing relative incomes if they have high accessibility, than if they have low accessibility. As we should expect from what has been said above, however, this tendency is far from significant.

The table also shows that the peripheral regions have a greater tendency to have increasing incomes relative to the national average than the consolidated regions. This tendency is significant at an 89% level.

These South American data on *per capita* income changes are inconclusive, but at least they do not contradict our model.

8.7 SUMMARY

Based on a simple model assuming that the level of economic development in the consolidated regions is determined basically by the level of information accessibility, we have simulated the process by which income differences increase and diminish.

The simulation shows that if our basic hypothesis holds good we should expect the relative regional income differences to follow an inverted U-shaped curve as development takes place. This corresponds to the empirical findings of, among others, Williamson (1965).

Around 1960 South America on the average appears to have been located at just about the maximum of the inverted U so that income differences between the consolidated regions of South America should decrease in the future.

To the extent to which our model is correct we can influence the regional income differences by changing the spatial accessibility structure. The accessibility structure is sensitive to growth of the urban population, improvement of the transport and communication networks, and international integration. Of the total accessibility increase more than 50% is due to growth of the urban population. Of the two other factors, network improvements appears to be slightly less important than integration. Unfortunately this means that the factor which we have at present the best chance of influencing through policy decisions, namely, network improvement, is that which is least important.

The development effort, therefore, should be concentrated on the social sectors and on local development rather than on the interregional linkages. The local aspects of development should be emphasized both because they are important in themselves and because the effect of the interregional linkages will be larger the larger the level of local participation.

One of the difficulties in reducing income differences through network improvements is that improvements of a link in a network always improve the accessibility at both ends of the network. When we attempt to improve the accessibility of the periphery by linking it to the centre, the accessibility will go up both at the centre and on the periphery. The effect of such a link in the network will generally be larger on the periphery (which is linked to the large population in the centre), than at the centre (which is only linked to the thinly populated periphery). The accessibility differences between centre and periphery, therefore, will generally be reduced, but never eliminated. This is likely to be one of the reasons for the high stability of the rank of towns in the urban system found in chapter 5, and for the persistence of regional income differences even in highly developed countries.

PART IV

Socio-economic feed-backs to the
process of innovation diffusion

Introduction to part IV

The population of the most accessible regions tends to invent or adopt innovations from outside before the population of less accessible regions. Therefore, the population of the most accessible regions will tend to have access to better techniques for the production of existing products, and be in a monopoly position for new products. This makes the centre better able to absorb growth. Secondly, it creates a permanent structural difference between the centre and the periphery, giving the periphery a disproportionately large share of the low income, stagnating industries. If no migration took place, the innovation diffusion process would, therefore, lead to very marked regional *per capita* income differences.

Regional income differences will also be created where the natural population growth rate varies from region to region. Regional differences in the natural growth rates, however, are the result of regional differences in death and birth rates, and these differences appear to result from ordinary diffusion processes by which education and health institutions are spread from region to region. They will therefore tend to aggravate the income differences created by the innovation diffusion processes.

The migration process tends to reduce these regional income differences by drawing people from the low opportunity regions to the high opportunity regions. The migration process can thus be considered a feed-back mechanism which responds to the negative effects of the innovation diffusion process. However, the migration process is always delayed and it does not therefore eliminate the income differences.

On the other hand, even if innovation diffusion and migration were simultaneous processes, it is unlikely that the regional income differences would disappear, because both innovation diffusion and migration are selective processes. The innovation diffusion process leads, as was shown in chapter 5, to a concentration of low productivity, stagnating industries in the periphery; and selective migration leads to uneven distribution of the active population, thus giving the peripheral regions the heaviest burden of unproductive population, children and old people.

In the chapters of part IV, on the basis of the same data as those used in the factor analysis in chapter 2, we shall investigate these interactions between urbanization, economic development, and the demographic processes.

First, we shall in chapter 9 analyse regional variations in the birth rate and show how these are related to the variations in education and urbanization. The reasons for concentrating on the birth rate are first, that variations in the death rate have generally been recognized to have much less influence on poulation structure than variations in the birth rate, and secondly, that no reliable data on death rates are available.

In chapter 10 the migration process will be discussed. Unfortunately, detailed migration data are not available. Chapter 10, therefore, only contains a general discussion of the relations between migration, un- and underemployment, and urbanization.

The demographic processes influence the *per capita* income in a region first of all through their influence on the proportion of the population in the active age group. In chapter 11 the determinants of the proportion of economically active people in the population will be investigated, and their importance for variations in *per capita* income will be discussed.

The ecological data which have been used in the analyses presented in the following chapters are not suited to test cause-and-effect relations, and though the existence of such cause-and-effect relations will be postulated in the following pages, often based on reference to other research, we shall not be able to test them. The virtue of the analysis presented is that it is based on many more observations covering wider value intervals than most earlier studies. We are thus able to show that a number of inconsistencies in earlier findings based on simple linear correlations of national data are due to the non-linearity of the relations. In other cases, the large number of observations enables us to introduce multivariant explanations.

CHAPTER 9

Urbanization and the regional variation
in birth rate and education

9.1 MEASUREMENT OF BIRTH RATES

As a measure of fertility we shall use the child-women relation (children 0–4 years/women 15–49 years) which is one of the most commonly used measures. Where birth registration is incomplete, this fertility index has the advantage of being based on census data only. Its disadvantage is that it does not measure real fertility, because only those children who survive at the census date are registered. It therefore contains an element of infant mortality.

It has also been claimed that rural-urban migration would tend to reduce the child-women relation in the urban areas and increase it in the rural areas because young childless women are over-represented among the migrants to the towns; the child-women relation should therefore lead to higher urban-rural fertility differences than are obtained by more direct fertility measures. Carleton (1965), however, has shown that this effect of migration disappears where migration is a continuous process.

That the child-women relation contains an element of infant mortality is, of course, a serious deficiency when fertility is analysed for purposes of birth control. For problems of economic development, however, the child-women relation might be more relevant than the direct fertility measures, because only those children who survive cause economic problems as they grow up and find that there are no schools for them and no jobs; and they alone will contribute to economic growth.

9.2 DETERMINANTS OF THE BIRTH RATE

There is no general agreement on how fertility changes are brought about. The two causes most commonly cited are urbanization and education, but other causes have been analysed as well; for instance, social class, female employment, marital status, migration, and biological factors (Stycos, 1968, pp. 279–283 and Miro and Rath, 1965). Most of these variables, however, are like education, highly correlated with urbanization, and we might consider them all as aspects of urbanization. This high multi-colinearity makes it very difficult to judge the importance of the different variables on the basis of ecological data. Simple linear correlations between child-women relation, percentage of illiteracy and of urban population, however, indicate that the educational level as a single variable is more relevant than urbanization (see Table 9.1). This might, however, be simply because the educational level functions as an indicator of the availability of a whole series of public services, such as educational and health facilities.

Table 9.1   *Linear correlations between child-women relation, percentage illiteracy, and urbanization*

	Year	No. of regions	% urban	% illiterate	Correlation between % urban and % illiterate
Child-women	1960	55	− 0.49	0.69	− 0.56
relation	1950	66	− 0.51	0.66	− 0.49

The importance of education as a determinant of fertility is confirmed by a number of studies of data for individuals. Miro and Rath (1965), who interviewed women in Panama City, Rio de Janeiro, and San José (Costa Rica), found a very regular reduction in fertility when educational level increased, and they conclude that educational level is a far better measure than socio-economic status of the socio-economic and cultural influences on fertility. For Puerto Rico, Stycos (1968, p. 279) showed that the same strong correlation between education and fertility was operative through all levels of education. His data indicate that fertility decreases especially rapidly after 4–6 years of schooling. If a single measure of education is to be used, the illiteracy rate, therefore, seems to be relevant, because lifelong literacy is probably not achieved until after 4–6 years of school.

Stycos' data also show that rural-urban fertility differences are not completely accounted for by rural-urban differences in education. Part of this unexplained difference is likely to be due to demographic variables, such as the percentage of single women and of women in the labour force, which both tend to result in lower urban fertility. However, even after accounting for these variables rural-urban fertility differences still exist. These rural-urban fertility differences decrease inversely to educational level, so that they are large for women with a low level of education and very small for women with a high level of education.

The picture offered by the Puerto Rican data can be reasonably explained if we consider the spread of family planning practice as an innovation diffusion process. This diffusion process can take place either through personal contacts or through mass media, in the first place through written material. Highly educated women, who will often actively seek written information themselves, are likely to find it both in urban and in rural areas. Less educated, but literate women might well be influenced by written material, but they are not likely to look for it themselves and have therefore a larger chance of getting the information if they live in urban areas where public health services are more readily available. Finally, illiterate women, who have to rely on personal contacts are unlikely to get information on family planning if they live outside the urban areas. This view is borne out by the Puerto Rican data, which show that although the use of birth control methods both in urban and in rural areas is more common among highly educated women than among women with little or no education, the difference between the educational groups is larger in rural than in urban areas (Stycos, 1968, p. 267). It is further supported by a Bolivian investigation (Centro de Estudios de Población, 1969).

Thus it appears that education is a more relevant single determinant of fertility than urbanization, although urbanization especially in the least developed areas, ought to be considered as well.

However, this result – that education seems to be a relevant determinant of the level of fertility – only scratches the surface. There are still many possible explanations of the mechanism by which the level of fertility changes. Frederiksen (1969) distinguishes between two explanations: a Neo-Malthusian one, which explains the reduction in fertility as a result of increasing efficiency of family planning; and one, which he advocates, that explains the reduction in fertility as a result of the increased expectation of survival of the children consequent on improved health services and decreasing mortality. Both of these situations are likely to lead to a high correlation between education and fertility, literacy in the first case increasing the efficiency of family planning, and in the second case tending to improve the efficiency of the health services.

9.3 BIRTH RATE AND EDUCATION IN SOUTH AMERICA

One of the reasons for the uncertainty of the conclusions of many of the ecological investigations of fertility is that they use linear correlations. Figure 9.1 shows clearly that these do not hold; rather the relation between child-women relation and illiteracy has the shape of an inverted U. This U-shaped relation is not apparent from studies of individual countries, because the range of illiteracy rates is insufficient to reveal the shape of the curve.

A possible explanation of the U-shaped relation is, that while real fertility increases with the illiteracy rate, the proportion of the children, who survive to the census date, will tend to decrease with illiteracy rate (and/or increase with urbanization).

If we assume that both fertility (F) and survival rate (S) are linear functions of illiteracy (I), and that the survival rate is 1.0 for zero illiteracy, which is not much for the developed countries, then the resulting child-women relation (C) can be estimated by a quadratic expression:

Survival rate $\qquad : S = 1.0 - a\,I$

Fertility $\qquad\qquad : F = b + c\,I$

Child-women relation $\quad : C = F \times S = (b + c\,I)(1.0 - a\,I)$

$$= -ac\,I^2 + (c - ab)I + b \qquad (9.1)$$

From the empirical data we can by regression analysis estimate the coefficients in (9.1), $(-ac)$, $(c - ab)$, and b. From these estimates the values of a, b and c can be computed. The results of these computations are shown both for 1950 and for 1960 in Table 9.2 and in Figure 9.1.

From Table 9.2 we can draw the following conclusions:

1. The correlation coefficients are reasonably large, and increased from 1950 to 1960;
2. One of the arguments most often advanced in the debate on the fertility problem is that, because fertility tends to be lower in urban areas where illiteracy is low, we should expect fertility to decrease as the population becomes urbanized and the educational level increases. Figure 9.1 shows that this reasoning must be modified. Only when the illiteracy rates decrease below 20–30 % can sizable decreases in the child-women relation be expected, and this is a state of affairs which currently exists in few areas outside Argentina, Chile, and Uruguay;

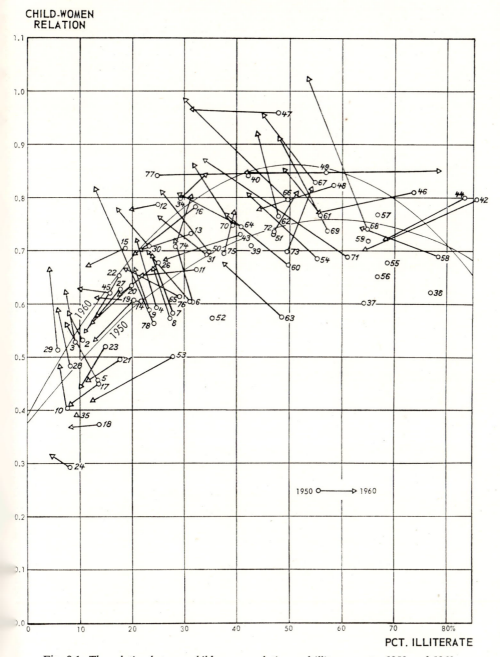

Fig. 9.1. *The relation between child-women relation and illiteracy rate, 1950 and 1960*

Table 9.2 *Regression equations (quadratic) between child-women relation (C) and illiteracy rate (I), 1950 (71 regions) and 1960 (55 regions)*

1950	$C = 37.50 + 1.30\,I - 0.011\,I^2$	$(R = 0.72;\ R^2 = 0.52)$
	(0.21) (0.0024)	
	$F = 37.5 + 1.56\,I$	
	$S = 1.00 - 0.07\,I$	
1960	$C = 39.02 + 1.85\,I - 0.018\,I^2$	$(R = 0.80;\ R^2 = 0.64)$
	(0.26) (0.0036)	
	$F = 39.0 + 2.18\,I$	
	$S = 1.00 - 0.08\,I$	

The differences between 1950 and 1960 are for both coefficients significantly different at a 98 % level.

3. The argument must be modified still further, because the inverted U-curve for the illiteracy and child-women relation is not stable in time. In the illiteracy interval in which most of the regions are found, the child-women relation has been increasing for a given illiteracy rate. This change in the curve can be at least partly explained by the proportion of single women, which was found to be lower in 1960 than in 1950. For instance among Chilean women above 15 years of age the proportion classified as *single women* in the census decreased from 37.2% in 1950 to 35.8% in 1960 and among Venezuelan women the proportion of single women decreased from 42.9% in 1950 to 36.8% in 1961.

9.4 THE SPREAD OF EDUCATION IN SOUTH AMERICA

No matter which theory one favours, it appears that the reduction of death and birth rates is directly or indirectly related to the diffusion of the basic urban services such as sanitary installations, health services and education. To link the demographic processes with the process of urbanization we shall, therefore, investigate the distribution of one of these services, namely, education.

Education, as well as other basic services which modern society wants to provide for its citizens, is subject to scale economies. Installations such as sewage, running water, and electricity are very much more expensive to provide for isolated houses than for houses in a town or village; the optimal size of a school is such that only villages or towns above a certain size have a sufficient number of children to support it. In rural areas and where villages are small, students must be recruited from a large area. But where no special transportation is provided, the distance students will be willing to travel to school is very limited. In such areas schools will be either less effective or more expensive, if they are provided at all. We should therefore expect the level of school attendance and the level of education to be a function of urbanization. This trend is reinforced by the low incomes often found in rural areas, which mean that people cannot afford to lose the children's work during school hours.

The diagram Figure 9.2 shows that such a relation between urbanization and education (here measured as the percentage of the population which is illiterate) really exists. The diagram, however, also indicates that the relation is non-linear, and not very clear. A regression equation in the form of a power function gives for

$$1960 \ (55 \ \text{regions}) : \log I = 2.96 - 0.98 \log U \quad (R = 0.58; R^2 = 0.34)$$
$$(0.19)$$

$$1950 \ (65 \ \text{regions}) : \log I = 2.89 - 0.88 \log U \quad (R = 0.60; R^2 = 0.36)$$
$$(0.15)$$

or

$$1960 : I = 906 \ U^{0.98}$$
$$1950 : I = 776 \ U^{0.88}$$

These equations are not significantly different even at a 75% level.

Closer inspection of Figure 9.2 reveals that the deviations from the curves are ordered nationally. It has therefore been attempted to add eight dummy variables to the equations, one for each of the countries: Argentina (X_1), Chile (X_2), Paraguay (X_3), Ecuador (X_4), Peru (X_5), Brazil (X_6), Venezuela (X_7), and Colombia (X_8). These dummy variables are given the value 1 for regions within the respective countries and the value 0 for all other regions. The regression equation for 1960 resulting from this procedure becomes:

$$\log I = 2.75 - 0.81 \log U - 0.28X_1 - 0.17X_2 + 0.27X_7 + 0.18X_8$$

$$(R = 0.85; R^2 = 0.73)$$

Here only dummy variables with regression coefficients significant at a 97.5% level are included.

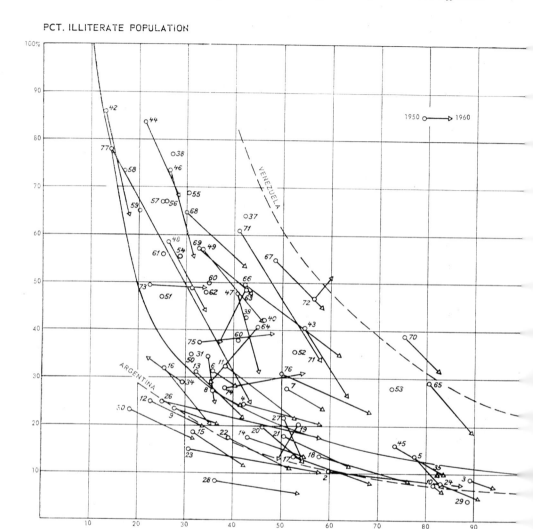

Fig. 9.2. *The relation between illiteracy rate and urbanization, 1950 and 1960*

This equation can be divided into seven equations, one for each country. In a log *I* – log *U* diagram these equations represent parallel lines, the lowest of which corresponds to Argentina and the highest to Venezuela. The distance between these parallel lines indicates that illiteracy in Venezuela for a given level of urbanization is 3.5 times higher than in Argentina.

A detailed account of national differences in illiteracy is shown in Table 9.3 for both 1950 and 1960.

These national differences in educational levels for given levels of urbanization can, of course, be due to national differences in the definition of urbanization. However, when the same dummy variables were used in chapter 7 in the equation between *per capita* income and urbanization, only the dummy for Argentina was significant; it seems, therefore, that the dummy variables represent real national differences in education.

One explanation of these national differences is that both the cost of providing education and the ability to pay for it will vary from country to country. A measure of the economic burden of education, namely, the number of children 5–14 years per inhabitant in the active age group, is shown in the first column of table 9.4.

Figure 9.3 shows that this measure of the economic burden tends to decrease when urbanization increases, but that Argentina has a lower economic burden than corresponding to its level of urbanization, while Colombia and Venezuela have higher economic burdens.

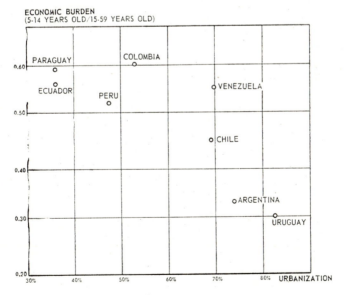

Fig. 9.3. *The economic burden of education as a function of urbanization, 1960*

Table 9.3　*Regression equations for the relation between* log illiteracy *and* log urbanization, *showing national differences in illiteracy for given level of urbanization, 1950 (65 regions) and 1960 (55 regions)*

		Regression coefficients (and Std. errors)		Number of times illiteracy for given U is larger than in Argentina	
		1950 (1)	1960 (2)	1950 (3)	1960 (4)
Constant		2.83	2.75	–	–
Log percentago urban population	(U)	−0.76 (0.09)	−0.81 (0.14)	–	–
Argentina	(X_1)	−0.36 (0.04)	−0.28 (0.07)	1.00	1.00
Chile	(X_2)	−0.29 (0.05)	−0.17 (0.08)	1.16	1.30
Paraguay	(X_3)	−0.19 (0.09)	...	1.48	(1.92)
Ecuador	(X_4)	–	...	–	(1.92)
Peru	(X_5)	...	...	(2.27)	(1.92)
Brazil	(X_6)	...	–	(2.27)	–
Venezuela	(X_7)	0.13 (0.05)	0.27 (0.09)	3.08	3.54
Colombia	(X_8)	...	0.18 (0.09)	(2.27)	2.90
R		0.90	0.85		
R^2		0.82	0.73		

− = country not included in analysis owing to lack of data.
... = regression coefficients not significant at a 85% level.
All other coefficients are significant at a 97.5% level. None of the 1960 regression coefficients are significantly different from the 1950 coefficients.

The national differences in education might also result from the long term trends in the importance attached to education in the national budgets. Table 9.4 shows some characteristics of the primary-secondary school systems in the South American countries around 1960. These data indicate that Argentina has higher quality school systems than would be expected from the level of urbanization, while Venezuela has lower

Table 9.4 · *Quality of the primary and secondary school systems, and the economic burden of education in the South American countries around 1960*

| | Economic burden of education. Children 5–14 years per adult 15–59 | Quality of the school system | | | | |
		Teachers per school	Students per teacher	Students per school	Children per student	% urban population
Argentina 1960	0.33	8.4	20	167	1.35	74
Bolivia 1960	–	–	28	–	–	–
Brazil 1961	–	2.9	29	85	–	45
Chile 1961	0.46	–	–	188	1.31	69
Colombia 1960	0.60	2.8	32	89	2.77	53
Ecuador 1961	0.56	3.5	32	111	1.91	36
Paraguay 1960	0.59	5.2	26	137	1.61	36
Peru 1959	0.52	3.2	33	105	1.71	47
Uruguay 1959	0.30	4.2	39	166	1.23	82
Venezuela 1961	0.55	3.7	34	126	1.48	68

– = No data available.

Source: *United Nations Statistical Yearbooks.*

quality systems. The national differences in educational level can thus to some extent be considered as a political input to our model.

The level of illiteracy thus appears to be determined (1) in part by the level of urbanization, because this is correlated both with the cost of providing education and with the ability to pay for it; (2) in part by the economic burden of providing education expressed as the number of children per economically active inhabitant and (3) finally, by the national policy for investment in the educational infrastructure.

9.5 SUMMARY

Although the birth rate as measured by the child-women relation is not a function of the educational level alone, education at least seems to be one of the most important single determinants of the child-women relation. The relation between the child-women relation and education, however, is not linear but rather has the shape of an inverted U, where the maximum child-women relation is found for 50–60% illiteracy. Only for the higher educational levels should we therefore expect to find the negative often relation assumed to exist between education and birth rate.

The level of illiteracy is in turn a function (1) of the degree of urbanization, which determines both the cost of providing education and the ability to pay for it; (2) the proportion of the economically active popula-

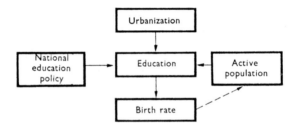

Fig. 9.4. *Determinants of regional variations in birth rate*

tion, which influences the ability to pay for education, and (3) the long term trend of national education policy, which indicates the willingness of the nation to allocate money to education. The fact that the illiteracy-urbanization relation is the only one of the relations investigated for which significant national differences were found points to the importance of educational planning as an instrument for developmental planning.

The relation between urbanization and illiteracy is not linear either. The reductions in illiteracy for every 1 per cent increase in urbanization become smaller and smaller as the level of urbanization increases, and when the level of illiteracy comes down to the level where it is positively related to the birth rate, its relation to urbanization is only weak. Thus, although a relation between urbanization, education, and birth rate does exist, it is probably only over a short range of values, from 20–50% urbanization and illiteracy, that it can be used effectively as an instrument to reduce the birth rate.

The relation between urbanization, education and birth rate are summarized in the flow chart in Figure 9.4.

CHAPTER 10

The process of migration

10.1 THE ECONOMIC OPPORTUNITIES AND THEIR PERCEPTION

Migration is a response to the perception of a changed regional distribution of economic opportunities. This accords with the findings from both Lima (Matos Mar, 1961) and Santiago de Chile (Elizaga 1966) that more than 60 per cent of all migrants move for economic reasons.

Changes in the regional distribution of economic opportunities result either from termination or rationalization of economic activities in depressed regions, from the opening up of new natural resources in the periphery, from the creation or growth of economic opportunities in the core region, or from an uneven distribution of the natural growth of population.

Of these possibilities the reduction of the number of jobs in the depressed areas plays only a limited role. Except in the central parts of Argentina the agricultural population shows remarkable stability. Widespread adoption of land reforms might change this picture, but this is far from certain. In Chile the recent division of large estates has resulted in some reduction of the agricultural labour force, but in Bolivia, Burke (1970) found that the population living on the *haciendas* doubled after their subdivision. However, rationalization of Peruvian *haciendas* without subdivision has led to a reduction of the population.

With respect to manufacturing, in only a few regions in central Chile and in the mountain regions of Peru was there a decline in employment, but at the same time employment in services increased, so that in no region was total employment reduced. On the other hand, there are many regions in which the increase in employment has been very limited and far from sufficient to keep up with the natural growth of population.

In a number of peripheral regions investments in mines have led to increased employment in mining; and in others road construction, for example in the interior of Brazil, has opened up large regions for agricultural settlement. In absolute terms this settlement might not be large, but for the regions in question the resulting flows of migrants are very important.

Finally, in the core regions new jobs have been created in the manufacturing industries and services. Manufacturing employment, however, has only grown at the same rate as the total population of the countries, and the majority of the new jobs have been in services. As the number of service jobs in the regions are highly correlated with the total of the regional population ($R = 0.90$), it appears that they are created by the migration flow rather than in advance of it. From the point of view of the migrant, however, this is less important. What generates his move is not necessarily real conditions, but his perception of them.

Peter Gould has in a number of countries analysed the image which school leavers and thus potential migrants have of the regions of their respective countries (see, for instance, Gould, 1967, and Gould and White, 1968). His results indicate that the image consists of two overlapping pictures – a national image on which the capital regions, and sometimes some physically attractive regions are favoured, and a local image on which the areas surrounding the place of living are favoured. There is no reason to believe that this picture is very different from what one could find in South America, because, in South America as elsewhere, it is strongly supported by the existence of a national system of mass communication and a local system of person-to-person communication.

It also corresponds closely to the actual migration patterns found in South America. For instance, the migration statistics in the Chilean census show that the two largest groups of migrants from practically all the provinces left for Santiago and a neighbouring province respectively. And in an analysis of the migrants from a rural community in the mountain regions of Peru, Montoya Rojas (1967) found that the largest group moved to Lima, the second-largest to the nearest provincial town, and the third-largest to peripheral mining communities.

10.2 UN- AND UNDEREMPLOYMENT AS A REGULATOR OF THE MIGRATION FEED-BACK

If migration is a feed-back mechanism responding to changes in the distribution of economic opportunities, then unemployment can be considered a measure of the success of this feed-back mechanism. In Western Europe and the United States the migration process has most often resulted in unemployment rates which are much higher in the peripheral than in the core regions.[1] This indicates that new jobs were created by industrialization in the core regions more rapidly than migrants arrived to take them up.

In many developing countries this picture is reversed, and the rate of urbanization has drastically exceeded the rate of industrialization. The fact that employment in manufacturing industries has only grown at the same rate as the total population has not stopped rural-urban migration, and as a result an increasing part of the urban population is either unemployed or employed in personal services, petty trades, and traditional handicrafts with very low productivity and income. Consequently, the most urbanized areas have both the highest *per capita* incomes and the highest unemployment rates, and the rural areas have both the lowest incomes and the lowest unemployment rates. This pattern, as shown in Figure 10.1, is characteristic for all the South American countries for which data are available, except Argentina, which shows the same picture as the United States and Western Europe.

This reversed unemployment pattern found in many less developed countries is often argued to be artificial. As unemployment benefit only exists in the modern sector, it is only here that unemployment is registered. Consequently, most of the unemployment does not appear in the statistics, but is rather distributed among the active population in the form of low productivity work and fewer than normal working hours.

ILPES (1968) has estimated the percentages of open unemployment that are equivalent to this combined un- and underemployment in different economic sectors in Latin America.[2] These equivalents of open unemployment are shown in Table 10.1.

[1] There are exceptions to this. These, however, are generally due not to rural unemployment rates which are lower than urban rates on an average, but rather to excessive unemployment rates in stagnating or contracting industries in specific regions such as the coal mining areas in Belgium or textile areas in France. See, *e.g.* for Europe *Area Redevelopment Administration* (1965), for Canada, Wood and Thomas (1965), and for the United States the correlations presented in Matilla and Floncannon (1964).

[2] In these estimates it is assumed that all the active population who produce less than a certain income, which varies from country to country according to general level of development, are underemployed. The unemployment corresponding to this underemployment is computed as that labour force which would have to be taken away to enable the rest of the labour force, by sharing the present product, to obtain an average income equal to that which was chosen as the lower limit for the fully employed.

It should be made clear that this definition of underemployment is different from the usually given theoretical definition, that underemployment exists when the marginal productivity of labour is zero or negative.

Also it should be made clear that the data given in Table 10.1 for equivalent unemployment cannot be compared to data on open unemployment in the United States and Europe because the underemployment according to this definition is likely to be sizeable in the developed countries as well.

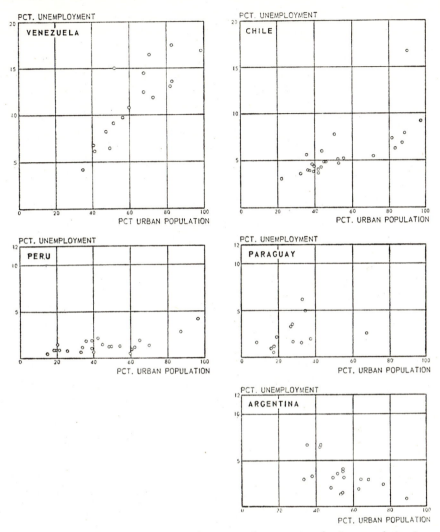

Fig. 10.1. *The relation between unemployment and percentage of urban population in five South American countries. (Each point represents an administrative area). Argentina deviates markedly from the other countries*

The table shows that the combined un- and underemployment is larger in agriculture than in the urban trades, and therefore the cross-section picture between urbanization and unemployment known in the more developed countries also exists in Latin America, if underemployment is taken into account.

Table 10.1   *Un- and underemployment in Latin America*

Sector	% of total unemployment in sector	% unemployment in sector	
Agriculture	47	32.6	
Mining	1.8	19.0	
Manufacturing industry	13.2	16.7	
Construction	3.9	6.4	only open
Electricity, gas, and water	3.9	2.0	unemployment
Transportation	5.7	no data	
Commerce	6.9	19.0	
Services	17.5	35.7	
Total	100	25.7	
Total non-agricultural activities	53	21.4	

Source: ILPES (1968).

The existence of this underemployment is important from an economic point of view, because it should at least theoretically make it possible to transfer labour from the traditional sectors to more productive work in the modern sectors, with little or no loss of production in the traditional sectors.

This argument, that geographic unemployment structure is the same in the developed and the less developed country when underemployment is taken into account is not, however, very helpful in explaining the differences between the rural-urban migration processes in the developed and less developed countries, which are often supposed to exist.

One reason for this is that the underemployment concept is generally stated in macro-economic terms, while a theory of migration must be based on micro-economic, behavioural processes.

Theoretically, underemployment is considered to exist when the marginal productivity of labour is zero or negative. In many cases, however, the marginal productivity worker works as hard or harder than the high productivity worker, and is therefore not very likely to consider himself as marginal to the group in which he lives. It is rather the rural group which is marginal to the rest of society.

An unemployment concept useful for a migration theory must be a measure of the desire for more employment, rather than a measure of low productivity. Such a measure is offered by a Chilean investigation. This investigation offers information on two empirical underemployment definitions. The first considers as underemployed those who are active but work less than normal working hours. The second considers as underemployed those who work less than normal working hours but would work more if jobs were available. Both definitions result in higher underemployment in the urban that in the rural areas, though the difference is not very large (see Table 10.2). Thus, when using these definitions, underemployment supports the picture found for open unemployment, namely that unemployment is larger in the urban than in the rural areas.

Table 10.2 *Urban-rural unemployment differences in Chile*

	Urban	Rural	Agri-culture	Non-agri-culture
% open unemployment	7.6	4.5	2.2	
% of those working who work				
1–14 hours per week	2.4	1.5	0.6	2.6
15–34 hours per week	10.3	10.8	8.5	11.2
35–40 hours per week	13.3	13.5	13.3	13.4
41–48 hours per week	38.9	41.3	44.0	38.4
49+ hours per week	35.1	33.0	33.8	34.4
Total	100.0	100.1	100.2	100.0
% of those working less than 30 hours per week who would like to work more			40.3	54.0
% of inactive population wanting to work more				
Yes	4.9	4.0		
Possible	4.4	3.7		
No	90.7	92.3		
% of the unemployed who have been so for less than				
–5 weeks	32.1	38.0		
5–14 weeks	29.6	31.3		
15–26 weeks	15.1	17.5	24.1	15.3
27 weeks or more	21.9	10.5	15.2	18.1
Without information	1.3	2.7		

Source: Dirección de Estadística y Censo (1966).

10.3 CONCLUSION

Migration is a feed-back mechanism responding to the changed distribution of economic opportunities. Because the economic opportunities have tended to shift from rural to urban activities, migration has led in most cases to increased urbanization; only in a few peripheral areas has this not been the case.

Un- and underemployment can be considered a measure of the success of this feed-back mechanism. Its size will depend on the speed of the closing down of rural jobs, the speed of the opening up of new urban jobs, and the speed of migration. These relations are shown in Figure 10.2.

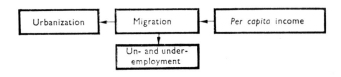

Fig. 10.2. *The migration syndrome*

In developing countries, where the rural areas are characterized by low income and low unemployment and the urban areas are characterized by high income and high unemployment, the situation which confronts the potential rural-urban migrant can be conceived as a type of gaming situation, where by migrating to the city he can increase his income, but only at the risk of unemployment, *i.e.* at the risk of earning nothing or less than before.

Without the underemployed sectors of the economy, the stake in this game would be even larger than now. Thus the underemployment sector functions as a buffer – a waiting room – where the migrants have to wait some time – up to several generations – before they are let in to the modern economic sectors.

The usual policy proposed to relieve un- and underemployment in the core regions has been industrialization. So far, however, this policy has not been very successful, and even if it should become more successful in the future, it appears very unlikely that manufacturing employment will ever reach levels as high as those found in the developed countries, because production techniques now are much less labour intensive than when the cities in Europe and the United States developed. Even if successful, therefore, industrialization will not solve the underemployment problem. The underemployment problem is fundamentally not a problem of insufficient income generation, but rather an insufficient solution to the problem of income distribution. Consequently it has to be solved, not through industrialization alone but rather through deliberate development of the service industries.

CHAPTER 11

The selectivity of migrants

11.1 INCOME *per capita*: THE EFFECT OF VARIATION IN ACTIVITY RATES

The age and sex selectivity of migrants together with the regional variation in birth rates lead to regional variations in the proportion of economically active population ranging from 25–50% of the total population.
This again influences the regional variation in *per capita* income. This
influence can be expressed by the following identity:

Income/*capita* = income/worker × worker/population in active age group
(15–59 years) × active age group (15–59 years)/*capita*

In chapter 7 where the regional variation in *per capita* income was analysed it might, therefore, have been more relevant to analyse income per
worker.

To make up for this deficiency we shall in this chapter (1) discuss the
selectivity of migrants with regard to both economic and demographic
characteristics, (2) investigate the causes of the regional variation in the
two activity rates *active population as a percentage of the active age group*
and *the active age group (15–59 years) as a percentage of the total population,* and (3) investigate how this variation in the activity rates influences
per capita income.

11.2 ECONOMIC AND EDUCATIONAL CHARACTERISTICS OF MIGRANTS

If migrants deviate from the average for the population they leave or
move into, the migration will give rise to regional differences in population structure. Several investigations indicate that the economically active
migrant to a city is not worse off economically than the native urban
worker, *i.e.* an investigation in Lima in 1967 *(Población Economicamente*

Activa de Lima Metropolitana, 1967) found the following un- and under-employment rates for native citizens and migrants, respectively:

	Among natives %	Among migrants %
Unemployed	7	3
Underemployed	22	28
Adequate employment	71	69
Total	100	100

Here, those are considered underemployed who work less than 35 hours a week and those who work more than 35 hours a week, but earn less than the official minimum salary. Mattelard (1965) and Herrick (1965) present data for Santiago de Chile which show that migrants have a slightly lower level of education and also lower income level than the natives, but the difference between natives and migrants is very small and migrants who have stayed more than 10 years in Santiago have practically the same income as the natives.

Information about the migrants in their rural environment prior to migration is much more scarce, but there are indications that they have a level of education above the average for the population they leave (Herrick, 1965).

Buenos Aires appears to be one of the exceptions to the rule that differences in economic status between migrants and natives are generally small. Germani (1963) reports on very large status differences between natives and migrants in Buenos Aires. This is in accordance with the inverse relation between unemployment and urbanization found in Argentina (see Section 10.2 and Figure 10.1). Because of the relatively large rural and small-town unemployment found in Argentina, the pressure to leave rural areas is larger than in other countries, and the migration is, therefore, less selective. While migrants in many of the South American countries come from the provincial towns rather than from rural areas, such selectivity is not pronounced in Argentina. At the same time, the natives of Buenos Aires with whom the migrant should be compared have a higher socio-economic status than in most other large cities in South America.

11.3 AGE AND SEX CHARACTERISTICS OF MIGRANTS

The most marked way in which migrants deviate from the rest of the population, however, is with regard to age and sex. With regard to age migrants are recruited mostly from the 15–35 years age group.

With regard to sex we must distinguish between two types of migration flow – the flow towards the large urban areas and flow towards the periphery. The flow towards the large urban areas contains slightly more women than men. This is due to the numbers of women seeking employment in personal services, as housemaids. Consequently, the predominance of women in the large cities tends to be largest in the low income regions. As migrants to the town will in the short run be few relative to the large mass of the urban population, this female predominance, however, will only have a limited impact on the population structure.

In the flow of migrants towards the periphery, on the other hand, male migrants clearly predominate, and this is likely to have a much larger impact on the peripheral population than the rural-urban migration has on the urban population, because migration to the periphery, though small in number, is large relatively to peripheral population.

The percentage of women in the population, therefore, can be expressed as a function of the population density (D). This gives the following estimates of the percentage of women (W) in the regions:

1960 (54 regions) : $\log W = 1.668 + 0.0272 \log D$ (0.0052)

$$(R = 0.59; R^2 = 0.34)$$

1950 (66 regions) : $\log W = 1.667 + 0.0302 \log D$ (0.0041)

$$(R = 0.68; R^2 = 0.47)$$

or

1960 : $W = 46.6 \, D^{0.027}$

1950 : $W = 46.5 \, D^{0.030}$

The regression coefficients in these equations are statistically significant at a 99% level, and they are not significantly different even at a 75% level.

11.4 PERCENTAGE OF POPULATION IN THE ACTIVE AGE GROUP

On the basis of the age selectivity of migrants it has often been claimed that migration in emigration areas will lead to an age structure which is unfavourable to economic development, because it is especially people in the productive age groups who leave these emigration areas. The problem, however, is extremely complex because the emigration of young people also reduces the number of children born in the years after the emigration, and later also the number of old people. What the outcome of this process will be is not at all simple. Lowry (1967) showed by simulation of the development of a theoretical population from which emigration took place that the percentage of people in the productive age group (15–59 years) only decreased with increased emigration to the extent to which emigration reduced the birth rate.

To see if this conclusion is true of South America we have in Figure 11.1 plotted the percentage of population in the productive age group as a function of the child-women relation. The figure shows that there is a high linear correlation between population in the active age group and the child-women relation. This supports the view that the population in the active age group is largely a function of the birth rate, and that migration, therefore, only influences the percentage of the population in the active age group in so far as it influences the birth rate.

It appears from Figure 11.1 that there is an exception to this rule. A larger active population than would be expected from the child-women relation is found in the jungle areas of Peru, Colombia, Venezuela, Bolivia, and Brazil, at the extreme ends of Chile, and in southern Argentina, *i.e.* in the economic periphery of the continent with low population density and very high, but basically male, immigration.

In these areas the child-women relation is determined by a basically rural and indigenous population, while the active population is dominated by the male immigrants, because immigration is large in proportion to the original population.

The active age group can thus be determined as a function of both the child-women relation (C) and the percentage of women (W), or by the following regression equation ($\%$ 15–59 years):

$$1950 \ (66 \ \text{regions}) : 114.6 - 0.877W - 0.261C \quad (R = 0.97; R^2 = 0.93)$$
$$(0.044) \quad (0.015)$$

$$1960 \ (55 \ \text{regions}) : 120.1 - 0.998W - 0.264C \quad (R = 0.98; R^2 = 0.96)$$
$$(0.052) \quad (0.010)$$

The correlation coefficient between the two independent variables is very small, $R = 0.051$, so there is no multi-colinearity problem. The regression coefficient of the child-women relation is seen to be stable in time, while the regression coefficient of the percentage of women increased between 1950 and 1960. This change in the regression coefficient is probably

14*

due to the decrease in the proportion of single women, which seems to have taken place in the decade (see chapter 9.3).

11.5 PROPORTION OF ACTIVE POPULATION IN THE ACTIVE AGE GROUP (15–59 YEARS)[1]

Because male activity rates are generally larger than the female rates, the proportion of active population in the active age group could be expected to vary with the sex-ratio. The relation, however, is a rather subtle one.

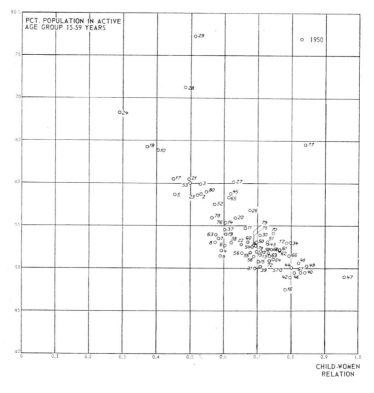

Fig. 11.1.a *The relation between child-women relation and population in the active age group, 1950*

---

[1] Active population covers all the active population above 15 years of age, not only active population between 15–59 years.

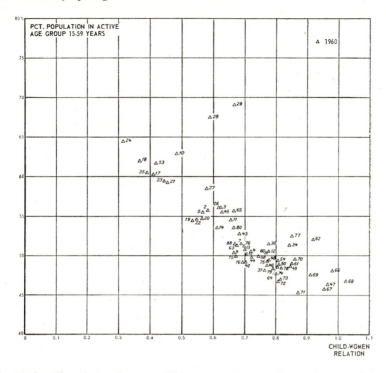

Fig. 111.b. *The relation between child-women relation and population in the active age group, 1960*

The variation in the sex-ratio is an outcome of selective migration. As we have seen, we must distinguish between two different flows of migrants; rural-urban migration and migration to the periphery. Rural-urban migration tends to result in a surplus of women in the urban areas and a deficit in the rural areas. As the female activity rate is generally much lower than the male rate this should result in lower activity rates in the urban areas. On the other hand, both male and female activity rates vary from rural to urban areas, male activity rates tending to be higher in rural than in urban areas, and female activity rates higher in urban than in rural areas. These two opposed tendencies tend to neutralize each other so that the urban-rural differences in activity rates become of minor significance.

The other important stream of migrants, going from the densely populated areas to the periphery, is composed predominantly of male migrants. This stream of migrants, therefore, leads to high activity rates in the thinly populated periphery.

The result is a high negative correlation between the proportion of economically active population in the active age group and per cent women (W). For 1960 the following regression equation is obtained:

$$1960 \text{ (55 regions)} : (\% \text{ active}) = 118.0 - 1.276W \quad (R = 0.87; \ R^2 = 0.76)$$
$$(0.099)$$

For 1950, the correlation coefficient is much smaller ($R = 0.27$; $R^2 = 0.07$). A dot diagram (not shown) reveals that the reason for the poor correlation found in 1950 is that the regions of Bolivia and Andean Peru in 1950 showed much higher activity rates than expected. For the other regions the relation appears to be at least as strong in 1950 as in 1960.

The difference between the 1950 and 1960 activity rates found in Bolivia and in the Peruvian mountain regions might be due to increased labour costs (for instance, due to introduction of a minimum wage rate) which in Peru have led the *hacienda* owners to reduce their work force by dismissing the female workers (Burke, 1970).

11.6 INCOME PER WORKER

In chapter 7 only the *per capita* income index was analysed. To the extent to which the activity rates vary from region to region we should expect income per worker to be a more relevant variable.

To judge how the variation in the activity rate influences *per capita* income one can include the logarithms to the *per cent of population in the active age group* and to the *per cent of active age group* as independent variables in the equation in Table 7.3, which attempts to explain the variation in the *per capita* income as a function of accessibility, mining employment and population density. This improves the multiple correlation coefficient of the equation from $R = 0.65$ to $R = 0.88$; but the regression coefficients obtained for the two new variables are numerically much larger (3.4 and 2.9 respectively) than the value ($+1.0$) we should expect. The reason for this must be that the activity rates are correlated with some of the other independent variables in the equation.

The regression equations obtained in sections 11.4 and 11.5 prove that this is true. Here the activity rates were found to be functions of the child-women relation and the percentage of women. Of these two variables the percentage of women was in section 11.3 found to be related to population density, and the child-women relation was in chapter 9 shown indirectly to be related to urbanization, which in turn is related to the accessibility index. Accessibility and population density thus indirectly account for the variation in activity rates.

To force the regression coefficients to take on the value 1.0 income per worker can be used directly as a dependent variable. This new dependent variable can be obtained by dividing the *per capita* income first by the percentage of population in the active age group to obtain *income per capita* (*15–59 years old*), and then by the percentage active in the active age group to obtain *income per worker*. By using these new dependent variables in the equation in Table 7.3 we get for 1960 (54 regions):

log income *per capita* =

$$1.54 + 0.195 \log M + 0.561 \log A - 0.145 \log D \quad (R = 0.65; R^2 = 0.42)$$

$$(0.047) \qquad (0.119) \qquad (0.06)$$

log income *per capita* (15–59 years) =

$$-0.08 + 0.190 \log M + 0.501 \log A - 0.113 \log D$$

$$(0.042) \qquad (0.106) \qquad (0.052) \qquad (R = 0.66; R^2 = 0.44)$$

log income *per worker* =

$$-1.84 + 0.185 \log M + 0.503 \log A - 0.089 \log D$$

$$(0.039) \qquad (0.098) \qquad (0.048) \qquad (R = 0.69; R^2 = 0.47)$$

For purposes of comparison the equation from table 7.3 is also shown. It can be seen that there is only a small improvement in the multiple correlation when income per worker is used as a dependent variable rather than *per capita* income. As would be expected from the analysis in sections 11.4 and 11.5, introduction of population in the active age group reduces the regression coefficients for both accessibility (related to child-women relation) and density (related to per cent women), while introduction of the active population in the active age group only reduces the regression coefficient of the population density. The changes in the regression coefficients, however, are not significant.

In numerical terms regional differences in the proportion of economically active population account for a regional difference in *per capita* income of about 50% from the regions with the highest activity rate to those with the lowest.

11.7 SUMMARY

The demographic processes, especially birth and migration, lead to regional variations in the proportion of the economically active population,
which in turn lead to regional variations in *per capita* income. These
relations are outlined in Figure 11.2.

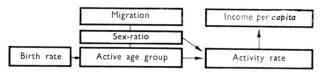

Fig. 11.2. *Income per capita and the demographic processes*

Variations in the activity rate account for approximately 50% variation
in the regional *per capita* incomes. Most of this variation, however, has
already been accounted for by the accessibility index and population
density, which are both correlated with the activity rate.

CHAPTER 12

Conclusions

12.1 THE ROLE OF INFORMATION ACCESSIBILITY IN ECONOMIC DEVELOPMENT

Traditional models of interregional development have emphasized the physical flows of capital, goods, and migrants as determinants of economic development. Here the weight has been placed on the information flows. This is not because the physical flows are considered unimportant, but because the physical flows are usually contingent upon flows of information; investors do not invest in projects they know nothing about, goods are not shipped before they are ordered and not ordered before they are known, and migrants need lots of persuasion before they break away from the place where they are established.

However, telecommunication alone would seldom be sufficient to secure information accessibility. First, because goods and people in themselves are important carriers of information. Secondly, because a large part of all communication takes place to prepare the ground for physical flows of goods and persons, which cannot be brought about by telecommunication alone, but only through physical contact. The measure of interregional information accessibility used here is therefore based on the road network rather than on the telecommunication networks.

Contrary to the traditional models of regional economic development, information accessibility and innovation have here been considered the main factor of production, while capital and labour are treated as residuals.

Although information accessibility is clearly not the only factor in regional development, the analysis in chapter 7 indicates that it is able to explain about 50% of the regional variation in the *per capita* income of those regions which are closely linked to the urban system, *i.e.* the consolidated regions. This, of course, does not mean that capital is unimportant in the consolidated regions; it only means that capital in these regions tends to be distributed in proportion to the accessibility of the regions.

201

12.2 THE ECONOMIC PERIPHERY: THE ROLE OF CAPITAL

On the other hand, in the thinly populated peripheral regions, which have less diversified economies based on one or a few natural resources, information accessibility does not seem to be of much importance. In these regions availability of natural resources and direct capital inputs seem to play a role in themselves. Capital inputs can be either mining investment or more or less direct government subsidies, for instance in the form of grants of free port status, large military establishments, or large service sectors.

12.3 CHANGES IN THE REGIONAL INCOME DIFFERENCES

In chapter 8 some of the dynamic consequences of the hypothesized relationship between information accessibility and regional income differences have been investigated.

If information accessibility can be considered the most important factor of regional economic development, as the analysis in chapter 7 indicates for the consolidated regions, then we can draw an income-accessibility curve, analogous to the economists' production curve. In chapter 7 we found that such an income-accessibility curve is probably S-shaped.

If such an S-shaped income-accessibility curve exists, changes in regional income differences will depend on the location of the regions on the curve and on the changes in the regional accessibilities.

An investigation of the development of the regional accessibility differences resulting from network improvements, international integration and urban growth shows that the absolute differences are steadily increasing, while the relative differences have followed an inverted U-shaped curve.

By inserting the changes in accessibility into the S-shaped income-accessibility curve, regional *per capita* income differences were found to follow much the same pattern as the accessibility differences. The maximum relative differences in *per capita* income seem to correspond roughly to an income level at US $ 100 to US $ 400 *per capita* in 1960. South America as a whole should thus have past the maximum now and be experiencing decreasing relative income differences between the regions.

12.4 THE SOCIO-DEMOGRAPHIC PROCESSES: THE ROLE OF LABOUR

The socio-demographic processes, especially birth and migration, influence regional variations in *per capita* income by creating regional differences in the proportion of the economically active population. The proportion of active population varies between 25 and 50%, but in most regions it is around 30%. It is thus able to explain at most a regional variation in *per capita* income of about 50%. The socio-demographic processes have been investigated in part IV, and the findings both from chapter 7 and part IV have been summarized in Figure 12.1.

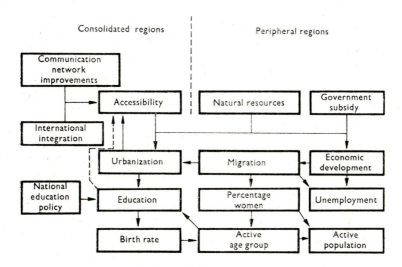

Fig. 12.1. *The process of regional development. A flow chart*

The findings in part IV show that the proportion of the population in the active age group (15–59 years) can be explained as a result of regional variations in the birth rate, as expressed by the child-women relation (children 0–5 years/women 15–49 years), except in a few thinly populated peripheral regions with very large predominantly male immigration. In these peripheral regions the active age groups tend to be larger than would be expected from their birth rate. That the size of the active age groups in most regions depends only on the child-women relation indicates that it is in general independent of migration, except in so far as migration influences the child-women relation. This conflicts with, or at least modifies, the often repeated postulate that heavy emigration from a region leads to an unfavourable age structure.

The proportion of active population within the active age group is basically determined by the sex ratio, here expressed as the percentage of women. The variation in this activity rate, however, is not very large, except in the same peripheral regions with very large male immigration mentioned above.

In brief, the proportion of active population can be expressed as a function of the child-women relation and the proportion of women, or of birth-rate and migration to the peripheral areas. Of these, migration to the peripheral areas is correlated with population density, and the birth-rate is related to education and urbanization, which in turn are correlated with information accessibility. In the regression analysis on *per capita* income carried out in chapter 7, accessibility and population density, therefore, have already accounted for most of the variation due to the activity rates.

Finally, the relation between birth-rate (child-women relation), education (percentage illiteracy), and urbanization has been analysed in chapter 9. It has often been stated that the birth-rate tends to decrease with increasing urbanization and a higher level of education. This could only be verified subject to modification. The child-women relation was found to be better explained by education than by urbanization, but none of the relations were found to be linear. The relation between the child-women relation and illiteracy has the shape of an inverted U with its maximum for an illiteracy rate of 50–60%. Only for illiteracy rates lower than this was the child-women relation positively related to illiteracy.

The illiteracy rates and urbanization were in turn found to be negatively correlated, but the relation was hyperbolic rather than linear, so that the decrease in illiteracy corresponding to a 1% increase in urbanization is much larger at low than at high levels of urbanization. Consequently, in the interval where illiteracy is positively related to the child-women relation, the relation between illiteracy and urbanization is only weak. This explains why urbanization does not very effectively lead to reduced birth-rates.

12.5 THE NATIONAL DIFFERENCES

Much of the literature on Latin American development emphasizes the national differences between the Latin American countries, it is, therefore, interesting that only in one case deviations from the structural relations were found to vary systematically with the nationality of the regions. The national differences which clearly exist are not structural differences, but appear to be due to differences in the composition of regions with different positions in the multi-dimensional development space.

The only significant national differences found were in the relation between the levels of urbanization and illiteracy, where the level of illiteracy corresponding to a given level of urbanization varies from country to country. These national differences might be due to differences in the definition of illiteracy, but are most likely due to different educational policies.

12.6 POLICIES OF REGIONAL DEVELOPMENT

Most, if not all, forms of planning are directed towards the attainment of two often conflicting goals, namely, efficiency and equity. In the case of regional planning the two goals can be formulated as follows:

1. To utilize the nation's resources, no matter in which region they are located, to the best advantage of the nation;
2. To reduce interregional differences in levels of living.

In terms of the four-group typology of regions developed in chapter 2, the first of these two goals corresponds to integration of the natural resource regions and the core regions, while the second goal rather corresponds to the integration of the densely populated, low income, depressed areas and the core regions.

Actual policy in the South American countries has for the most part been geared to the attainment of the first of these goals. The policies favoured have sought to develop the natural resources in the peripheral regions through direct investments in mines and land settlement schemes, through the construction of transport and communication links between the resources and the core regions and through attempts to build manufacturing industries on the basis of the natural resources. Many examples of such schemes can be mentioned, for instance the Carretera Marginal in Peru, the highway to the Chilean north, agricultural settlement schemes in nearly all the countries, and Ciudad Guayana in Venezuela.

This is in accordance with the pattern of change observed in chapter 2. Here we found that the only regions, which tended to become more industrialized were – except for the core regions – the natural resource regions. The efficacy of these very costly resource development projects as a tool for regional development, however, is doubtful, because only few industries today are likely to have their optimal location near the natural resources.

Goal number 2, the reduction of regional differences in levels of living, would be much better satisfied by integration of the densely populated, depressed regions and the core regions, i.e. by integration of the already consolidated regions. Such policies, however, have been much weaker, and according to our analysis in chapter 2, none of the regions classified as depressed, became more industrialized in the decade 1950–60; they all became more dependent on the extraction of natural resources and on services.

This process of integration between the depressed regions and the core regions, however, is the one which is described by our accessibility income model. According to the model the *per capita* income of a region is, other things being equal, a function of the information accessibility of the region, and this accessibility can be increased by improving the transport and communication networks, by international integration and by increased local participation.

All these three elements are at least partly subject to policy decisions. They are, however, not equally acceptable politically, nor are they equally effective.

The simulations in chapter 8 indicate that policies of urbanization, social development and education – aimed at increasing local participation – would be much more effective tools in the planning of economic development, than policies of network improvement and international integration. In practice, however, it has been easier to reach agreement on policies of network improvement, which are the least effective, than on the two others. Consequently, the communication and transportation networks of South America have been developing rapidly since 1950.

However, the long distance links, both between the metropolitan areas and to the peripheral regions have developed much more rapidly than the local links within the already consolidated regions. While the Pan-American highway network is nearing completion, most local roads even close to the large cities are still dirt roads; and while long distance telephone connexions are being created via satellites, many villages have no or only a single telephone, and the telephone networks of the large cities are hopelessly overloaded. As both ends of the communication lines are equally important, this is very unfortunate; the more so because development of the local network would be much more effective in increasing local participation.

To improve the accessibility of the depressed areas, policies of regional development must be geared directly to the improvement of local participation.

However, it will in any case be difficult to reduce interregional accessibility differences because improvement of accessibility in one region will necessarily improve accessibility in the other regions as well.

12.7 EXTENSION OF THE RESULTS TO OTHER WORLD REGIONS

The issues treated in this volume are all keenly discussed by regional planners and economists throughout the world. In all world regions, policies of social, national, and international integration have been discussed or attempted with more or less vigour. (See Mouton/ UNRISD's publication series on experiences in and prospects for regional development: USA (Cumberland, 1971), South and Southeast Asia (Lefeber and Datta-Chaudhuri, 1971), Latin America (Stöhr, 1974) and Eastern Europe (Mihailovic, 1972). It might therefore be of interest to see to what extent the conclusions of this volume are valid for other continents than South America.

There are many reasons why the conclusions should not hold elsewhere. The cultural and historical traditions of Asia and Africa and of Europe and North America, are very different from those of Latin America, and the cultural variation from country to country or even from region to region is much larger. Many of the empirical findings, therefore, might not be true in general. In Latin America the common cultural background has been an important factor in the uniformity of both the birth rate and the migration structure, and the common language certainly facilitates trade, migration, and information flows. Also the educational level, which is the only one of the analysed variables which showed large national differences in South America, is likely to show still larger differences in other parts of the world.

But even if the cultural differences did not matter, one should not extrapolate the model to areas with levels of urbanization and economic development much lower or much higher than those of South America.

The process of urbanization and economic development is a transition period during which society develops from a set of isolated villages into an integrated urban system. It is this period of spatial integration which is depicted by our model. Development before and during the very early stages of the period of spatial integration is poorly depicted by the model, because the interregional flows are non-existent or so small that the index of information accessibility based on the gravity concept is too gross. Here Ivo Barbarovic's (1971) study of rural development in Brazil, in which he distinguishes between rural-to-urban accessibility and interurban accessibility, might prove to be a fruitful improvement.

Development in the last phases of the transition period and in the fully integrated urban system is also poorly depicted by the model. Here the interregional flows can be carried out almost instantaneously. The flows, however, also become specialized, because their volume becomes too large for single individuals to handle them. The multi-purpose, gravity-type flow index, therefore, is no longer sufficient. Only certain types of information are important for the regional development process, and it will be necessary to develop new specialized indices based on content analysis of the information flows.

Finally, it should be remembered that the information accessibility model even in South America only holds good within the consolidated regions. The model, therefore, should be expected to fit better in densely populated, consolidated countries, than in countries with large thinly populated peripheries.

Appendices

APPENDIX A

Census data for 74 regions in South America

A.1 INTRODUCTION

This appendix presents the data matrix used in the present investigation. It contains a number of demographic variables corresponding to 74 subnational geographic units, or regions, covering the whole of South America. Each of the regions consists of one or more administrative areas (provinces, departments, or states) of the South American countries. It has been attempted to create regions consisting of a large city and its hinterland; however, this has not been possible in all cases. Lists of the administrative areas are given in appendix C, and a list of the 74 regions, their code numbers and the administrative areas of which they consist is given in appendix D.

One of the problems of international research on regional (subnational) problems is that regional data, if they exist at all, are comparable neither from country to country nor from census to census, because census definitions vary from country to country and from census to census.

In cases where the census definition of a variable does not correspond to the definition chosen here, it has, therefore, been necessary either to recompute the variable if finer cross tabulations exist, or where cross tabulations of the data do not exist to estimate it.

The most common deviation between census definitions and the definitions here chosen is that active and illiterate population, which here have been counted among population 15 years old and more, in many censuses are presented for population 7, 10 or 12 years old or more. We have thus needed to estimate the active or illiterate population in the age groups below 15 years.

In section A.2 and A.3 of this appendix we shall describe in detail two estimation methods which have been applied several times, namely:

211

- The method applied to estimate the distribution of the economically active population in the age group below 15 years among economic sectors and geographical areas;
- The method applied to estimate the unemployment 15 years old and more when it is only known for the age group 10 (or 12) years old and more.

Also some data will be presented which give an impression of the error involved in the estimations. (The exact procedure applied in each case where estimation has been necessary is stated for each country and year in the notes after the tables.)

Another variable for which census definitions vary from census to census is urban population. To correct these data on urban population has not been possible, but we shall in section A.4 present some data which indicate the size of the error involved in using different definitions. The exact definitions applied by the different censuses are given in the notes after the tables.

In evaluating the data it must be kept in mind that they are never better than the published censuses and in many cases they are of lower quality because estimation has been necessary to achieve comparable data.

A.2 DISTRIBUTION OF THE ECONOMICALLY ACTIVE POPULATION 15 YEARS OLD AND MORE AMONG ECONOMIC SECTORS AND GEOGRAPHICAL AREAS

For the whole country information on the total active population 15 years old and more distributed in economic sectors is given in most censuses, but in many cases the distribution of the active population in geographical areas has only been given for the age group 12 (or 10) years old and more. We must therefore distribute in geographical areas the known national active population in each of the economic sectors and in the age group 12–14 (or 10–14) years. (*i.e.* the column sums of the matrix in Table A.1).

The estimation method to be described here requires that also the total active population 12–14 (or 10–14) years old in each of the geographical areas (*i.e.* row sums in the matrix in Table A.1) is known. This is the case in some countries; in others we have estimated these figures as described in the notes below the tables.

The problem can thus be stated in the following way: We have the matrix of active population 12 years old and more distributed in economic sectors and geographical areas. We want the elements of the same matrix for the age group 12–14 years. Of this second matrix we only know the row and column sums (either directly or estimated).

To utilize this information as well as possible, the elements of the matrix of 12–14 years old active population has been estimated by an iterative procedure with the following steps:

1. The national active population 12–14 years old in each economic sector (the column sums of matrix Table A.1), is distributed among the geographical areas in proportion to the known distribution of the active population 12 years old and more in the sector. This results in the matrix in Table A.2;

2. When we, row by row, add the values of the matrix elements obtained in this way, the sums will not necessarily be equal to the known (or previously estimated) 'real' row sums – the total active population 12–14 years old in each geographical area. To achieve this correspondence between the 'real' and the computed row sums, we divide each row by its computed sum and multiply it by its 'real' sum;

3. Now the column sums do not fit any more, but the deviations will be smaller than before for the row sums. Then the column sums are adjusted by dividing all the elements in a column by their computed sum and multiplying them by their 'real' sum. Now the column sum will fit, but the row sums need not fit any more. The differences between the computed and the 'real' sums, however, will be smaller than before;

4. By continuing these alternating adjustments of row and column sums the deviations become smaller and smaller. Empirically 5–8 adjustments are sufficient to bring the deviations below 1;

5. The matrix obtained in this way (Table A.3) has been used as an estimate of the active population 12–14 years old in each sector in each geographical area. By subtracting these estimates from the corresponding active population 12 years old and more we have obtained an estimate of the active population 15 years old and more.

The example shown in the Tables A.1, A.2 and A.3 refer to Paraguay, 1950. For this example the real values of the active population 15 years old and more exist so that we can have an impression of the error involved in the estimation method. Only in a few cases was the error larger than 1 per cent and in most cases it was smaller than 1/3 of a per cent of the active population 15 years old and more (the average error was $1688/425,262 = 0.4\%$). Of the active population 12–14 years old the error was $1688/11,888 = 14.2\%$.

Table A.1 *Economically active population 12–14 years old. Real values. Paraguay, 1950*

Province	(0) Agriculture	(1) Mining	(2/3) Manufacturing	(4) Construction	(5) Elec., gas, water	(6) Commerce	(7) Transport	(8) Services	Total active population
Asunción	33	–	469	51	1	214	48	2,469	3,285
Concepción	151	3	47	2	–	16	5	192	416
San Pedro	188	–	19	1	–	6	6	166	386
Caaguazú	496	–	17	2	1	14	1	142	673
Amambay	68	–	6	–	–	4	2	48	128
Cordillera	640	–	42	–	–	9	6	242	939
Paraguarí	715	–	113	2	–	15	10	345	1,200
Central	436	–	399	11	1	36	14	459	1,356
Guairá	537	–	27	3	–	10	4	203	784
Caazapá	608	–	5	1	–	7	2	156	779
Misiones	158	–	8	3	–	5	7	148	329
Ñeembucú	148	–	12	2	–	2	4	106	274
Alta Paraná	52	–	4	–	–	2	1	24	83
Itapúa	605	–	37	2	–	24	11	251	930
Pdte. Hayes	69	–	12	–	–	3	1	63	148
Boquerón	111	–	2	–	–	1	1	35	150
Olimpo	10	–	–	–	–	–	–	18	28
Total Paraguay	5,025	3	1,219	80	3	368	123	5,067	11,888

Table A.2 *First iteration in the estimation of the economically active population 12–14 years old. Paraguay, 1950*

Province	(0) Agri-culture	(1) Mining	(2/3) Manufac-turing	(4) Construc-tion	(5) Elec., gas, water	(6) Commerce	(7) Trans-port	(8) Services	Total active population Esti-mated	Total active population 'Real'
Asunción	61	–	385	47	3	158	62	2,499	3,215	3,285
Concepción	209	2	54	2	–	13	6	247	533	416
San Pedro	287	–	37	1	–	7	7	145	484	386
Caaguazú	377	–	33	1	–	11	2	95	519	673
Amambay	73	–	13	–	–	5	1	57	149	128
Cordillera	703	–	77	4	–	24	5	246	1,059	939
Paraguarí	734	–	103	4	–	24	4	297	1,166	1,200
Central	625	1	261	10	–	57	9	377	1,340	1,356
Guairá	423	–	63	3	–	14	4	214	721	784
Caazapá	353	–	22	1	–	7	2	107	492	779
Misiones	164	–	23	2	–	7	1	134	331	329
Ñeembucú	210	–	37	1	–	9	3	112	372	274
Alta Paraná	51	–	10	–	–	1	–	28	90	83
Itapúa	484	–	70	3	–	24	11	236	828	930
Pdte. Hayes	115	–	21	1	–	4	3	92	236	140
Boquerón	145	–	8	–	–	2	2	155	312	150
Olimpo	11	–	2	–	–	1	1	26	41	28
Total Paraguay	5,025	3	1,219	80	3	368	123	5,067	11,888	11,888

Table A.3 *Final estimation of the economically active population 12–14 years old. Paraguay, 1950*

Province	(0) Agri-culture	(1) Mining	(2/3) Manufac-turing	(4) Construc-tion	(5) Elec., gas, water	(6) Commerce	(7) Trans-port	(8) Services	Total active population
Asunción	60	–	400	36	3	160	64	2,562	3,285
Concepción	160	2	43	1	–	10	5	195	416
San Pedro	227	–	31	1	–	5	5	117	386
Caaguazú	485	–	44	1	–	14	3	126	673
Amambay	63	–	–	8	–	4	1	52	128
Cordillera	615	–	70	3	–	21	5	225	939
Paraguarí	744	–	109	3	–	25	4	315	1,200
Central	618	1	271	8	–	57	9	392	1,356
Guairá	455	–	70	2	–	15	4	228	784
Caazapá	555	–	36	1	–	11	3	173	779
Misiones	161	–	23	1	–	7	1	136	329
Ñeembucú	153	–	28	1	–	7	2	83	274
Alta Paraná	48	–	–	7	–	1	–	27	83
Itapúa	535	–	81	2	–	27	13	272	930
Pdte. Hayes	71	–	13	1	–	2	2	59	148
Boquerón	68	–	–	3	–	1	1	77	150
Olimpo	7	–	–	1	–	1	1	18	28
Total Paraguay	5,025	3	1,219	80	3	368	123	5,067	11,888

The sum of numerical differences between the elements in tables A.1 and A.3 is 1688.

A.3 ESTIMATION OF THE UNEMPLOYMENT FOR POPULATION 15 YEARS OLD
AND MORE

In many cases unemployment figures were only available for age groups
12 (or 10) years old or more, sometimes even at the national level only.

When data exist on national unemployment in the age group 12–14
(or 10–14) years they are distributed among the geographical areas in
proportion to the total active population in the age group.

Where data on national unemployment are not available the unemployment in the age group 15 years old and more is for each geographical
area computed by the formula:

Unemployed (15 years+) area i

$$= \frac{(\text{Unemployed (12 years}+)\text{ area } i)\times(\text{population (15 years}+)\text{ area } i)}{\text{Population (12 years}+)\text{ area } i}$$

The unemployment figures for the geographical areas obtained by this
formula do not necessarily add up to the national total obtained by the
formula. To achieve this, all the provincial estimates are divided by their
sum and multiplied by the estimate obtained for the country as a whole

A.4 URBAN POPULATION

The data on urban population in all the tables are for urban population as defined in the respective censuses. Unfortunately the definition
varies from country to country. In some countries the urban population
is defined as the population in urban places of more than a certain size;
for instance 2,000 inhabitants, as in Argentina. In other countries, and
this is the most common, urban population is defined as the population
of the administrative centres of the lowest order administrative areas.

There is no way of correcting the data for the differences in definition,
but for a few countries the information is given according to two definitions, which makes it possible to get some idea of the probable error
resulting from the use of different definitions of urban population.

For Colombia information is available both for a size criterion (1,500
inhabitants) and for an administrative criterion. To get a rough idea of
the differences between the two definitions we have in Figure A.1 shown
the relationship between the percentages of urban population according
to the two definitions. The administrative criterion is seen to result in

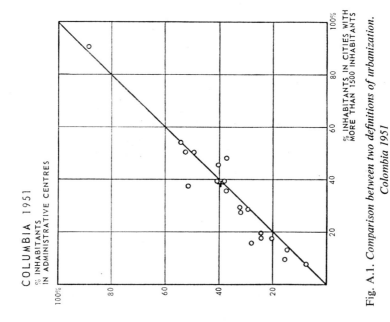

Fig. A.1. *Comparison between two definitions of urbanization.*
Colombia 1951

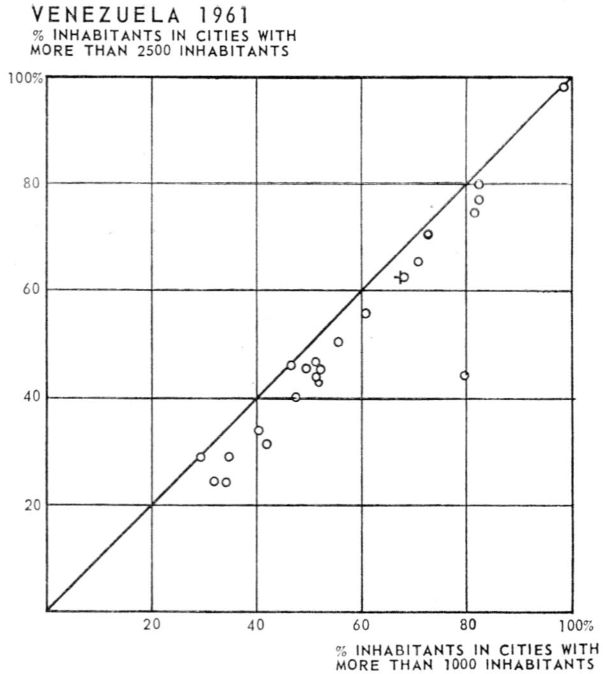

Fig. A.2. *Comparison between two definitions of urbanization.*
Venezuela 1961

larger values of urbanization than the size criterion in areas with low level of urbanization, but smaller values in areas with high level of urbanization. The reason is that the administrative centres in little urbanized areas are often smaller than the fixed size of 1,500 inhabitants, while towns of more than 1,500 inhabitants in highly urbanized areas are not necessarily administrative centres.

For Venezuela we have information about urban population according to two different size criteria, 1,000 inhabitants and 2,500 inhabitants. This corresponds as far as we can judge to the maximum range of the definitions in different countries. If, therefore, we assume that the lower end of the rank-size curve has the same slope in all the South American countries (this of course need not be true), the differences between the percentages of urban population according to the two size criteria should give us an impression of the error involved in using different definitions. In Figure A.2 we have compared the percentages of urban population according to the two definitions. The relationship between the two percentages, $U_{1,000}$ and $U_{2,500}$, is on the average given by the equation:

$$U_{2,500} = 1{,}07 \, U_{1,000} - 10$$

This means that the differences in degree of urbanization obtained by the two definitions vary between 3 and 10 per cent when the degree of urbanization varies between 0 and 100 per cent, the error being smallest for low levels of urbanization.

Finally, a note on the size criteria should be made. Many studies of urbanization use a size criterion of 20,000 or even 100,000 inhabitants. Such a definition is relevant where only the urban population is to be studied because urban characteristics are sure to be found here. Where urban and rural population are to be compared, such a definition, however, is not likely to be good because a great part of the rural population will have urban characteristics. Central place studies in European countries indicate that the size criterion involved in the census definitions (1,000–2,000 inhabitants), is reasonable. For South America, however, it is likely to be too small, so that a size criteria of 5,000 inhabitants, if available, might have been preferable.

Another reason for avoiding the big-size criteria is that we are concerned with small sub-national units in which inclusion or not of a small city close to the limit (19,900 $\sim$ 20,100) will have a very large impact on the degree of urbanization.

TABLES 1960: 1–6, AND 1950: 1–6

In the following tables 0 and 0.00 mean that no data has been available, except for region 29 (Tierre del Fuego) in 1950 where the urban population was 0 and the percentage of urban population 0.00.

Regional codes. The first 8 ciphers on each line of the tables are the regional codes:

Cipher:

1–2	Number of region	(see appendix D)
3	Country code	(see appendix D)
4–5	Letter code for region	(see appendix D)
6	Table number	
7–8	Year	

1960: Table 1 *Population*

Code No C Re T Ye	Area km²	Total pop.	Urban pop.	Census pop.	Urb. census pop.	Women	Pop. 0–4 years	Women 15–49 years
02 4 IQ 1 60	58,073	123,070	107,211	123,070	107,211	59,555	16,795	28,838
03 4 AN 1 60	125,306	215,219	203,997	215,219	203,997	104,712	31,707	50,843
04 4 SE 1 60	117,915	425,226	245,607	425,226	245,226	213,764	68,520	95,328
05 4 SA 1 60	48,110	3,613,457	3,008,586	3,613,457	3,008,586	1,885,235	526,758	931,702
06 4 TA 1 60	30,518	563,042	227,206	563,042	227,206	278,620	86,506	120,664
07 4 CO 1 60	50,102	1,257,638	726,856	1,257,638	726,856	631,568	196,636	285,366
08 4 VD 1 60	46,086	798,453	333,459	798,453	333,459	397,364	121,955	182,850
09 4 PM 1 60	148,802	304,652	112,269	304,652	112,269	156,942	47,247	71,061
10 4 PA 1 60	132,033	73,156	60,869	73,156	60,869	33,548	8,596	17,748
11 1 SA 1 60	207,994	654,316	345,564	654,316	345,564	317,996	98,963	151,351
12 1 FO 1 60	72,066	178,526	59,948	178,526	59,948	86,989	30,514	39,337
13 1 CR 1 60	187,832	1,076,532	452,775	1,076,532	452,775	534,820	167,575	239,091
14 1 TU 1 60	22,524	773,972	420,837	773,972	420,837	384,323	109,804	179,538
15 1 LR 1 60	192,149	296,451	125,228	296,451	125,228	150,904	44,204	65,746
16 1 ES 1 60	135,254	476,503	167,944	476,503	167,944	243,591	72,190	104,100
17 1 CD 1 60	168,766	1,753,840	1,196,190	1,753,840	1,196,190	876,912	185,090	452,495
18 1 RO 1 60	133,007	1,884,918	1,436,799	1,884,918	1,436,799	938,750	181,088	493,662
19 1 PA 1 60	76,216	805,357	398,314	805,357	398,314	402,568	101,094	189,378
20 1 SJ 1 60	86,137	352,387	191,388	352,387	191,388	177,157	48,332	85,660
21 1 ME 1 60	150,839	824,036	527,421	824,036	527,421	411,564	97,135	213,382
22 1 SL 1 60	76,748	174,316	90,232	174,316	90,232	86,619	22,229	40,564
23 1 SR 1 60	143,440	158,746	91,565	158,746	91,565	74,666	16,930	38,080
24 1 BA 1 60	308,004	9,732,742	8,850,629	9,732,742	8,850,629	4,912,452	824,654	2,623,052
26 1 NE 1 60	297,091	303,182	175,494	303,182	175,494	143,137	43,172	70,005
27 1 RA 1 60	224,686	142,412	77,500	142,412	77,500	65,336	19,160	33,130
28 1 SC 1 60	243,943	52,908	28,353	52,908	28,353	19,161	5,885	10,020
29 1 US 1 60	20,392	7,995	7,064	7,955	7,064	2,676	922	1,385
30 1 PO 1 60	29,801	361,440	115,096	361,440	115,096	175,021	61,629	79,383
31 7 AS 1 62	159,827	1,744,974	635,410	1,744,974	635,410	890,241	298,769	391,581
34 7 ME 1 62	246,925	74,129	16,459	74,129	16,459	34,698	13,150	15,591
35 0 MO 1 63	187,000	2,592,600	2,132,000	2,592,600	2,132,000	1,300,900	254,200	651,400
42 8 PU 1 62	67,386	727,309	0	686,260	124,147	355,338	112,818	160,325

43 8 AR 1 62	94,467	528,223		0	506,519	321,364	244,709	77,284	113,082
44 8 CU 1 62	175,283	977,085		0	915,085	259,240	462,443	150,468	208,165
45 8 LI 1 62	55,174	2,573,981		0	2,500,521	2,094,856	1,236,406	385,647	615,173
46 8 HU 1 62	165,813	1,798,259		0	1,702,087	536,055	872,946	296,292	383,959
47 8 IQ 1 62	531,400	581,796		0	498,857	225,903	245,236	100,503	104,128
48 8 TR 1 62	152,817	2,483,912		0	2,372,664	804,991	1,205,030	415,451	533,991
49 8 PI 1 62	37,785	749,792		0	724,753	331,622	359,120	133,063	156,926
50 3 PA 1 60	95,483	2,129,252	688,358	688,358	2,129,252	688,358	1,050,147	379,317	468,310
51 3 CU 1 60	199,060	4,277,763	1,327,982	1,327,982	4,277,763	1,327,982	0	0	0
52 3 SP 1 60	247,898	12,974,699	8,149,979	8,149,979	12,974,699	8,149,979	0	0	0
53 3 RJ 1 60	1,171	3,281,908	3,198,591	3,198,591	3,281,908	3,198,591	1,687,909	384,219	921,109
54 3 BH 1 60	39,368	1,169,553	370,075	370,075	1,169,553	370,075	575,130	209,368	259,913
55 3 RE 1 60	257,314	9,343,516	3,724,086	3,724,086	9,343,516	3,724,086	0	0	0
56 3 SA 1 60	559,951	5,990,605	2,083,716	2,083,716	5,990,605	2,083,716	0	0	0
57 3 FO 1 60	149,323	3,337,856	1,124,829	1,124,829	3,337,856	1,124,829	0	0	0
58 3 TE 1 60	576,857	3,726,571	735,417	735,417	3,726,571	735,417	1,853,225	636,176	855,934
59 3 BR 1 60	647,807	2,096,604	689,102	689,102	2,096,604	689,102	0	0	0
60 3 BE 1 60	1,367,938	1,606,713	659,057	659,057	1,606,713	659,057	797,089	280,716	365,488
61 3 MA 1 60	1,943,020	902,497	282,648	282,648	902,497	282,648	435,938	167,651	196,928
62 3 CI 1 60	243,044	70,232	30,626	30,626	70,232	30,626	31,194	13,253	14,408
63 6 QU 1 62	166,309	1,761,349	653,831	653,831	1,761,349	653,831	889,969	280,249	414,768
64 6 GU 1 62	117,252	2,712,267	957,515	957,515	2,712,267	957,515	1,348,489	481,965	598,819
65 9 CA 1 61	16,920	2,063,999	1,850,198	1,850,198	2,063,999	1,850,198	1,014,050	330,008	495,428
66 9 CB 1 61	453,950	259,279	160,244	160,244	259,279	160,244	123,932	51,170	52,125
67 9 BA 1 61	85,150	1,119,703	651,781	651,781	1,119,703	651,781	555,071	220,191	230,458
68 9 AP 1 61	176,690	501,814	212,055	212,055	501,814	212,055	242,804	102,727	100,383
69 9 SC 1 61	22,400	669,831	290,803	290,803	669,831	290,803	329,710	126,258	138,635
70 9 MA 1 61	50,230	919,863	760,094	760,094	919,863	760,094	449,869	170,903	198,578
71 9 BQ 1 61	93,470	1,989,510	1,148,670	1,148,670	1,989,510	1,148,670	986,843	372,779	422,565
72 5 BA 1 64	132,235	3,246,017	1,946,102	1,946,102	3,246,017	1,946,102	1,640,043	580,048	717,484
73 5 BU 1 64	143,005	2,617,999	883,816	883,816	2,617,999	883,816	1,333,421	469,089	573,688
74 5 ME 1 64	123,145	4,115,034	2,228,752	2,228,752	4,115,034	2,228,752	2,091,907	739,591	922,668
75 5 CA 1 64	241,855	2,130,728	2,130,728	2,130,728	4,463,576	2,130,728	2,242,630	781,327	1,010,829
76 5 BO 1 64	109,730	2,985,054	2,035,552	2,035,552	2,985,054	2,035,552	1,534,976	505,783	725,541
77 5 CM 1 64	388,900	40,097	5,636	5,636	40,097	5,636	18,533	7,362	8,650
78 0 GE 1 60	214,969	560,330	0	0	560,330	0	281,202	98,177	120,257
79 0 PM 1 64	142,822	324,211	0	0	324,211	0	162,356	53,513	67,708
80 0 CA 1 61	91,000	33,535	18,000	18,000	33,535	18,000	16,496	4,666	7,019

1960: Table 2 *Population*

Code No C Re T Ye	Pop. 0–14 years	Pop. 60+ years	Pop. 15+ years	Illit. pop. 15+ years	Active pop. 15+ years	Unempl. pop.
02 4 IQ 2 60	45,536	8,911	77,534	6,110	41,940	2,883
03 4 AN 2 60	81,250	13,261	133,969	9,650	71,799	6,643
04 4 SE 2 60	181,706	28,566	243,520	50,027	125,425	8,887
05 4 SA 2 60	1,358,189	249,935	2,255,268	167,342	1,194,326	161,811
06 4 TA 2 60	236,420	43,062	326,622	92,102	171,289	6,995
07 4 CO 2 60	531,218	78,788	726,420	172,123	376,226	21,287
08 4 VD 2 60	335,993	51,101	462,460	111,149	244,397	12,552
09 4 PM 2 60	129,972	21,311	174,680	35,710	93,653	3,628
10 4 PA 2 60	22,234	4,865	50,922	3,114	30,384	1,907
11 1 SA 2 60	267,162	30,813	387,154	82,963	228,165	7,039
12 1 FO 2 60	81,191	7,056	97,335	19,372	54,990	1,586
13 1 CR 2 60	468,941	62,103	607,591	131,936	341,527	10,882
14 1 TU 2 60	312,423	47,027	461,549	60,806	252,824	10,023
15 1 LR 2 60	127,503	21,193	168,948	19,686	94,526	6,105
16 1 ES 2 60	211,354	31,223	265,149	53,919	140,381	9,242
17 1 CD 2 60	551,661	145,670	1,202,179	96,714	643,750	18,619
18 1 RO 2 60	534,320	182,672	1,350,598	112,535	690,301	16,829
19 1 PA 2 60	299,720	67,516	505,637	65,647	272,575	8,761
20 1 SJ 2 60	138,831	21,038	213,556	26,451	115,530	4,362
21 1 ME 2 60	281,616	54,620	542,420	62,411	292,449	8,460
22 1 SL 2 60	66,094	13,032	108,222	11,945	61,057	2,136
23 1 SR 2 60	50,589	13,860	108,157	11,031	62,028	808
24 1 BA 2 60	2,409,083	1,045,995	7,323,659	352,662	3,853,379	75,451
26 1 NE 2 60	118,068	15,004	185,114	32,404	109,948	2,131
27 1 RA 2 60	51,664	7,482	90,748	12,109	57,063	867
28 1 SC 2 60	14,259	2,917	38,649	2,233	28,682	379
29 1 US 2 60	2,174	289	5,781	248	4,276	35
30 1 PO 2 60	158,715	16,666	202,725	34,727	121,073	1,597
31 7 AS 2 62	801,933	104,029	943,041	236,395	537,785	23,073
34 7 ME 2 62	32,790	3,332	41,339	14,031	23,863	1,308
35 0 MO 2 63	721,500	303,300	1,854,800	179,500	997,100	116,700

42 8 PU 2 62	293,539	56,625	392,721	252,599	217,532	1,853
43 8 AR 2 62	207,303	31,991	299,216	78,479	177,398	3,134
44 8 CU 2 62	383,343	76,536	531,742	363,010	282,532	2,659
45 8 LI 2 62	989,295	122,127	1,511,226	151,933	886,264	24,582
46 8 HU 2 62	758,351	114,495	943,736	523,627	482,175	5,220
47 8 IQ 2 62	250,765	16,892	248,092	77,675	132,920	1,942
48 8 TR 2 62	1,070,669	131,046	1,301,995	576,144	660,687	6,502
49 8 PI 2 62	336,819	36,549	387,934	162,176	205,457	3,061
50 6 PA 2 60	999,674	88,949	1,129,578	290,073	0	0
51 3 CU 2 60	0	0	0	0	0	0
52 3 SP 2 60	0	0	0	0	0	0
53 3 RJ 2 60	1,036,700	220,836	2,245,208	278,152	0	0
54 3 BH 2 60	545,738	47,190	623,815	263,586	0	0
55 3 RE 2 60	0	0	0	0	0	0
56 3 SA 2 60	0	0	0	0	0	0
57 3 FO 2 60	0	0	0	0	0	0
58 3 TE 2 60	1,722,263	147,935	2,004,308	1,277,803	0	0
59 3 BR 2 60	0	0	0	0	0	0
60 3 BE 2 60	728,546	69,556	878,167	333,871	0	0
61 3 MA 2 60	428,832	31,753	473,665	231,726	0	0
62 3 CI 2 60	31,784	1,882	38,448	16,838	0	0
63 6 QU 2 62	744,390	113,801	1,016,959	381,658	560,824	113,265
64 6 GU 2 62	1,268,998	127,048	1,443,269	417,810	793,504	10,223
65 9 CA 2 61	825,014	89,526	1,238,985	231,298	738,440	35,235
66 9 CB 2 61	124,126	10,406	135,153	47,270	75,568	10,759
67 9 BA 2 61	561,557	45,405	558,146	250,887	296,125	10,507
68 9 AP 2 61	246,945	20,083	254,869	136,089	141,297	45,027
69 9 SC 2 61	316,669	34,511	353,162	168,980	190,853	58,605
70 9 MA 2 61	429,986	34,657	489,877	154,912	257,299	0
71 9 BQ 2 61	935,000	94,846	1,054,510	509,814	562,081	0
72 5 BA 2 64	1,576,013	153,428	1,670,004	857,434	831,688	0
73 5 BU 2 64	1,242,986	144,193	1,375,013	674,824	726,513	37658
74 5 ME 2 64	1,951,573	202,429	2,163,461	672,271	1,073,090	48963
755 CA 364	673032 21016	175109 53155	3262 106584	45331	210040	0
765 BO 364	251370 15428	155098 56628	3627 104758	45579	250137	13,400
77 5 CM 2 64	17,739	1,304	22,358	17,478	12,213	0
78 0 GE 2 60	259,228	29,987	301,102	38,694	170,500	0
79 0 PM 2 64	147,927	19,678	176,284	0	0	
80 0 CA 2 61	12,358	3,243	21,177	0	11,981	

16

1960: Table 3. *Active population. Income per capita*

Code No C Re T Ye	(0) Agriculture	(1) Mining	(2/3) Manufacturing	(4) Construction	(5) Elec., gas, water	(6) Commerce	(7) Transport	(8) Services	(9) No specification
02 4 IQ 3 60	5,847	3,203	5,979	4,491	321	5,137	4,865	10,322	1,775
03 4 AN 3 60	2,162	22,140	8,139	5,660	604	6,467	7,668	14,019	4,940
04 4 SE 3 60	35,895	25,404	12,239	5,850	711	10,808	7,772	19,845	6,901
05 4 SA 3 60	181,298	15,705	281,112	69,536	11,845	154,133	62,389	332,287	86,021
06 4 TA 3 60	94,971	297	16,852	7,620	1,177	11,360	4,788	27,500	6,724
07 4 CO 3 60	146,058	20,054	59,414	21,107	2,265	27,395	14,414	67,062	18,457
08 4 VD 3 60	123,611	585	28,987	13,559	1,280	16,048	9,781	39,038	11,508
09 4 PM 3 60	49,910	530	10,034	5,168	379	5,142	4,019	14,911	3,560
10 4 PA 3 60	5,175	2,978	3,625	2,322	256	2,803	1,989	10,527	709
11 1 SA 3 60	69,329	4,642	42,121	13,038	1,998	19,221	12,780	44,053	20,983
12 1 FO 3 60	24,870	38	6,445	2,163	191	4,359	1,909	9,354	5 661
13 1 CR 3 60	133,481	439	49,139	16,526	2,034	27,934	15,124	64,399	32,451
14 1 TU 3 60	74,606	249	54,369	10,162	2,387	25,240	15,712	47,366	22,733
15 1 LR 3 60	22,671	993	15,007	7,174	1,770	6,948	4,976	23,645	11,342
16 1 ES 3 60	40,613	375	31,201	6,098	1,555	11,376	7,561	28,272	13,330
17 1 CD 3 60	141,247	4,842	140,370	35,602	6,361	76,680	41,467	130,460	66,721
18 1 RO 3 60	142,685	463	172,204	34,124	6,200	88,151	60,690	124,207	61,577
19 1 PA 3 60	81,697	1,360	45,157	15,887	2,114	28,968	17,936	53,765	25,693
20 1 SJ 3 60	39,359	1,538	16,269	8,614	1,116	11,963	4,040	25,229	7,402
21 1 ME 3 60	87,123	2,164	53,880	18,367	3,328	32,906	15,134	54,043	25,504
22 1 SL 3 60	13,534	2,087	8,809	4,042	1,036	5,153	4,863	13,940	7,593
23 1 SR 3 60	24,178	179	7,664	4,038	348	6,196	3,480	10,529	5,416
24 1 BA 3 60	310,767	4,195	1,171,948	233,647	49,762	543,494	299,024	842,412	398,135
26 1 NE 3 60	37,882	3,093	14,669	5,900	1,390	8,955	6,392	20,851	10,816
27 1 RA 3 60	14,689	7,729	6,905	3,597	508	4,628	4,005	11,155	3,847
28 1 SC 3 60	7,266	5,868	2,220	2,855	234	1,824	1,853	4,856	1,706
29 1 US 3 60	905	63	858	363	48	401	258	1,207	173
30 1 PO 3 60	57,049	126	16,759	4,230	338	9 083	4,361	18,384	10,743
31 7 AS 3 62	290,964	460	81,700	18,631	1,202	39,735	13,737	80,030	11,326
34 7 ME 3 62	12,185	10	5,117	712	2	893	683	3,615	646
35 0 MO 3 63	177,500	2,400	209,500	48,800	17,700	129,700	61,300	274,700	75,500
42 8 PU 3 62	155,454	4,166	19,825	4,450	162	13,564	2,521	13,098	4,292

43 8 AR 3 62	68,183	6,984	24,825	9,686	665	16,917	8,692	32,806	8,640
44 8 CU 3 62	185,450	2,531	30,567	5,655	380	20,745	3,362	26,103	7,739
45 8 LI 3 62	157,762	14,291	177,487	53,689	4,859	140,945	48,976	230,001	58,254
46 8 HU 3 62	322,073	25,059	38,953	8,924	557	27,369	7,814	38,446	12,980
47 8 IQ 3 62	85,147	439	10,186	1,892	203	8,555	2,748	19,543	4,207
48 8 TR 3 62	427,665	6,856	81,022	15,024	1,257	36,027	14,406	57,744	20,686
49 8 PI 3 62	113,588	5,872	25,425	5,041	456	15,539	5,253	26,337	7,946
50 3 PA 3 60	0	0	0	0	0	0	0	0	0
51 3 CU 3 60	0	0	0	0	0	0	0	0	0
52 3 SP 3 60	0	0	0	0	0	0	0	0	0
53 3 RJ 3 60	0	0	0	0	0	0	0	0	0
54 3 BH 3 60	0	0	0	0	0	0	0	0	0
55 3 RE 3 60	0	0	0	0	0	0	0	0	0
56 3 SA 3 60	0	0	0	0	0	0	0	0	0
57 3 FO 3 60	0	0	0	0	0	0	0	0	0
58 3 TE 3 60	0	0	0	0	0	0	0	0	0
59 3 PR 3 60	0	0	0	0	0	0	0	0	0
60 3 BE 3 60	0	0	0	0	0	0	0	0	0
61 3 MA 3 60	0	0	0	0	0	0	0	0	0
62 3 CI 3 60	0	0	0	0	0	0	0	0	0
63 6 QU 3 62	291,820	1,063	97,770	22,958	1,588	31,067	16,166	84,187	14,205
64 6 GU 3 62	448,288	2,366	105,365	23,975	3,029	64,464	26,581	94,723	24,613
65 9 CA 3 61	67,914	6,083	130,028	49,535	13,573	121,661	47,491	254,324	47,831
66 9 CB 3 61	25,591	6,461	6,662	5,410	467	7,366	3,212	15,239	5,160
67 9 BA 3 61	125,656	11,237	30,606	13,732	2,196	32,316	14,236	51,001	15,145
68 9 AP 3 61	80,976	1,098	8,033	5,363	630	11,847	3,512	24,352	5,486
69 9 SC 3 61	100,324	420	13,912	8,047	1,048	16,029	7,095	39,554	4,424
70 9 MA 3 61	59,146	22,254	29,924	19,000	1,652	38,999	18,724	48,256	19,344
71 9 BQ 3 61	240,839	5,917	65,072	29,373	3,731	65,132	23,048	101,468	27,501
72 5 BA 3 64	408,619	6,492	100,808	34,390	2,369	79,362	37,358	129,841	32,449
73 5 BU 3 64	420,012	10,426	70,797	27,285	1,642	48,354	20,932	112,516	14,549
74 5 ME 3 64	510,705	25,600	142,239	45,751	2,271	92,961	40,769	174,353	38,441
75 5 CA 3 64	673,032	21,016	175,109	53,155	3,262	106,584	45,331	210,040	37,658
76 5 BO 3 64	251,370	15,428	155,098	56,628	3,627	104,758	45,579	250,137	48,963
77 5 CM 3 64	9,262	5	336	189	2	355	105	1,876	83
78 0 GE 3 60	63,270	6,425	27,785	13,600	975	19,320	8,140	30,820	165
79 0 PM 3 64	0	0	0	0	0	0	0	0	0
80 0 CA 3 61	3,271	629	1,354	1,050	0	1,172	397	3,824	284

1960: Table 4 *Percentage population*

Code No C Re T Ye	Census pop.	Urban pop.	Women	Pop. 0-14 years	Pop. 60+ years	Pop. 15-59 years	Illit. pop. 15+ years	Active pop. 15+ years	Child-women relation	Pop. density per km²
02 4 IQ 4 60	100.00	87.11	48.39	37.00	7.24	55.76	7.88	54.09	58.24	2.12
03 4 AN 4 60	100.00	94.79	48.65	37.75	6.16	56.09	7.20	53.59	62.36	1.72
04 4 SE 4 60	100.00	57.76	50.27	42.73	6.72	50.55	20.54	51.51	71.88	3.61
05 4 SA 4 60	100.00	83.26	52.17	37.59	6.92	55.50	7.42	52.96	56.54	75.11
06 4 TA 4 60	100.00	40.35	49.48	41.99	7.65	50.36	28.20	52.44	71.69	18.45
07 4 CO 4 60	100.00	57.80	50.22	42.24	6.26	51.50	23.69	51.79	68.91	25.10
08 4 VD 4 60	100.00	41.76	49.77	42.08	6.40	51.52	24.03	52.85	66.70	17.33
09 4 PM 4 60	100.00	36.85	51.52	42.66	7.00	50.34	20.44	53.61	66.49	2.05
10 4 PA 4 60	100.00	83.20	45.86	30.39	6.65	62.96	6.12	59.67	48.43	0.55
11 1 SA 4 60	100.00	52.81	48.60	40.83	4.71	54.46	21.43	58.93	65.39	3.15
12 1 FO 4 60	100.00	33.58	48.73	45.48	3.95	50.57	19.90	56.50	77.57	2.48
13 1 CR 4 60	100.00	42.06	49.68	43.56	5.77	50.67	21.71	56.21	70.09	5.73
14 1 TU 4 60	100.00	54.37	49.66	40.37	6.08	53.56	13.17	54.78	61.16	34.36
15 1 LR 4 60	100.00	42.24	50.90	43.01	7.15	49.84	11.65	55.95	67.23	1.54
16 1 ES 4 60	100.00	35.25	51.12	44.36	6.55	49.09	20.34	52.94	69.35	3.52
17 1 CD 4 60	100.00	68.20	50.00	31.45	8.31	60.24	8.04	53.55	40.90	10.39
18 1 RO 4 60	100.00	76.23	49.80	28.35	9.69	61.96	8.33	51.11	36.68	14.17
19 1 PA 4 60	100.00	49.46	49.99	37.22	8.38	54.40	12.98	53.91	53.38	10.57
20 1 SJ 4 60	100.00	54.31	50.27	39.40	5.97	54.63	12.39	54.10	56.42	4.09
21 1 ME 4 60	100.00	64.00	49.94	34.18	6.63	59.20	11.51	53.92	45.52	5.46
22 1 SL 4 60	100.00	51.76	49.69	37.92	7.48	54.61	11.04	56.42	54.80	2.27
23 1 SR 4 60	100.00	57.68	47.03	31.87	8.73	59.40	10.20	57.35	44.46	1.11
24 1 BA 4 60	100.00	90.94	50.47	24.75	10.75	64.50	4.82	52.62	31.44	31.60
26 1 NE 4 60	100.00	57.88	47.21	38.94	4.95	56.11	17.50	59.39	61.67	1.02
27 1 RA 4 60	100.00	54.42	45.88	36.28	5.25	58.47	13.34	62.88	57.83	0.63
28 1 SC 4 60	100.00	53.59	36.22	26.95	5.51	67.54	5.78	74.21	58.73	0.22
29 1 US 4 60	100.00	88.80	33.64	27.33	3.63	69.04	4.29	73.97	66.57	0.39
30 1 PO 4 60	100.00	31.84	48.42	43.91	4.61	51.48	17.13	59.72	77.64	12.13
31 7 AS 4 62	100.00	36.41	51.02	45.96	5.96	48.08	25.07	57.03	76.30	10.92
34 7 ME 4 62	100.00	22.20	46.81	44.23	4.49	51.27	33.94	57.73	84.34	0.30
35 0 MO 4 63	100.00	82.23	50.18	27.83	11.70	60.47	9 68	53.76	39.02	13.86
42 8 PU 4 62	94.36	18.09	51.78	42.77	8.25	48.98	64.32	55.39	70.37	10.79

43 8 AR 4 62	95.89	63.45	48.31	40.93	6.32	52.76	26.23	59.29	68.34	5.59
44 8 CU 4 62	93.65	28.33	50.54	41.89	8.36	49.74	68.27	53.13	72.28	5.57
45 8 LI 4 62	97.15	83.78	49.45	39.56	4.88	55.55	10.05	58.65	62.69	46.65
46 8 HU 4 62	94.65	31.49	51.29	44.55	6.73	48.72	55.48	51.09	77.17	10.85
47 8 IQ 4 62	85.74	45.28	49.16	50.27	3.39	46.35	31.31	53.58	96.52	1.09
48 8 TR 4 62	95.52	33.93	50.79	45.13	5.52	49.35	44.25	50.74	77.80	16.25
49 8 PI 4 62	96.66	45.76	49.55	46.47	5.04	48.48	41.81	52.96	84.79	19.84
50 3 PA 4 60	100.00	32.33	49.32	46.95	4.18	48.87	25.68	0.00	81.00	22.30
51 3 CU 4 60	100.00	31.04	0.00	0.00	0.00	0.00	0.00	0.00	0.00	21.49
52 3 SP 4 60	100.00	62.81	0.00	0.00	0.00	0.00	0.00	0.00	0.00	52.34
53 3 RJ 4 60	100.00	97.46	51.43	31.59	6.73	61.68	12.39	0.00	41.71	2,802.65
54 3 BH 4 60	100.00	31.64	49.18	46.66	4.03	49.30	42.25	0.00	80.55	29.71
55 3 RE 4 60	100.00	39.86	0.00	0.00	0.00	0.00	0.00	0.00	0.00	36.31
56 3 SA 4 60	100.00	34.78	0.00	0.00	0.00	0.00	0.00	0.00	0.00	10.70
57 3 FO 4 60	100.00	33.70	0.00	0.00	0.00	0.00	0.00	0.00	0.00	22.35
58 3 TE 4 60	100.00	19.73	49.73	46.22	3.97	49.81	63.75	0.00	74.33	6.46
59 3 BR 4 60	100.00	32.87	0.00	0.00	0.00	0.00	0.00	0.00	0.00	3.24
60 3 BE 4 60	100.00	41.02	49.61	45.34	4.33	50.33	38.02	0.00	76.81	1.17
61 3 MA 4 60	100.00	31.32	48.30	47.52	3.52	48.97	48.92	0.00	85.13	0.46
62 3 CI 4 60	100.00	43.61	44.42	45.26	2.68	52.06	43.79	0.00	91.98	0.29
63 6 QU 4 62	100.00	37.12	50.53	42.26	6.46	51.28	37.53	55.15	67.57	10.59
64 6 GU 4 62	100.00	35.30	49.72	46.79	4.68	48.53	28.95	54.98	80.49	23.13
65 9 CA 4 61	100.00	89.64	49.13	39.97	4.34	55.69	18.67	59.60	66.61	121.99
66 9 CB 4 61	100.00	61.80	47.80	47.87	4.01	48.11	34.98	55.91	98.17	0.57
67 9 BA 4 61	100.00	58.21	49.57	50.15	4.06	45.79	44.95	53.06	95.54	13.15
68 9 AP 4 61	100.00	42.26	48.39	49.21	4.00	46.79	53.40	55.44	102.34	2.84
69 9 SC 4 61	100.00	43.41	49.22	47.28	5.15	47.57	47.85	54.04	91.07	29.90
70 9 MA 4 61	100.00	82.63	48.91	46.74	3.77	49.49	31.62	52.52	86.06	18.31
71 9 BQ 4 61	100.00	57.74	49.60	47.00	4.77	48.23	48.35	53.30	88.22	21.29
72 5 PA 4 64	100.00	59.95	50.52	48.55	4.73	46.72	51.34	49.80	80.84	24.55
73 5 BU 4 64	100.00	33.76	50.93	47.48	5.51	47.01	49.08	52.84	81.77	18.31
74 5 ME 4 64	100.00	54.16	50.84	47.43	4.92	47.66	31.07	49.60	80.16	33.42
75 5 CA 4 64	100.00	47.74	50.24	45.72	5.05	49.23	39.29	54.70	77.30	18.46
76 5 BO 4 64	100.00	68.19	51.42	44.23	4.57	51.20	22.94	55.96	69.71	27.20
77 5 CM 4 64	100.00	14.06	46.22	44.24	3.25	52.51	78.17	54.62	85.11	0.10
78 0 GE 4 60	100.00	0.00	50.19	46.26	5.35	48.38	12.85	56.63	81.64	2.61
79 0 PM 4 64	100.00	0.00	50.08	45.63	6.07	48.30	0.00	0.00	79.03	2.27
80 0 CA 4 61	100.00	53.68	49.19	36.85	9.67	53.48	0.00	56.58	66.48	0.37

1960: Table 5. *Percentage active population 15 years+ in the economic sectors*

Code No C Re T Ye	(0) Agriculture	(1) Mining	(2/3) Manufacturing	(4) Construction	(5) Elec., gas, water	(6) Commerce	(7) Transport	(8) Services	(9) No specification
02 4 IQ 5 60	13.94	7.64	14.26	10.71	0.77	12.25	11.60	24.61	4.23
03 4 AN 5 60	3.01	30.84	11.34	7.88	0.84	9.01	10.68	19.53	6.88
04 4 SE 5 60	28.62	20.25	9.76	4.66	0.57	8.62	6.20	15.82	5.50
05 4 SA 5 60	15.18	1.31	23.54	5.82	0.99	12.91	5.22	27.82	7.20
06 4 TA 5 60	55.44	0.17	9.84	4.45	0.69	6.63	2.80	16.05	3.93
07 4 CO 5 60	38.82	5.33	15.79	5.61	0.60	7.28	3.83	17.82	4.91
08 4 VD 5 60	50.58	0.24	11.86	5.55	0.52	6.57	4.00	15.97	4.71
09 4 PM 5 60	53.29	0.57	10.71	5.52	0.40	5.49	4.29	15.92	3.80
10 4 PA 5 60	17.03	9.80	11.93	7.64	0.84	9.23	6.55	34.65	2.33
11 1 SA 5 60	30.39	2.03	18.46	5.71	0.88	8.42	5.60	19.31	9.20
12 1 FO 5 60	45.23	0.07	11.72	3.93	0.35	7.93	3.47	17.01	10.29
13 1 CR 5 60	39.08	0.13	14.39	4.84	0.60	8.18	4.43	18.86	9.50
14 1 TU 5 60	29.51	0.10	21.50	4.02	0.94	9.98	6.21	18.73	8.99
15 1 LR 5 60	23.98	1.05	15.88	7.59	1.87	7.35	5.26	25.01	12.00
16 1 ES 5 60	28.93	0.27	22.23	4.34	1.11	8.10	5.39	20.14	9.50
17 1 CD 5 60	21.94	0.75	21.81	5.53	0.99	11.91	6.44	20.27	10.36
18 1 RO 5 60	20.67	0.07	24.95	4.94	0.90	12.77	8.79	17.99	8.92
19 1 PA 5 60	29.97	0.50	16.57	5.83	0.78	10.63	6.58	19.72	9.43
20 1 SJ 5 60	34.07	1.33	14.08	7.46	0.97	10.35	3.50	21.84	6.41
21 1 ME 5 60	29.79	0.74	18.42	6.28	1.14	11.25	5.17	18.48	8.72
22 1 SL 5 60	22.17	3.42	14.43	6.62	1.70	8.44	7.96	22.83	12.44
23 1 SR 5 60	38.98	0.29	12.36	6.51	0.56	9.99	5.61	16.97	8.73
24 1 BA 5 60	8.06	0.11	30.41	6.06	1.29	14.10	7.76	21.86	10.33
26 1 NE 5 60	34.45	2.81	13.34	5.37	1.26	8.14	5.81	18.96	9.84
27 1 RA 5 60	25.74	13.54	12.10	6.30	0.89	8.11	7.02	19.55	6.74
28 1 SC 5 60	25.33	20.46	7.74	9.95	0.82	6.36	6.46	16.93	5.95
29 1 US 5 60	21.16	1.47	20.07	8.49	1.12	9.38	6.03	28.23	4.05
30 1 PO 5 60	47.12	0.10	13.84	3.49	0.28	7.50	3.60	15.18	8.87
31 7 AS 5 62	54.10	0.09	15.19	3.46	0.22	7.39	2.55	14.88	2.11
34 7 ME 5 62	51.06	0.04	21.44	2.98	0.01	3.74	2.86	15.15	2.71
35 0 MO 5 63	17.80	0.24	21.01	4.89	1.78	13.01	6.15	27.55	7.57
42 8 PU 5 62	71.46	1.92	9.11	2.05	0.07	6.24	1.16	6.02	1.97

43 8 AR 5 62	4.87	18.49	4.90	9.54	0.37	5.46	13.99	3.94	38.44
44 8 CU 5 62	2.74	9.24	1.19	7.34	0.13	2.00	10.82	0.90	65.64
45 8 LI 5 62	6.57	25.95	5.53	15.90	0.55	6.06	20.03	1.61	17.80
46 8 HU 5 62	2.69	7.97	1.62	5.68	0.12	1.85	8.08	5.20	66.80
47 8 IQ 5 62	3.17	14.70	2.07	6.44	0.15	1.42	7.66	0.33	64.06
48 8 TR 5 62	3.13	8.74	2.18	5.45	0.19	2.27	12.26	1.04	64.73
49 8 PI 5 62	3.87	12.82	2.56	7.56	0.22	2.45	12.37	2.86	55.29
50 3 PA 5 60	0.00	0.00	0.00	0.00	0.00	0.00	0.00	0.00	0.00
51 3 CU 5 60	0.00	0.00	0.00	0.00	0.00	0.00	0.00	0.00	0.00
52 3 SP 5 60	0.00	0.00	0.00	0.00	0.00	0.00	0.00	0.00	0.00
53 3 RJ 5 60	0.00	0.00	0.00	0.00	0.00	0.00	0.00	0.00	0.00
54 3 BH 5 60	0.00	0.00	0.00	0.00	0.00	0.00	0.00	0.00	0.00
55 3 RE 5 60	0.00	0.00	0.00	0.00	0.00	0.00	0.00	0.00	0.00
56 3 SA 5 60	0.00	0.00	0.00	0.00	0.00	0.00	0.00	0.00	0.00
57 3 FO 5 60	0.00	0.00	0.00	0.00	0.00	0.00	0.00	0.00	0.00
58 3 TE 5 60	0.00	0.00	0.00	0.00	0.00	0.00	0.00	0.00	0.00
59 3 BR 5 60	0.00	0.00	0.00	0.00	0.00	0.00	0.00	0.00	0.00
60 3 BE 5 60	0.00	0.00	0.00	0.00	0.00	0.00	0.00	0.00	0.00
61 3 MA 5 60	0.00	0.00	0.00	0.00	0.00	0.00	0.00	0.00	0.00
62 3 CI 5 60	0.00	0.00	0.00	0.00	0.00	0.00	0.00	0.00	0.00
63 6 QU 5 62	2.53	15.01	2.88	5.54	0.28	4.09	17.43	0.19	52.03
64 6 GU 5 62	3.10	11.94	3.35	8.12	0.38	3.02	13.28	0.30	56.49
65 9 CA 5 61	6.48	34.44	6.43	16.48	1.84	6.71	17.61	0.82	9.20
66 9 CB 5 61	6.83	20.17	4.25	9.75	0.62	7.16	8.82	8.55	33.86
67 9 BA 5 61	5.11	17.22	4.81	10.91	0.74	4.64	10.34	3.79	42.43
68 9 AP 5 61	3.88	17.23	2.49	8.38	0.45	3.80	5.69	0.78	57.31
69 9 SC 5 61	2.32	20.72	3.72	8.40	0.55	4.22	7.29	0.22	52.57
70 9 MA 5 61	7.52	18.75	7.28	15.16	0.64	7.38	11.63	8.65	22.99
71 9 BQ 5 61	4.89	18.05	4.10	11.59	0.66	5.23	11.58	1.05	42.85
72 5 BA 5 64	3.90	15.61	4.49	9.54	0.28	4.13	12.12	0.78	49.13
73 5 BU 5 64	2.00	15.49	2.88	6.66	0.23	3.76	9.74	1.44	57.81
74 5 ME 5 64	3.58	16.25	3.80	8.66	0.21	4.26	13.26	2.39	47.59
75 5 CA 5 64	2.84	15.85	3.42	8.04	0.25	4.01	13.21	1.59	50.79
76 5 BO 5 64	5.26	26.85	4.89	11.25	0.39	6.08	16.65	1.66	26.98
77 5 CM 5 64	0.68	15.36	0.86	2.91	0.02	1.55	2.75	0.04	75.84
78 0 GE 5 60	0.10	18.08	4.77	11.33	0.57	7.98	16.30	3.77	37.11
79 0 PM 5 64	0.00	0.00	0.00	0.00	0.00	0.00	0.00	0.00	0.00
80 0 CA 5 61	2.37	31.92	3.31	9.78	0.00	8.76	11.30	5.25	27.30

1960: Table 6 *Percentage active population 15 years and unemployment in the economic sectors*

Code No C Re T Ye	(4/5)	(6/7)	Economic sectors (8/9)	(4-9)	Unempl. % of active pop.
02 4 IQ 6 60	11.47	23.85	28.84	64.17	6.87
03 4 AN 6 60	8.72	19.69	26.41	54.82	9.25
04 4 SE 6 60	5.23	14.81	21.32	41.37	7.09
05 4 SA 6 60	6.81	18.13	35.02	59.97	13.55
06 4 TA 6 60	5.14	9.43	19.98	34.54	4.08
07 4 CO 6 60	6.21	11.11	22.73	40.06	5.66
08 4 VD 6 60	6.07	10.57	20.68	37.32	5.14
09 4 PM 6 60	5.92	9.78	19.72	35.43	3.87
10 4 PA 6 60	8.48	15.77	36.98	61.24	6.28
11 1 SA 6 60	6.59	14.03	28.50	49.12	3.09
12 1 FO 6 60	4.28	11.40	27.30	42.98	2.88
13 1 CR 6 60	5.43	12.61	28.36	46.40	3.19
14 1 TU 6 60	4.96	16.20	27.73	48.89	3.96
15 1 LR 6 60	9.46	12.61	37.01	59.09	6.46
16 1 ES 6 60	5.45	13.49	29.64	48.58	6.58
17 1 CD 6 60	6.52	18.35	30.63	55.50	2.89
18 1 RO 6 60	5.84	21.56	26.91	54.32	2.44
19 1 PA 6 60	6.60	17.21	29.15	52.96	3.21
20 1 SJ 6 60	8.42	13.85	28.24	50.52	3.78
21 1 ME 6 60	7.42	16.43	27.20	51.05	2.89
22 1 SL 6 60	8.32	16.40	35.27	59.99	3.50
23 1 SR 6 60	7.07	15.60	25.71	48.38	1.30
24 1 BA 6 60	7.35	21.86	32.19	61.41	1.96
26 1 NE 6 60	6.63	13.96	28.80	49.39	1.94
27 1 RA 6 60	7.19	15.13	26.29	48.61	1.52
28 1 SC 6 60	10.77	12.82	22.88	46.47	1.32
29 1 US 6 60	9.61	15.41	32.27	57.30	0.82
30 1 PO 6 60	3.77	11.10	24.06	38.93	1.32
31 7 AS 6 62	3.69	9.94	16.99	30.62	4.29
34 7 ME 6 62	2.99	6.60	17.86	27.45	5.48
35 0 MO 6 63	6.67	19.16	35.12	60.95	11.70
42 8 PU 6 62	2.12	7.39	7.99	17.51	0.85
43 8 AR 6 62	5.83	14.44	23.36	43.63	1.77

44	8	CU	6	62	2.14	8.53	11.98	22.65	0.94
45	8	LI	6	62	6.61	21.43	32.52	60.56	2.77
46	8	HU	6	62	1.97	7.30	10.67	19.93	1.08
47	8	IQ	6	62	1.58	8.50	17.87	27.95	1.46
48	8	TR	6	62	2.46	7.63	11.87	21.97	0.98
49	8	PI	6	62	2.68	10.12	16.69	29.48	1.49
50	3	PA	6	60	0.00	0.00	0.00	0.00	0.00
51	3	CU	6	60	0.00	0.00	0.00	0.00	0.00
52	3	SP	6	60	0.00	0.00	0.00	0.00	0.00
53	3	RJ	6	60	0.00	0.00	0.00	0.00	0.00
54	3	BH	6	60	0.00	0.00	0.00	0.00	0.00
55	3	RE	6	60	0.00	0.00	0.00	0.00	0.00
56	3	SA	6	60	0.00	0.00	0.00	0.00	0.00
57	3	FO	6	60	0.00	0.00	0.00	0.00	0.00
58	3	TE	6	60	0.00	0.00	0.00	0.00	0.00
59	3	BR	6	60	0.00	0.00	0.00	0.00	0.00
60	3	BE	6	60	0.00	0.00	0.00	0.00	0.00
61	3	MA	6	60	0.00	0.00	0.00	0.00	0.00
62	3	CI	6	60	0.00	0.00	0.00	0.00	0.00
63	6	QU	6	62	4.38	8.42	17.54	30.34	0.00
64	6	GU	6	62	3.40	11.47	15.04	29.92	0.00
65	9	CA	6	61	8.55	22.91	40.92	72.37	15.34
66	9	CB	6	61	7.78	14.00	26.99	48.77	13.53
67	9	BA	6	61	5.38	15.72	22.34	43.44	11.90
68	9	AP	6	61	4.24	10.87	21.12	36.23	7.61
69	9	SC	6	61	4.77	12.12	23.04	39.92	5.51
70	9	MA	6	61	8.03	22.43	26.27	56.73	17.50
71	9	BQ	6	61	5.89	15.69	22.94	44.52	10.42
72	5	BA	6	64	4.42	14.03	19.51	37.97	0.00
73	5	BU	6	64	3.98	9.54	17.49	31.01	0.00
74	5	ME	6	64	4.48	12.46	19.83	36.77	0.00
75	5	CA	6	64	4.26	11.46	18.69	34.41	0.00
76	5	BO	6	64	6.47	16.14	32.11	54.71	0.00
77	5	CM	6	64	1.56	3.77	16.04	21.37	0.00
78	0	GE	6	60	8.55	16.11	18.17	42.83	7.86
79	0	PM	6	64	0.00	0.00	0.00	0.00	0.00
80	0	CA	6	61	8.76	13.10	34.29	56.15	0.00

1950: Table 1 *Population*

Code No C Re T Ye	Area km²	Total pop.	Urban pop.	Census pop.	Urb. census pop.	Women	Pop. 0–4 years	Women 15–49 years
02 4 IQ 1 52	55,287	102,789	61,383	102,789	61,383	48,755	13,137	24,725
03 4 AN 1 52	123,063	184,824	165,005	184,824	165,005	86,074	23,416	44,281
04 4 SE 1 52	119,772	342,282	144,671	342,282	144,671	173,254	47,968	81,002
05 4 SA 1 52	47,987	2,745,710	2,124,990	2,745,710	2,124,990	1,429,902	342,251	751,562
06 4 TA 1 52	30,823	481,563	172,603	481,563	172,603	239,917	66,211	109,572
07 4 CO 1 52	51,193	1,032,908	527,730	1,032,908	527,730	519,654	143,442	245,946
08 4 VD 1 52	47,387	720,778	256,853	720,778	256,853	358,816	98,887	172,083
09 4 PM 1 52	130,837	266,935	74,966	266,935	74,966	138,681	38,235	65,004
10 4 PA 1 52	135,418	55,119	44,921	55,119	44,921	25,384	5,592	13,832
11 1 SA 1 47	207,994	457,526	176,559	457,526	176,559	217,700	69,404	104,404
12 1 FO 1 47	72,066	113,790	25,977	113,790	25,977	53,638	19,850	25,232
13 1 CR 1 47	187,832	956,018	309,581	956,018	309,581	466,430	157,610	215,123
14 1 TU 1 47	22,524	593,371	299,383	593,371	299,383	292,350	87,407	144,485
15 1 LR 1 47	192,149	257,959	82,065	257,959	82,065	131,286	41,670	59,193
16 1 ES 1 47	135,254	479,473	123,521	479,473	123,521	247,106	84,783	108,358
17 1 CD 1 47	168,766	1,497,987	787,295	1,497,987	787,295	737,467	178,823	397,839
18 1 RO 1 47	133,007	1,702,975	984,599	1,702,975	984,599	810,254	169,975	455,443
19 1 PA 1 47	76,216	787,362	421,314	787,362	421,314	389,748	113,221	186,682
20 1 SJ 1 47	86,137	261,229	120,114	261,229	120,114	128,353	40,363	63,700
21 1 ME 1 47	150,839	588,231	296,575	588,231	296,575	286,195	75,787	153,056
22 1 SL 1 47	76,748	165,546	64,669	165,546	64,669	83,016	25,427	38,986
23 1 SR 1 47	143,440	169,480	52,099	169,480	52,099	78,253	21,108	40,557
24 1 BA 1 47	308,004	7,254,917	6,030,225	7,254,917	6,030,225	3,554,661	606,798	2,087,556
26 1 NE 1 47	297,091	221,186	55,835	221,186	55,835	98,765	32,417	47,839
27 1 RA 1 47	270,883	110,754	47,596	110,754	47,596	46,885	14,643	23,294
28 1 SC 1 47	197,746	24,582	8,930	24,582	8,930	8,202	2,153	4,447
29 1 US 1 47	20,392	5,045	0	5,045	0	1,360	395	770
30 1 PO 1 47	29,801	246,396	45,796	246,396	45,796	116,983	39,575	55,811
31 7 AS 1 50	159,827	1,274,175	443,754	1,274,175	443,754	654,378	208,381	301,113
34 7 ME 1 50	246,925	54,277	15,972	54,277	15,972	24,965	9,259	11,601
37 2 LP 1 50	187,573	1,158,706	504,883	1,046,435	442,056	532,074	162,253	269,179
38 2 SU 1 50	262,996	1,434,606	372,041	1,325,152	360,248	679,103	205,503	329,841
39 2 SC 1 50	370,621	286,145	105,608	244,658	103,966	124,306	41,243	58,112

40 2 TR 1 50	277,391	139,574	40,833	87,920	40,386	42,583	16,664	19,811
42 8 PU 1 40	67,703	646,385	0	548,371	71,079	281,673	101,141	126,817
43 8 AR 1 40	83,979	344,217	0	333,578	182,769	165,027	56,875	77,854
44 8 CU 1 40	317,955	870,883	0	749,636	160,794	380,413	137,706	171,831
45 8 LI 1 40	64,400	1,078,156	0	1,051,483	773,666	507,583	164,409	265,028
46 8 HU 1 40	167,677	1,456,759	0	1,266,465	334,873	655,338	240,201	296,161
47 8 IQ 1 40	354,193	442,254	0	263,454	107,421	131,008	57,053	59,510
48 8 TR 1 40	145,082	1,726,497	0	1,560,666	410,557	803,154	306,049	371,816
49 8 PI 1 40	43,588	457,960	0	434,314	155,974	215,903	84,069	99,149
50 3 PA 1 50	363,011	5,725,323	1,784,697	5,725,323	1,784,697	2,854,851	964,840	1,383,426
51 3 CU 1 50	199,060	2,115,547	528,288	2,115,547	528,288	1,024,227	363,821	498,235
52 3 SP 1 50	247,898	9,134,423	4,804,211	9,134,423	4,804,211	4,485,817	1,337,566	2,331,692
53 3 RJ 1 50	43,305	4,674,645	3,394,422	4,674,645	3,394,422	2,351,418	631,090	1,260,405
54 3 BH 1 50	632,769	8,739,426	2,522,101	8,739,426	2,522,101	4,383,420	1,460,086	2,132,885
55 3 RE 1 50	257,314	7,813,863	2,369,244	7,813,863	2,369,244	4,029,616	1,306,683	1,921,743
56 3 SA 1 50	559,951	4,834,575	1,250,507	4,834,575	1,250,507	2,481,754	782,526	1,196,769
57 3 FO 1 50	149,323	2,695,450	679,604	2,695,450	679,604	1,373,521	483,213	627,954
58 3 TE 1 50	576,857	2,628,944	444,872	2,628,944	444,872	1,321,725	434,550	629,821
59 3 BR 1 50	647,807	1,214,921	245,667	1,214,921	245,667	596,847	205,909	286,030
60 3 BE 1 50	1,367,938	1,160,750	402,911	1,160,750	402,911	577,971	189,622	281,318
61 3 MA 1 50	1,943,020	646,970	164,140	646,970	164,140	310,998	114,652	149,723
62 3 CI 1 50	1,474,593	558,979	191,646	551,979	191,646	266,985	96,232	125,872
63 6 QU 1 50	166,309	1,391,819	592,940	1,391,819	592,940	708,197	193,367	336,063
64 6 GU 1 50	117,252	1,809,592	813,810	1,809,592	813,810	899,179	313,943	420,513
65 9 CA 1 50	16,920	1,176,545	946,228	1,176,545	946,228	577,727	181,332	294,985
66 9 CB 1 50	453,950	171,666	72,584	171,666	72,584	82,203	30,506	38,354
67 9 BA 1 50	85,150	827,124	400,562	827,124	400,562	410,128	155,586	187,575
68 9 AP 1 50	176,690	333,406	99,896	333,406	99,896	161,717	56,650	76,385
69 9 SC 1 50	22,400	515,291	169,401	515,291	169,401	254,451	86,678	117,452
70 9 MA 1 50	50,230	560,336	421,764	560,336	421,764	271,910	99,320	132,766
71 9 BQ 1 50	93,470	1,450,470	598,909	1,450,470	598,909	724,211	237,676	344,899
72 5 BA 1 51	129,190	1,814,927	1,027,214	1,814,927	1,027,214	917,247	319,234	433,730
73 5 BU 1 51	143,170	1,934,472	435,847	1,934,472	435,847	984,331	320,283	458,643
74 5 ME 1 51	125,750	2,731,852	1,046,218	2,731,852	1,046,218	1,372,662	465,241	655,805
75 5 CA 1 51	254,200	3,063,269	1,009,267	3,063,269	1,009,267	1,511,892	502,410	723,567
76 5 BO 1 51	108,810	1,673,981	843,103	1,673,981	843,103	858,694	264,475	437,421
77 5 CM 1 51	377,180	4,333	1,898	4,333	1,898	1,527	625	743
78 0 GE 1 46	214,969	375,701	0	369,678	0	186,599	51,933	91,963
79 0 PM 1 50	142,822	197,000	0	177,089	0	89,262	27,137	39,782
80 0 CA 1 54	91,000	27,863	0	23,308	0	11,450	2,961	5,393

1950: Table 2 *Population*

Code No C Re T Ye	Pop. 0–14 years	Pop. 60+ years	Pop. 15+ years	Illit. pop. 15+ years	Active pop. 15+ years	Unempl pop.
02 4 IQ 2 52	35,163	7,255	67,626	7,147	39,247	1,816
03 4 AN 2 52	62,897	11,240	121,927	11,033	73,065	2,969
04 4 SE 2 52	139,926	24,095	202,356	49,696	113,282	3,442
05 4 SA 2 52	946,172	190,331	1,799,538	242,603	1,052,561	43,030
06 4 TA 2 52	188,501	39,470	293,062	92,408	165,605	4,138
07 4 CO 2 52	413,375	66,356	619,533	171,891	349,336	11,436
08 4 VD 2 52	295,449	42,696	425,329	116,145	240,990	7,390
09 4 PM 2 52	110,906	18,729	156,029	36,258	92,298	2,533
10 4 PA 2 52	16,199	3,729	38,920	2,943	24,410	1,052
11 1 SA 2 47	177,200	30,024	280,326	90,829	168,319	0
12 1 FO 2 47	49,919	3,630	63,871	15,904	37,304	0
13 1 CR 2 47	414,094	46,568	541,924	169,150	312,098	0
14 1 TU 2 47	234,704	29,912	358,667	77,510	193,646	0
15 1 LR 2 47	111,480	15,571	146,479	27,323	80,571	0
16 1 ES 2 47	225,131	26,806	254,342	81,698	131,189	0
17 1 CD 2 47	501,435	90,207	996,552	134,744	544,237	0
18 1 RO 2 47	491,430	117,729	1,211,545	164,142	666,240	0
19 1 PA 2 47	313,595	48,580	473,767	95,925	243,961	0
20 1 SJ 2 47	102,622	12,638	158,607	31,298	85,446	0
21 1 ME 2 47	200,565	32,098	387,666	68,350	208,790	0
22 1 SL 2 47	68,914	9,224	96,632	16,855	52,286	0
23 1 SR 2 47	58,777	11,422	110,703	16,505	63,333	0
24 1 BA 2 47	1,701,739	600,567	5,553,178	448,374	3,173,059	0
26 1 NE 2 47	84,592	10,948	136,594	34,091	79,543	0
27 1 RA 2 47	38,093	6,036	72,661	12,803	43,811	0
28 1 SC 2 47	5,542	1,526	19,040	1,565	12,894	0
29 1 US 2 47	941	205	4,104	240	2,970	0
30 1 PO 2 47	103,679	9,903	142,717	33,147	83,517	0
31 7 AS 2 50	558,085	78,532	716,090	246,377	394,406	11,751
34 7 ME 2 50	23,255	2,264	31,022	9,034	18,868	420
37 2 LP 2 50	400,306	75,329	646,129	413,880	480,768	0
38 2 SU 2 50	523,077	99,527	802,075	616,759	629,974	0
39 2 SC 2 50	107,443	14,292	137,215	58,584	82,928	0
40 2 TR 2 50	40,026	4,400	47,894	20,162	29,950	0

42	8	PU	2	40	232,180	47,664	316,013	271,067	245,242	463
43	8	AR	2	40	135,015	22,450	198,435	80,540	129,933	3,196
44	8	CU	2	40	305,363	69,650	444,150	370,760	311,057	2,421
45	8	LI	2	40	388,287	45,557	642,999	104,042	387,890	24,280
46	8	HU	2	40	544,430	95,966	721,748	531,350	462,642	5,364
47	8	IQ	2	40	125,677	8,813	137,426	65,682	97,275	938
48	8	TR	2	40	683,680	87,673	876,423	512,074	530,676	6,288
49	8	PI	2	40	197,535	18,663	236,636	134,755	148,792	3,167
50	3	PA	2	50	2,435,498	255,551	3,289,825	1,142,568	1,771,625	194,156
51	3	CU	2	50	917,138	75,527	1,198,409	562,406	645,270	86,785
52	3	SP	2	50	3,461,635	414,431	5,672,788	2,010,627	3,221,801	283,648
53	3	RJ	2	50	1,620,999	248,408	3,053,646	848,164	1,656,569	180,341
54	3	BH	2	50	3,819,016	338,253	4,920,410	2,724,872	2,544,568	356,765
55	3	RE	2	50	3,385,117	377,544	4,428,746	3,038,688	2,297,502	366,253
56	3	SA	2	50	2,093,102	239,116	2,741,473	1,833,062	1,416,924	248,169
57	3	FO	2	50	1,224,307	129,221	1,471,143	981,576	741,703	127,658
58	3	TE	2	50	1,165,738	110,343	1,463,206	1,071,887	733,297	120,025
59	3	BR	2	50	544,524	39,325	670,397	436,312	334,830	60,870
60	3	BE	2	50	494,334	49,874	666,416	331,773	352,150	42,150
61	3	MA	2	50	286,824	23,365	360,146	201,300	190,863	30,858
62	3	CI	2	50	246,551	21,007	312,428	149,334	163,002	25,922
63	6	QU	2	50	557,768	83,419	834,051	404,552	0	0
64	6	GU	2	50	801,388	84,534	1,008,204	410,747	0	0
65	9	CA	2	50	433,883	56,900	742,662	216,505	406,556	37,305
66	9	CB	2	50	75,633	7,608	96,033	47,674	48,673	3,879
67	9	BA	2	50	383,403	34,563	443,721	242,913	221,272	180,032
68	9	AP	2	50	145,024	13,910	188,382	121,867	97,749	4,724
69	9	SC	2	50	223,941	25,945	291,350	166,421	159,524	4,056
70	9	MA	2	50	235,080	21,931	325,256	127,207	158,322	16,717
71	9	BQ	2	50	612,824	73,118	837,646	511,265	429,125	19,952
72	5	BA	2	51	803,439	88,213	1,011,488	475,565	530,383	8,587
73	5	BU	2	51	839,639	109,684	1,094,833	541,240	610,409	3,271
74	5	ME	2	51	1,173,786	135,865	1,558,066	434,346	835,596	9,883
75	5	CA	2	51	1,292,886	158,540	1,770,383	663,814	1,033,285	10,346
76	5	BO	2	51	664,978	82,506	1,009,003	313,226	586,324	10,223
77	5	CM	2	51	1,463	76	2,870	708	1,822	31
78	0	GE	2	46	139,283	23,569	230,395	55,356	143,648	0
79	0	PM	2	50	70,532	12,230	96,731	0	0	0
80	0	CA	2	54	7,076	2,500	16,232	0	0	0

1950: Table 3 *Active population.*

Code No C Re T Ye	(0) Agri- culture	(1) Mining	(2/3) Manufac- turing	(4) Construc- tion	(5) Elec., gas, water	(6) Commerce	(7) Transport	(8) Services	(9) No speci- fication
02 4 IQ 3 52	5,183	9,175	4,043	1,561	346	3,695	3,731	8,881	2,632
03 4 AN 3 52	1,705	31,608	7,076	3,789	366	5,487	6,632	12,839	3,563
04 4 SE 3 52	33,691	18,806	11,547	7,957	1,928	9,603	5,865	18,746	5,139
05 4 SA 3 52	180,378	16,413	260,384	59,544	11,909	137,103	50,421	280,574	55,835
06 4 TA 3 52	88,334	636	17,969	6,072	2,254	12,377	4,068	26,377	7,518
07 4 CO 3 52	139,373	20,445	54,985	12,191	2,199	27,651	11,091	63,991	17,410
08 4 VD 3 52	120,516	1,068	35,613	6,641	978	18,012	7,959	38,293	11,910
09 4 PM 3 52	54,512	440	9,730	2,800	220	4,820	2,933	13,167	3,676
10 4 PA 3 52	5,380	2,407	3,776	1,275	228	2,193	2,329	6,401	421
11 1 SA 3 47	59,312	4,366	35,929	6,395	331	13,096	10,000	33,876	5,014
12 1 FO 3 47	19,973	13	3,621	1,435	40	3,740	1,369	6,826	287
13 1 CR 3 47	166,310	168	36,312	10,309	534	26,467	11,797	52,769	7,432
14 1 TU 3 47	56,854	151	51,127	8,738	344	21,960	12,254	37,390	4,828
15 1 LR 3 47	31,086	984	11,710	2,933	150	5,709	3,189	21,712	3,098
16 1 ES 3 47	53,735	111	20,352	3,852	143	10,654	6,779	25,336	10,227
17 1 CD 3 47	185,714	3,633	76,804	36,311	2,032	72,675	30,324	117,980	18,764
18 1 RO 3 47	238,992	354	119,743	27,503	2,919	91,393	48,848	122,384	14,104
19 1 PA 3 47	93,897	314	32,811	9,127	565	28,005	13,037	53,844	12,361
20 1 SJ 3 47	30,121	875	11,975	7,820	293	9,107	3,140	19,297	2,818
21 1 ME 3 47	64,794	3,223	38,647	17,575	1,201	25,069	13,249	42,447	2,585
22 1 SL 3 47	18,921	817	6,079	2,543	98	4,852	3,833	12,829	2,314
23 1 SR 3 47	33,314	210	6,590	2,268	148	6,484	2,970	9,866	1,483
24 1 BA 3 47	446,204	6,038	931,149	190,282	21,472	509,160	215,701	748,214	104,839
26 1 NE 3 47	34,972	3,049	7,419	4,562	220	6,774	4,373	15,910	2,264
27 1 RA 3 47	15,174	7,363	2,844	1,784	98	3,483	2,281	8,702	2,082
28 1 SC 3 47	5,810	248	1,795	363	19	969	654	2,699	337
29 1 US 3 47	975	7	299	56	6	146	34	1,369	73
30 1 PO 3 47	42,183	48	14,509	2,590	60	6,357	2,701	12,955	2,114
31 7 AS 3 50	218,097	349	65,231	12,515	618	29,373	9,153	59,070	0
34 7 ME 3 50	12,500	3	1,739	179	1	552	380	3,514	0
37 2 LP 3 50	307,438	19,347	50,373	13,206	0	30,646	8,427	45,712	5,620
38 2 SU 3 50	483,003	22,787	46,517	9,463	0	20,551	9,037	36,907	1,708
39 2 SC 3 50	51 154	745	8,035	2,125	0	3,978	3,107	12,681	1,103

40 2 TR 3 50	19,902	15	2,422	403	0	1,490	497	4,657	564
42 8 PU 3 40	190,183	3,343	31,654	1,535	37	6,160	1,376	8,537	2,417
43 8 AR 3 40	67,594	3,207	16,711	5,000	172	9,835	5,905	18,875	2,634
44 8 CU 3 40	214,690	2,946	53,623	4,464	86	10,050	2,715	19,492	2,991
45 8 LI 3 40	127,960	5,179	64,150	19,823	1,391	43,714	22,176	93,190	10,307
46 8 HU 3 40	329,611	15,389	60,131	5,851	430	14,706	5,634	24,045	6,845
47 8 IQ 3 40	69,600	1,104	9,725	579	32	3,211	999	9,496	2,529
48 8 TR 3 40	347,035	5,952	103,974	5,739	248	16,281	7,636	35,240	8,571
49 8 PI 3 40	81,667	7,048	28,335	2,214	66	6,674	4,154	16,297	2,337
50 3 PA 3 50	1,038,932	38,830	166,405	50,529	3,404	110,006	70,199	284,174	9,146
51 3 CU 3 50	425,730	9,879	52,070	21,854	908	31,259	25,433	76,508	1,629
52 3 SP 3 50	1,295,280	42,537	603,275	153,843	12,241	282,544	196,142	630,248	5,691
53 3 RJ 3 50	293,556	25,222	275,006	115,774	10,347	200,905	143,406	582,942	9,411
54 3 BH 3 50	1,699,777	48,870	144,813	81,138	3,987	121,356	84,995	355,143	4,489
55 3 RE 3 50	1,557,053	35,315	169,363	48,185	2,713	121,567	62,676	296,238	4,392
56 3 SA 3 50	972,515	34,978	71,374	49,067	1,139	70,261	39,376	174,778	3,436
57 3 FO 3 50	534,423	8,168	39,740	10,885	596	39,486	15,854	90,633	1,918
58 3 TE 3 50	553,218	43,035	17,141	10,554	447	26,063	15,453	63,831	3,555
59 3 PR 3 50	269,592	6,409	7,951	6,929	159	9,509	4,873	28,224	1,184
60 3 BE 3 50	160,783	70,740	15,887	8,468	622	24,034	18,715	52,147	754
61 3 MA 3 50	65,148	76,005	6,347	3,987	323	10,400	6,762	21,581	310
62 3 CI 3 50	94,173	19,294	5,200	4,701	143	7,227	7,749	23,922	593
63 6 QU 3 50	0	0	0	0	0	0	0	0	0
64 6 GU 3 50	0	0	0	0	0	0	0	0	0
65 9 CA 3 50	77,211	4,719	67,483	40,766	2,837	53,915	17,930	129,671	12,024
66 9 CB 3 50	25,208	3,083	3,231	2,112	120	3,317	1,413	8,988	1,201
67 9 BA 3 50	116,742	12,053	20,598	8,081	456	17,741	7,310	33,219	5,072
68 9 AP 3 50	63,358	1,793	4,502	2,923	121	6,033	1,285	15,417	2,317
69 9 SC 3 50	98,048	242	10,178	5,869	202	8,975	2,831	31,154	2,025
70 9 MA 3 50	43,503	20,967	19,917	8,909	552	20,492	10,573	29,331	4,078
71 9 BQ 3 50	229,593	6,205	38,532	21,637	903	36,404	10,474	76,186	9,012
72 5 BA 3 51	274,036	3,572	67,649	17,300	1,161	44,200	27,669	76,215	18,581
73 5 BU 3 51	392,847	8,266	55,906	17,972	1,187	21,908	12,687	85,166	14,470
74 5 ME 3 51	460,297	24,375	100,333	27,317	3,476	41,157	29,521	112,336	36,784
75 5 CA 3 51	597,288	15,376	139,111	34,605	2,003	51,220	32,410	132,720	28,552
76 5 BO 3 51	219,507	8,098	85,413	33,106	2,629	40,935	25,544	141,383	29,709
77 5 CM 3 51	1 159	15	114	42	4	53	46	311	78
78 0 GE 3 46	65,701	4,031	22,182	7,059	431	11,624	6,135	24,097	2,388
79 0 PM 3 50	0	0	0	0	0	0	0	0	0
80 0 CA 3 54	0	0	0	0	0	0	0	0	0

1950: Table 4   *Percentage population*

Code No C Re T Ye	Census pop.	Urban pop.	Women	Pop. 0-14 years	Pop. 60+ years	Pop. 15-59 years	Illit. pop. 15+years	Active pop. 15+years	Child-women relation	Pop. density per km²
02 4 IQ 4 52	100.00	59.72	47.43	34.21	7.06	58.73	10.57	58.04	53.13	1.86
03 4 AN 4 52	100.00	89.28	46.57	34.03	6.08	59.89	9.05	59.93	52.88	1.50
04 4 SE 4 52	100.00	42.27	50.62	40.88	7.04	52.08	24.56	55.98	59.22	2.86
05 4 SA 4 52	100.00	77.39	52.08	34.46	6.93	58.61	13.48	58.49	45.54	57.22
06 4 TA 4 52	100.00	35.84	49.82	39.14	8.20	52.66	31.53	56.51	60.43	15.62
07 4 CO 4 52	100.00	51.09	50.31	40.02	6.42	53.56	27.75	56.39	58.32	20.18
08 4 VD 4 52	100.00	35.64	49.78	40.99	5.92	53.09	27.31	56.66	57.46	15.21
09 4 PM 4 52	100.00	28.08	51.95	41.55	7.02	51.44	23.24	59.15	58.82	2.04
10 4 PA 4 52	100.00	81.50	46.05	29.39	6.77	63.85	7.56	62.72	40.43	0.41
11 1 SA 4 47	100.00	38.59	47.58	38.73	6.56	54.71	32.40	60.04	66.48	2.20
12 1 FO 4 47	100.00	22.83	47.14	43.87	3.19	52.94	24.90	58.41	78.67	1.58
13 1 CR 4 47	100.00	32.38	48.79	43.31	4.87	51.81	31.21	57.59	73.27	5.09
14 1 TU 4 47	100.00	50.45	49.27	39.55	5.04	55.40	21.61	53.99	60.50	26.34
15 1 LR 4 47	100.00	31.81	50.89	43.22	6.04	50.75	18.65	55.01	70.40	1.34
16 1 ES 4 47	100.00	25.76	51.54	46.95	5.59	47.46	32.12	51.58	78.24	3.54
17 1 CD 4 47	100.00	52.56	49.23	33.47	6.02	60.50	13.52	54.61	44.95	8.88
18 1 RO 4 47	100.00	57.82	47.58	28.86	6.91	64.23	13.55	54.99	37.32	12.80
19 1 PA 4 47	100.00	53.51	49.50	39.83	6.17	54.00	20.25	51.49	60.65	10.33
20 1 SJ 4 47	100.00	45.98	49.13	39.28	4.84	55.88	19.73	53.87	63.36	3.03
21 1 ME 4 47	100.00	50.42	48.65	34.10	5.46	60.45	17.63	53.86	49.52	3.90
22 1 SL 4 47	100.00	39.06	50.15	41.63	5.57	52.80	17.44	54.11	65.22	2.16
23 1 SR 4 47	100.00	30.74	46.17	34.68	6.74	58.58	14.91	57.21	52.05	1.18
24 1 BA 4 47	100.00	83.12	49.00	23.46	8.28	68.27	8.07	57.14	29.07	23.55
26 1 NE 4 47	100.00	25.24	44.65	38.24	4.95	56.81	24.96	58.23	67.76	0.74
27 1 RA 4 47	100.00	42.97	42.33	34.39	5.45	60.16	17.62	60.30	62.86	0.41
28 1 SC 4 47	100.00	36.33	33.37	22.54	6.21	71.25	8.22	67.72	48.41	0.12
29 1 US 4 47	100.00	0.00	26.96	18.65	4.06	77.28	5.85	72.37	51.30	0.25
30 1 PO 4 47	100.00	18.59	47.48	42.08	4.02	53.90	23.23	58.52	70.91	8.27
31 7 AS 4 50	100.00	34.83	51.36	43.80	6.16	50.04	34.41	55.08	69.20	7.97
34 7 ME 4 50	100.00	29.43	46.00	42.85	4.17	52.98	29.12	60.82	79.81	0.22
37 2 LP 4 50	90.31	42.24	50.85	38.25	7.20	54.55	64.06	74.41	60.28	6.18
38 2 SU 4 50	92.37	27.19	51.25	39.47	7.51	53.02	76.90	78.54	62.30	5.45
39 2 SC 4 50	85.50	42.49	50.81	43.92	5.84	50.24	42.70	60.44	70.97	0.77
40 2 TR 4 50	62.99	45.93	48.43	45.53	5.00	49.47	42.10	62.53	84.11	0.50

42 8 PU 4 40	84.84	12.96	51.37	42.34	8.69	48.97	85.78	77.61	79.75	9.55
43 8 AR 4 40	96.91	54.79	49.47	40.47	6.73	52.80	40.59	65.48	73.05	4.10
44 8 CU 4 40	86.08	21.45	50.75	40.73	9.29	49.97	83.48	70.03	80.14	2.74
45 8 LI 4 40	97.53	63.58	48.27	36.93	4.33	58.74	15.69	58.51	62.03	16.74
46 8 HU 4 40	86.94	26.44	51.75	42.99	7.58	49.43	73.62	64.10	81.10	8.69
47 8 IQ 4 40	59.57	40.77	49.73	47.70	3.35	48.95	47.79	70.78	95.87	1.25
48 8 TR 4 40	90.39	26.31	51.46	43.81	5.62	50.58	58.43	60.55	82.31	11.90
49 8 PI 4 40	94.84	35.91	49.71	45.48	4.30	50.22	56.95	62.88	84.79	10.51
50 3 PA 4 50	100.00	31.17	49.86	42.54	4.46	53.00	34.73	53.85	69.74	15.77
51 3 CU 4 50	100.00	24.97	48.41	43.35	3.57	53.08	46.93	53.84	73.02	10.63
52 3 SP 4 50	100.00	52.59	49.11	37.90	4.54	57.57	35.44	56.79	57.36	36.85
53 3 RJ 4 50	100.00	72.61	50.30	34.68	5.31	60.01	27.78	54.25	50.07	107.95
54 3 BH 4 50	100.00	28.86	50.16	43.70	3.87	52.43	55.38	51.71	68.46	13.81
55 3 RE 4 50	100.00	30.32	41.57	43.32	4.83	51.85	68.61	51.88	67.99	30.37
56 3 SA 4 50	100.00	25.87	51.33	43.29	4.95	51.76	66.86	51.68	65.39	8.63
57 3 FO 4 50	100.00	25.21	50.96	45.42	4.79	49.78	66.72	50.42	76.95	18.05
58 3 TE 4 50	100.00	16.92	50.28	44.34	4.20	51.46	73.26	50.12	69.00	4.56
59 3 BR 4 50	100.00	20.22	49.13	44.82	3.24	51.94	65.08	49.95	71.99	1.88
60 3 BE 4 50	100.00	34.71	49.79	42.59	4.30	53.12	49.78	52.84	67.40	0.85
61 3 MA 4 50	100.00	25.37	48.07	44.33	3.61	52.06	55.89	53.00	76.58	0.33
62 3 CI 4 50	100.00	34.29	47.76	44.11	3.76	52.13	47.80	52.17	76.45	0.38
63 6 QU 4 50	100.00	42.60	50.88	40.07	5.99	53.93	48.50	0.00	57.54	8.37
64 6 GU 4 50	100.00	44.97	49.69	44.29	4.67	51.04	40.74	0.00	74.66	15.43
65 9 CA 4 50	100.00	80.42	49.10	36.88	4.84	58.29	29.15	54.74	61.47	69.54
66 9 CB 4 50	100.00	42.28	47.89	44.06	4.43	51.51	49.64	50.68	79.54	0.38
67 9 BA 4 50	100.00	48.43	49.58	46.35	4.18	49.47	54.74	49.87	82.95	9.71
68 9 AP 4 50	100.00	29.96	48.50	43.50	4.17	52.33	64.69	51.89	74.16	1.89
69 9 SC 4 50	100.00	32.87	49.38	43.46	5.04	51.51	57.12	54.75	73.80	23.00
70 9 MA 4 50	100.00	65.27	48.53	41.95	3.91	54.13	39.11	48.68	74.81	11.16
71 9 BQ 4 50	100.00	41.29	49.93	42.25	5.04	52.71	61.04	51.23	68.91	15.52
72 5 BA 4 51	100.00	56.60	50.54	44.27	4.86	50.87	47.02	52.44	73.60	14.05
73 5 BU 4 51	100.00	22.53	50.88	43.40	5.67	50.93	49.44	55.75	69.83	13.51
74 5 ME 4 51	100.00	38.30	50.25	42.97	4.97	52.06	27.88	53.63	70.94	21.72
75 5 CA 4 51	100.00	32.95	49.36	42.21	5.18	52.62	37.50	58.37	69.44	12.05
76 5 BO 4 51	100.00	50.37	51.30	39.72	4.93	55.35	31.04	58.11	60.46	15.38
77 5 CM 4 51	100.00	43.80	35.24	33.76	1.75	64.48	24.67	63.48	84.12	0.01
78 0 GE 4 46	98.40	0.00	50.48	37.68	6.38	55.95	24.03	62.35	56.47	1.75
79 0 PM 4 50	89.89	0.00	50.41	39.83	6.91	53.27	0.00	0.00	68.21	1.38
800 CA 4 54	83.65	0.00	49.12	30.36	10.73	58.92	0.00	0.00	54.90	0.31

1950: Table 5 *Percentage active population 15 years+ in the economic sectors*

Code No C Re T Ye	(0) Agriculture	(1) Mining	(2/3) Manufacturing	(4) Construction	(5) Elec., gas, water	(6) Commerce	(7) Transport	(8) Services	(9) No specification
02 4 IQ 5 52	13.21	23.38	10.30	3.98	0.88	9.41	9.51	22.63	6.71
03 4 AN 2 52	2.33	43.26	9.68	5.19	0.50	7.51	9.08	17.57	4.88
04 4 SE 5 52	29.74	16.60	10.19	7.02	1.70	8.48	5.18	16.55	4.54
05 4 SA 5 52	17.14	1.56	24.74	5.66	1.13	13.03	4.79	26.66	5.30
06 4 TA 5 52	53.34	0.38	10.85	3.67	1.36	7.47	2.46	15.93	4.54
07 4 CO 5 52	39.90	5.85	15.74	3.49	0.63	7.92	3.17	18.32	4.98
08 4 VD 5 52	50.01	0.44	14.78	2.76	0.41	7.47	3.30	15.89	4.94
09 4 PM 5 52	59.06	0.48	10.54	3.03	0.24	5.22	3.18	14.27	3.98
10 4 PA 5 52	22.04	9.86	15.47	5.22	0.93	8.98	9.54	26.22	1.72
11 1 SA 5 47	35.24	2.59	21.35	3.80	0.20	7.78	5.94	20.13	2.98
12 1 FO 5 47	53.54	0.03	9.71	3.85	0.11	10.03	3.67	18.30	0.77
13 1 CR 5 47	53.29	0.05	11.63	3.30	0.17	8.48	3.78	16.91	2.38
14 1 TU 5 47	29.36	0.08	26.40	4.51	0.18	11.34	6.33	19.31	2.49
15 1 LR 5 47	38.58	1.22	14.53	3.64	0.19	7.09	3.96	26.95	3.85
16 1 ES 5 47	40.96	0.08	15.51	2.94	0.11	8.12	5.17	19.31	7.86
17 1 CD 5 47	34.12	0.67	14.11	6.67	0.37	13.35	5.57	21.68	3.45
18 1 RO 5 47	35.87	0.05	17.97	4.13	0.44	13.72	7.33	18.37	2.12
19 1 PA 5 47	38.49	0.13	13.45	3.74	0.23	11.48	5.34	22.07	5.07
20 1 SJ 5 47	35.25	1.02	14.01	9.15	0.34	10.66	3.67	22.58	3.30
21 1 ME 5 47	31.03	1.54	18.51	8.42	0.58	12.01	6.35	20.33	1.24
22 1 SL 5 47	36.19	1.56	11.63	4.86	0.19	9.28	7.33	24.54	4.43
23 1 SR 5 47	52.60	0.33	10.41	3.58	0.23	10.24	4.69	15.58	2.34
24 1 BA 5 47	14.06	0.19	29.35	6.00	0.68	16.05	6.80	23.58	3.30
26 1 NE 5 47	43.97	3.83	9.33	5.74	0.28	8.52	5.50	20.00	2.85
27 1 RA 5 47	34.64	16.81	6.49	4.07	0.22	7.95	5.21	19.86	4.75
28 1 SC 5 47	45.06	1.92	13.92	2.82	0.15	7.52	5.07	20.93	2.61
29 1 US 5 47	32.83	0.24	10.07	1.89	0.20	4.92	1.14	46.09	2.46
30 1 PO 5 47	50.51	0.06	17.37	3.10	0.07	7.61	3.23	15.51	2.53
31 7 AS 5 50	55.30	0.09	16.54	3.17	0.16	7.45	2.32	14.98	0.00
34 7 ME 5 50	66.25	0.02	9.22	0.95	0.01	2.93	2.01	18.42	0.00
37 2 LP 5 50	63.95	4.02	10.48	2.75	0.00	6.37	1.75	9.51	1.17
38 2 SU 5 50	76.67	3.62	7.38	1.50	0.00	3.26	1.43	5.86	0.27
39 2 SC 5 50	61.68	0.90	9.69	2.56	0.00	4.80	3.75	15.29	1.33
40 2 TR 5 50	66.45	0.05	8.09	1.35	0.00	4.97	1.66	15.55	1.88

42	8	PU	5	40	77.55	1.36	12.91	0.63	0.02	2.51	0.56	3.48	0.99
43	8	AR	5	40	52.02	2.47	12.86	3.85	0.13	7.75	4.54	14.53	2.03
44	8	CU	5	40	69.02	0.95	17.24	1.44	0.03	3.23	0.87	6.27	0.96
45	8	LI	5	40	32.99	1.34	16.54	5.11	0.36	11.27	5.72	24.02	2.66
46	8	HU	5	40	71.25	3.33	13.00	1.26	0.09	3.18	1.22	5.20	1.48
47	8	IQ	5	40	71.55	1.13	10.00	0.60	0.03	3.30	1.03	9.76	2.60
48	8	TR	5	40	65.39	1.12	19.59	1.08	0.05	3.07	1.44	6.64	1.62
49	8	PI	5	40	54.89	4.74	19.04	1.49	0.04	4.49	2.79	10.95	1.57
50	3	PA	5	50	58.64	2.19	9.39	2.85	0.19	6.21	3.96	16.04	0.52
51	3	CU	5	50	65.98	1.53	8.07	3.39	0.14	4.84	3.94	11.86	0.25
52	3	SP	5	50	40.20	1.32	18.72	4.78	0.38	8.77	6.09	19.56	0.18
53	3	RJ	5	50	17.72	1.52	16.60	6.99	0.62	12.13	8.66	35.19	0.57
54	3	BH	5	50	66.80	1.92	5.69	3.19	0.16	4.77	3.34	13.96	0.18
55	3	RE	5	50	67.77	1.54	7.37	2.10	0.12	5.29	2.73	12.89	0.19
56	3	SA	5	50	68.64	2.47	5.04	3.46	0.08	4.96	2.78	12.34	0.24
57	3	FO	5	50	72.05	1.10	5.36	1.47	0.08	5.32	2.14	12.22	0.26
58	3	TE	5	50	75.44	5.87	2.34	1.44	0.06	3.55	2.11	8.70	0.48
59	3	BR	5	50	80.52	1.91	2.37	2.07	0.05	2.84	1.46	8.43	0.35
60	3	BE	5	50	45.66	20.09	4.51	2.40	0.18	6.82	5.31	14.81	0.21
61	3	MA	5	50	34.13	39.82	3.33	2.09	0.17	5.45	3.54	11.31	0.16
62	3	CI	5	50	57.77	11.84	3.19	2.88	0.09	4.43	4.75	14.68	0.36
63	6	QU	5	50	0.00	0.00	0.00	0.00	0.00	0.00	0.00	0.00	0.00
64	6	GU	5	50	0.00	0.00	0.00	0.00	0.00	0.00	0.00	0.00	0.00
65	9	CA	5	50	18.99	1.16	16.60	10.03	0.70	13.26	4.41	31.89	2.96
66	9	CB	5	50	51.79	6.33	6.64	4.34	0.25	6.81	2.90	18.47	2.47
67	9	BA	5	50	52.76	5.45	9.31	3.65	0.21	8.02	3.30	15.01	2.29
68	9	AP	5	50	64.82	1.83	4.61	2.99	0.12	6.17	1.31	15.77	2.37
69	9	SC	5	50	61.46	0.15	6.38	3.68	0.13	5.63	1.77	19.53	1.27
70	9	MA	5	50	27.48	13.24	12.58	5.63	0.35	12.94	6.68	18.53	2.58
71	9	BQ	5	50	53.50	1.45	8.98	5.04	0.21	8.48	2.44	17.75	2.10
72	5	BA	5	51	51.67	0.67	12.75	3.26	0.22	8.33	5.22	14.37	3.50
73	5	BU	5	51	64.36	1.35	9.16	2.94	0.19	3.59	2.08	13.95	2.37
74	5	ME	5	51	55.09	2.92	12.01	3.27	0.42	4.93	3.53	13.44	4.40
75	5	CA	5	51	57.80	1.49	13.46	3.35	0.19	4.96	3.14	12.84	2.76
76	5	BO	5	51	37.44	1.38	14.57	5.65	0.45	6.98	4.36	24.11	5.07
77	5	CM	5	51	63.61	0.82	6.26	2.31	0.22	2.91	2.52	17.07	4.28
78	0	GE	5	46	45.74	2.81	15.44	4.91	0.30	8.09	4.27	16.78	1.66
79	0	PM	5	50	0.00	0.00	0.00	0.00	0.00	0.00	0.00	0.00	0.00
80	0	CA	5	54	0.00	0.00	0.00	0.00	0.00	0.00	0.00	0.00	0.00

1950: Table 6   Percentage active population 15 + years and unemployed in the economic sectors

Code						Economic sectors				Unempl. % of active pop.
No	C	Re	T	Ye	(4/5)	(6/7)	(8/9)	(4-9)		
02	4	IQ	6	52	4.86	18.92	29.33	53.11		4.63
03	4	AN	6	52	5.69	16.59	22.45	44.72		4.06
04	4	SE	6	52	8.73	13.65	21.08	43.46		3.04
05	4	SA	6	52	6.79	17.82	31.96	56.57		4.09
06	4	TA	6	52	5.03	9.93	20.47	35.43		2.50
07	4	CO	6	52	4.12	11.09	23.30	38.51		3.27
08	4	VD	5	52	3.16	10.78	20.83	34.77		3.07
09	4	PN	6	52	3.27	8.40	18.25	29.92		2.74
10	4	PA	6	52	6.61	18.53	27.95	52.63		4.31
11	1	SA	6	47	4.00	13.72	23.10	40.82		0.00
12	1	FO	6	47	3.95	13.70	19.07	36.72		0.00
13	1	CR	6	47	3.47	12.26	19.29	35.02		0.00
14	1	TU	6	47	4.69	17.67	21.80	44.16		0.00
15	1	LR	6	47	3.83	11.04	30.79	45.66		0.00
16	1	ES	6	47	3.05	13.29	27.11	43.44		0.00
17	1	CD	6	47	7.05	18.93	25.13	51.10		0.00
18	1	RO	6	47	5.47	21.05	20.49	46.10		0.00
19	1	PA	6	47	3.97	16.82	27.14	47.93		0.00
20	1	SJ	6	47	9.49	14.33	25.88	49.71		0.00
21	1	ME	6	47	8.99	18.35	21.57	48.91		0.00
22	1	SL	6	47	5.05	16.61	28.96	50.62		0.00
23	1	SR	6	47	3.81	14.93	17.92	36.66		0.00
24	1	BA	6	47	6.67	22.84	26.88	56.40		0.00
26	1	NE	6	47	6.01	14.01	22.85	42.87		0.00
27	1	PA	6	47	4.30	13.16	24.61	42.07		0.00
28	1	SC	6	47	2.96	12.59	23.55	39.10		0.00
29	1	US	6	47	2.09	6.06	48.55	56.70		0.00
30	1	PO	6	47	3.17	10.85	18.04	32.06		0.00
31	7	AS	6	50	3.33	9.77	14.98	28.07		2.98
34	7	ME	6	50	0.15	4.94	18.62	24.52		2.23
37	2	LP	6	50	2.75	8.13	10.68	21.55		0.00
38	2	SU	6	50	1.50	4.70	6.13	12.33		0.00
39	2	SC	6	50	2.56	8.54	16.62	27.73		0.00
40	2	TR	6	50	1.35	6.63	17.43	25.41		0.00

42	8	PU	6	40	0.64	3.07	4.47	8.18	0.19
43	8	AR	6	40	3.98	12.11	16.55	32.65	2.46
44	8	CU	6	40	1.46	4.10	7.23	12.79	0.78
45	8	LI	6	40	5.47	16.99	26.68	49.14	6.26
46	8	HU	6	40	1.36	4.40	6.68	12.43	1.16
47	8	IQ	6	40	0.63	4.33	12.36	17.32	0.96
48	8	TR	6	40	1.13	4.51	8.26	13.89	1.18
49	8	PI	6	40	1.53	7.28	12.52	21.33	2.13
50	3	PA	6	50	3.04	10.17	16.56	29.77	10.96
51	3	CU	6	50	3.53	8.79	12.11	24.42	13.45
52	3	SP	6	50	5.16	14.86	19.74	39.75	8.80
53	3	RJ	6	50	7.61	20.78	35.76	64.16	10.89
54	3	BH	6	50	3.35	8.11	14.13	25.59	14.02
55	3	RE	6	50	2.22	8.02	13.09	23.32	15.94
56	3	SA	6	50	3.54	7.74	12.58	23.86	17.51
57	3	FO	6	50	1.55	7.46	12.48	21.49	17.21
58	3	TE	6	50	1.50	5.66	9.19	16.35	16.37
59	3	BR	6	50	2.12	4.30	8.78	15.20	18.18
60	3	BE	6	50	2.58	12.14	15.02	29.74	11.97
61	3	MA	6	50	2.26	8.99	11.47	22.72	16.17
62	3	CI	6	50	2.97	9.19	15.04	27.20	15.90
63	6	QU	6	50	0.00	0.00	0.00	0.00	0.00
64	6	GU	6	50	0.00	0.00	0.00	0.00	0.00
65	9	CA	6	50	10.72	17.67	34.85	63.25	9.18
66	9	CB	6	50	4.59	9.72	20.93	35.24	7.97
67	9	BA	6	50	3.86	11.32	17.30	32.48	8.15
68	9	AP	6	50	3.11	7.49	18.14	28.74	4.83
69	9	SC	6	50	3.81	7.40	20.80	32.01	2.54
70	9	MA	6	50	5.98	19.62	21.10	46.70	10.56
71	9	BQ	6	50	5.25	10.92	19.85	36.03	4.65
72	5	BA	6	51	3.48	13.55	17.87	34.90	1.62
73	5	BU	6	51	3.14	5.67	16.32	25.13	0.54
74	5	ME	6	51	3.69	8.46	17.85	29.99	1.18
75	5	CA	6	51	3.54	8.09	15.61	27.24	1.00
76	5	BO	6	51	6.09	11.34	29.18	46.61	1.74
77	5	CM	6	51	2.52	5.43	21.35	29.31	1.70
78	0	GE	6	46	5.21	12.36	18.44	36.01	0.00
79	0	PM	6	50	0.00	0.00	0.00	0.00	0.00
80	0	CA	6	54	0.00	0.00	0.00	0.00	0.00

NOTES ON THE DATA

Argentina 1947

The AREAS of Chubut, Comodore, Rivadavia and Santa Cruz are estimated on the basis of their total area, and the areas of the departments contained in the provinces Chubut and Santa Cruz, 1960. For maps on the provincial limits in 1947 and 1960 see: María Cristine Cacopardo (1967), *República Argentina, Cambios en los Límites Nacionales, Provinciales y Departementales a través de los Censos Nacionales de Población. Documento de Trabajo No 47.* Instituto Torcuato di Tella, Buenos Aires.

URBAN POPULATION is defined as the population of towns with more than 2,000 inhabitants.

Both illiterate and active population is in the census only given for the population 14 years old and more.

ILLITERATE POPULATION 14-year-olds is estimated by assuming that the rate of illiteracy among the 14-year-olds was the same in 1947 as in 1960; *i.e.* for each province:

Illiterates 14-year-olds in 1947 = Population 14-year-olds in 1947 × Illiteracy rate among 14-year-olds in 1960.

ECONOMICALLY ACTIVE POPULATION 14 years old is estimated for each economic sector by assuming that the rate of active population 14 years old in 1947 was the same as in 1960; *i.e.* for each province:

Active population in sector N, 14-year-olds in 1947 = Population 14 years old in 1947 × Active population in sector N, 14 years old in 1960/Population 14 years old in 1960.

These methods of estimation may give too small numbers of illiterate and active population among the 14-year-olds, because the rates of illiteracy and employment among the 14-year-olds have probably decreased over time. Therefore, the estimates of illiterate and active population 15 years old and more may be too high.

As the 14-year-olds in 1960 only made up 1 1/3 % of the total active population and only 3/4% of the illiterate population, the error is likely to be insignificant.

UNEMPLOYMENT data are not available.

Source: *IV Censo General de la Nación. Censo de Población.* Buenos Aires, Dirección Nacional del Servicio Estadístico.

Argentina 1960

URBAN POPULATION is defined as in 1947.

The data are complete.

Source: *Censo Nacional de Población 1960. Tomo I–IX.* Buenos Aires, Dirección Nacional de Estadística y Censos.

Bolivia 1950

Though the census does not specifically say so, the URBAN POPULATION is probably defined as the population in the administrative centres of the departments, provinces and cantons. This definition corresponds to a very small lower size limit for urban places (below 500 inhabitants).

The data given for the construction sector (4), contain also sector (5) electricity, water, gas, etc.

ECONOMICALLY ACTIVE POPULATION in each sector and province is in the census only given for the age group 10 years old and more. For the age group 10–14 years old the national total for each sector also exists. This is the column sums of the matrix equivalent to table A.1. The total active population in each province in the age group 10–14 years old (the row sums), has been estimated by assuming that the rate of active population among the 10–14 years old is the same in all the departments.

The first step in the iterative procedure described in section A.2 has been to distribute the national active population in each sector and 10–14 years old among the departments in proportion to the total active population 10 years old and more in the respective sector. Then adjust so that the row sums fit, etc.

The error involved in this estimation may be sizable, as the national total of the 10–14-year-olds accounts for 9.4% of the total active population. The 10–14 years old active population belong mostly to the agricultural and service sectors in which it constitutes 11.5% and 9.6% respectively. In the other sectors the 10–14 year-olds constitute less than 2.2% of the total.

Source: *Censo Demográfico 1950.* La Paz, Dirección General de Estadística y Censo, 1955.

Brazil 1950

URBAN POPULATION is defined as 'areas correspondentes as cidades (sedes municipais ou às vilas (sedes distritais))'.

The ECONOMIC SECTORS, manufacturing industry (2/3), construction (4), electricity, water, gas, etc. (5) are in the census combined to only one sector. However, for the active population 10 years old and more a finer industrial classification exists, which has made it possible to separate the three sectors.

To obtain an estimate of the active population 15 years old and more in each of the three sectors, its distribution between the 3 sectors is assumed to be the same as for active population 10 years old and more.

In the three sectors together the active population 10–14 years old constitutes 3.5% of the active population 15 years old and more.

The UNEMPLOYED 15 years old and more are estimated on the basis of the unemployment 10 years old and more, by using the method shown in section A.3.

Source: *Censo Demográfico. Volume VI–XXX.* Rio de Janeiro, IBGE – Conselho Nacional de Estadística, 1954–1957.

Brazil 1960

URBAN POPULATION is defined as in 1950.

EMPLOYMENT data are lacking completely.

Other information is available for 11 states only, except data on area, population, and urban population, which are available for all states based on a sample of the census.

Comparison between the real and the sample populations which have been possible for the 11 states where the censuses are published, indicate that the sample estimates are 1–2% too high, varying from state to state.

The 1960 data given for the regions 50, 53, 54, and 62 are not complete, and therefore they are not comparable to the 1950 data for these regions. The 1960 data given for

– region 50 correspond to the state of Santa Catarina and do not include Rio Grande do Sul
– region 53 correspond to the state of Guanabara and do not include Rio de Janeiro
– region 54 correspond to the state of Espírito Santo, and do not include

Minais Gerais and Sierra dos Amores

– region 63 correspond to the state of Rondonia and do not include Matto Grosso.

Source: *Sinopse Preliminar do Censo Demográfico. VII Recenseamento General do Brasil – 1960* (A volume for each state). Rio de Janeiro, IGBE – Servico Nacional de Recenseamento.

Chile 1952

URBAN POPULATION is defined as population in: (a) 'aquella área que está integrada por los centros poblados de cierta importancia demográfica y administrativa, generalmente cabeceras de comunas; (b) los centros poblados que sin tener categoria de ciudad o pueblo cuentan con servicios públicos o municipales suficientes para darles, funcionalmente, características urbanas y (c) a causa de no haberse establecido la diferenciación de las llamadas "zonas rurales no agrícolas", algunos minerales y centros industriales de esas zonas, que quentan con los mencionados servicios públicos (Chuquicamata, María Elena, Pedro de Valdivia, Sewell y Victoria)'.

Young UNEMPLOYED seeking work for the first time is in the census classified as inactive population. They have here been added to sector 9 and to the unemployed. Data for *those seeking work for the first time* and for *unemployed* only exist for the population 12 years old and more. In both cases data for the age group 15 years old and more has been estimated by the method shown in section A.3.

Source: *XII Censo General de Población y I de Vivienda. Tomo I–VI.* República de Chile, Servicio Nacional de Estadística y Censos.

Chile 1960

URBAN POPULATION is defined as in 1952.

The data are complete.

Source: *XIII Censo de Población (29 de Noviembre de 1960). Serie B. No. 1–25.* República de Chile, Dirección de Estadísticas y Censos.

Colombia 1951

URBAN POPULATION is defined as the population in towns of more than 1,500 inhabitants.

Data on ECONOMICALLY ACTIVE POPULATION 15 years old and more are available for the departments of Antioquia, Atlántico, Bolívar, Boyacá, Cauca, Cundinamarca, Chocó, Huila and Nariño.

For the departments of Caldas, Magdalena, Norte de Santander, Santander, Tolima and Valle de Cauca data on active population are only available for population 10 years old and more. Both row and column sums of the matrix of economically active population 10–14 years old in these 6 departments are available, so that the matrix of active population 15 years old and more could be estimated by means of the method described in section A.2.

The same procedure is applied for the three *intendencias*, Caquetá, Meta and San Andrés y Providencia, for which summarized data are available separately.

For the six *comisarías* in total, the distribution among economic sectors of the active population 15 years old and more is available (*i.e.* the column sums of the final matrix). For each of the *comisarías only* total active population 12 years old and more is available. The total active population 15 years old and more (*i.e.* the row sums in the final matrix) is estimated by distributing the total active population 12–14 years old among the *comisarías* in proportion to the total population 10–14 years old.

The active population 15 years old and more in each sector is then distributed among the *comisarías* in proportion to the total active population in each *comisaría*. (As nothing at all is known about the elements of the matrix, the method described in section A.2 could not be applied). This method implies that all *comisarias* have the same industrial structure, which obviously is doubtful.

UNEMPLOYMENT data are only available for population 12 years old and more. Unemployment 15 years old and more is estimated by the method described in section A.3.

Data on ILLITERATE POPULATION 15 years old and more are available for the departments of Antioquia, Atlántico, Bolívar, Boyacá, Cauca, Cundinamarca, Chocó, Huila and Nariño.

For the other departments (Caldas, Magdalena, Norte de Santander, Santander, Tolima and Valle de Cauca), for the *intendencias* (Caquetá, Meta, and San Andrés y Providencia) and for the *comisarías* (Amazonas, Arauca, Casanare, Guajira, Putumayo, Vaupéz and Vichada) data on illiterate population are only available for the age group 7 years old and more. For each of these three groups of areas in total information is also available for the age group 7–14 years old. The illiterate population 7–14 years old for each of the three groups (departments, *intendencias* and *comisarías*) has been distributed in proportion to the total illiterate population 7 years old and more.

This means that the proportion of all illiterates in the age group 7–14 years is assumed to be the same for all the departments, *intendencias* and *comisarías*, respectively. As the 7–14 year old illiterates constitute 52.5% of the total illiterate population 15 years old and more, the estimates are very uncertain.

Source: *Censo de Población de Colombia – 1951* (Summary and a volume for each department). Bogotá, Departamento Administrativo Nacional de Estadística.

Colombia 1964

URBAN POPULATION is defined as population in towns of more than 1,500 inhabitants.

ECONOMICALLY ACTIVE POPULATION distributed in sectors exists only for the population 12 years old and more, except that the national total in each sector also exists for population 12–15 years old (the column sums). Total active population in each province in the age group 12–15 years (the row sums) also exists at the national level. This total active population has been distributed among the departments, *intendencias* and *comisarías* in proportion to the total population 10–14 years old. Based on these data the active population 15 years old and more has been distributed among departments and sectors by means of the method described in section A.2.

UNEMPLOYMENT data do not exist, except for a national figure.

Source: *XIII Censo Nacional de Población (15 de Julio de 1964). Resúmen General*. Bogotá, Departamento Administrativo Nacional de Estadística. 1967.

Ecuador 1950

URBAN POPULATION is defined as the population in: 'la zona urbana, que comprende las areas que se encuentran dentro del perímetro de la ciudad capital o cabecera cantonal; y, la zona suburbana que comprende las áreas que se hallan fuera del perímetro urbano propiamente dicho y pertenecen al territorio juridiccional de las parroquias urbanas'.

Figures for the ECONOMICALLY ACTIVE POPULATION are available at the national level only (Source: *Demographic Yearbook* 1956). These national figures do not include unemployed active population, which is unknown.

The AREA is only available for the whole country (Source: *Demographic Yearbook*).

Source: *Primér Censo de Población del Ecuador 1950. Resúmen de Características. Volúmen Unico y Vol. V – Tomo I Población Alfabeta y Analfabeta.* Quito, Dirección General de Estadística y Censos, 1960.

Ecuador 1962

URBAN POPULATION is defined as: 'aquella que fué empadronada en las ciudades, capitales provinciales y cabeceras cantonales. Se dividió en urbana propiamenta tal y periférica, siendo esta última aquella que se encontraba dentro de los límites de la ciudad pero en conglomerados no urbanizados'.

The AREA is only available for the whole country (Source: *Demographic Yearbook*).

UNEMPLOYMENT data are lacking, except for the national total.

Source: *Segundo Censo de Población y Primer Censo de Vivienda. República del Ecuador. Tomo I–III.* Quito, Junta Nacional de Planificación y Coordinación Económica de Estadística y Censos.

Paraguay 1950

URBAN POPULATION is defined as: 'la que habitaba en ciudades o pueblos, cabeceras de departamentos y distritos, sin tomar en consideración su volúmen demográfico'.

The ECONOMICALLY ACTIVE POPULATION generally classified as sector 9, other activities, is distributed among the other sectors in an unknown way; sector 9 therefore is empty.

Except for this the data are complete.

Source: *Censo de Población y Vivienda 1950. Cuadros Generales y un volúmen per cada departamento.* Asunción, Dirección de Estadística y Censos. 1953–1962.

Paraguay 1962

No definition of URBAN POPULATION is given in the census, but it is probably defined as in 1950.

The UNEMPLOYMENT figures used are taken from the mimeographed provincial volumes of the census. The unemployment data given in the summary volume of the census are different.

The data are complete.

Source: *Censo de población y vivienda 1962* (Summary and a volume for each province). Asunción, Dirección General de Estadística y Censos. 1965-66.

Peru 1940

'Se consideró como POBLACION URBANA la que habita en las capitales de circunscripción territorial (departamento, provincia y distrito), asimismo la que vive en centros poblados cuyo número de habitantes excede del promedio aritmético del de dichas capitales, siempre que no tengan características tipicamente rurales (hacienda, fundo, comunidad, etc.).

LITERATE POPULATION is population which has attended schools rather than population which can actually read and write at the census day.

As the ECONOMICALLY ACTIVE POPULATION in the census does not include the unemployed, these have been added. The distribution of the unemployed among sectors and departments had to be estimated first. Both the total national unemployment in each sector (the column sums) and the total unemployment in each department (the row sums) are known. The distribution among sectors and departments is carried out by an iterative procedure equivalent to the one described in section A.2. The first step of the iteration was to distribute the column sums (each corresponding to a sector) among the departments in proportion to the employment in the sector.

The total unemployment was 2.0 % of the active population 15 years old and more.

In the census, manufacturing industry (2/3) and electricity, water, gas, etc. (5) are combined. A finer industrial classification, however, does exist so that it has been possible to separate the two sectors, except for the unemployment data which have been distributed among the two sectors in proportion to the active population in the sectors.

The unemployment in the two sectors combined is 2.0 %.

Source: *Censo Nacional de Población y Ocupación, 1940*. Lima, Dirección Nacional de Estadística, 1944.

Peru 1961

URBAN POPULATION is defined as population in: 'Capitales del distrito y otras ciudades con características urbanas como plazas, servicios de agua, desagüe, alumbrado, y el número de sus habitantes sea igual o mayor al de la capital del mismo distrito'.

The ECONOMICALLY ACTIVE POPULATION 15 years old and more is distributed among economic sectors on the basis of the distribution of the active population 6 years old and more and by means of the method described in section A.2.

For the population 6–14 years old both the national total of each sector (the column sums) and the total active population in each department (the row sums), are known.

The active population 6–14 years old constitutes 2.6% of the total active population 15 years old and more.

The UNEMPLOYED POPULATION 15 years old and more is estimated from the unemployed population 10 years old and more by distributing the known national unemployment in the age group 10–14 years old among the departments in proportion to the total unemployment in the departments.

The unemployed 10–14 years old constitute only 0.3% of the total unemployment.

Source: *VI Censo Nacional de Población. Tomo I–III–IV*. Lima, Dirección Nacional de Estadística y Censo. República del Perú, 1965–1966.

Venezuela 1950

URBAN POPULATION is defined as the population in towns with more than 1,000 inhabitants.

In the census the ECONOMICALLY ACTIVE POPULATION does not include the unemployed. They have therefore been added. However, unemployment figures distributed in both sectors and states are only available for the age group 10 years old and more; the distribution of the unemployed 10–14 years old, therefore, had to be estimated and subtracted first. For each state the total unemployment 10–14 years old is available; these figures have been distributed among the economic sectors in proportion to the total employment in the sectors.

The unemployment 10–14 years old constitutes 0.15% of the total active population 15 years old and more. The error in the estimation, therefore, is likely to be insignificant.

Source: *VIII Censo General de Población*. Caracas, Dirección General de Estadísticas y Censos Nacionales, 1955–1959.

Venezuela 1961

URBAN POPULATION is defined as in 1950.

For the states of Apure, Barinas, Nueva Esparta, Portuguesa, Amazonas, Delta Amacuro and for the 'dependencias federales' data on the ECONOMICALLY ACTIVE POPULATION are only available for the age group 10 years old and more. (Because the volumes of the census corresponding to these states have not been published yet).[1] For the total of the seven states the data are also available for the age group 10–15 years (*i.e.* the column sums).

The total active population in each of the seven states (*i.e.* the row sums) has been estimated by assuming that the rate of the active population among the 10–14 years old is the same in all the states. The distribution of states and economic sectors has been estimated by the method described in section A.2.

Total active population 10–14 years old in the seven states constitutes 6.3% of the total active population 15 years old and more.

Source: *IX Censo General de Población*. Caracas, Dirección General de Estadística y Censos Nacionales, 1964.

Uruguay 1963

The census does not specify any definition of URBAN POPULATION.

All the data are based on a sample of the census only.

Source: *IV Censo General de Población y II de Vivienda 1963. Muestra de Anticipación*. Dirección General de Estadística y Censos.

British Guyana (1946 and 1960), Surinam (1958 and 1964), and French Guyana (1954 and 1961)

The data are incomplete.

Sources: *Population Census 1960. British Guiana. Vol. II. Summary tables*. Central Statistical Office, Trinidad and Tobago. Port of Spain, 1964.

Demographic Yearbook for several years.

---

[1] January 1970.

Per capita income and accessibilities in 74 regions of South America

B.1 *Per capita* INCOME

A set of internationally comparable *per capita* income figures does not exist for regions in South America, and the income figures presented here rest on a very weak data base. They are estimated on the basis of regional income *per capita* figures for each of the countries.

Unfortunately the data used for the individual countries do not correspond to the same year; the Colombian data are from 1953, the Argentine from 1959, the Brazilian, Chilean and Peruvian are from 1960 and the Venezuelan from 1965.

There are also large differences in the way they are computed; for some countries the available data are product figures for others they are income figures.

To obtain some uniformity in the data, indices have been computed for the regions of each country by dividing the regional figures by the national average *per capita* income. These indices are then multiplied by the United Nations (1963) estimate of the national *per capita* income in 1961. These estimates are corrected for international differences in buying power.

Finally, the income *per capita* figures thus obtained for the administrative areas have been combined into income figures for the 74 regions, by using the census populations shown in appendix A as weights.

For Bolivia, Ecuador, Paraguay, and Uruguay only the national *per capita* income figures have been available.

The resulting regional income data are clearly not satisfactory but they are the best which can be produced at present.

They suffer from all the deficiencies which beset comparative national income data and which, for instance, Kuznets (1966) has discussed at length, namely:

1. Low reliability;
2. Limited scope of the income and product accounts, which only

measure money income, and therefore are likely to undervalue the income of rural areas;

3. Regional differences in price level. Though the international income figures used are corrected for buying power differences, these corrections are averages over all products, and as the product composition varies from region to region the corrections should also have varied.

Sources:

National *per capita* figures are obtained from:

El Desarrollo Económico en América Latina de la Postguerra. Naciones Unidas, 1963.

Sub-national *per capita* indices are obtained from:

Argentina
Relevamiento de la Estructura Regional de la Economía Argentina Vol. II. Buenos Aires, Consejo Federal de Inversiones and Instituto Torcuatto di Tella, 1965.

Brazil
S. H. Robock: *Brazil's Developing Northeast.* Washington, Brookings Institution, 1963.

Chile
I. Cardenas: *Estimación del Producto de Chile al Nivel Provincial.* Santiago, 1961.

Colombia
L. J. Lebret: *Estudio sobre las Condiciones del Desarrollo de Colombia.* Bogotá, Mision 'Economía y Humanismo', Comité Nacional de Planificación, 1958.

Peru
Renta Nacional del Peru 1942–60. Banco Central de Reserva del Perú, 1962.

Venezuela
Estimates of regional gross products by Alejandro Grajal (CENDES) on the basis of information from Banco Central and Censos Economías y Población (Unpublished).

B.2 ACCESSIBILITIES

A detailed account of computation procedures is given in chapter 7, sections 7.2 and 7.3.

Table **B.1** *Accessibility*

Region	Income *per capita* 1960	Accessibility (10^2 urban population per km)		
		1950	1960	1980?
02	462	11	68	562
03	780	13	73	588
04	370	21	135	664
05	560	153	298	1,014
06	271	74	221	818
07	315	64	170	672
08	283	33	119	560
09	298	20	94	496
10	902	3	37	318
11	526	51	148	690
12	359	28	129	778
13	432	45	199	874
14	492	83	202	796
15	329	63	187	788
16	272	81	204	832
17	655	162	305	984
18	783	262	448	1,272
19	519	132	345	1,070
20	583	58	209	830
21	759	62	212	856
22	471	75	249	872
23	1,070	75	254	822
24	892	526	816	1,990
26	640	48	134	634
27	1,150	40	99	496
28	1,868	22	59	370
29	2,586	16	43	282
30	248	28	112	824
31	196	20	98	834
34	116	2	52	634
35	561	90	214	1,074
37	157*	35	76	574
38	94*	13	59	536
39	133*	7	50	570
40	106*	1	2	484
42	124	16	69	572
43	338	21	85	548
44	144	15	56	496
45	553	80	229	768
46	154	35	107	544

Table **B.1** *Accessibility (continued)*

Region	Income *per capita* 1960	Accessibility (10² urban population per km)		
		1950	1960	1980?
47	79	2	4	8
48	206	35	109	506
49	342	26	95	480
50	418	89	292	892
51	415	211	447	1,140
52	666	279	712	1,650
53	716	447	833	1,868
54	254	198	422	1,042
55	212	80	215	604
56	210	53	241	666
57	169	49	158	554
58	121	27	112	498
59	206	51	248	724
60	210	4	38	452
61	255	2	15	398
62	292	34	108	550
63	230*	33	81	508
64	218*	26	87	476
65	872	121	282	808
66	578	33	97	440
67	432	44	138	522
68	388	30	119	482
69	224	24	128	596
70	1,340	48	150	602
71	350	64	171	612
72	273	49	165	602
73	210	44	155	594
74	434	63	206	632
75	296	62	206	642
76	707	103	296	638
77	80	0	68	418

*These figures have been produced from estimates of the national income by distributing the national income among regions in proportion to the urban population in the regions.

18*

Table B.2   *Accessibility increases 1950–1960*

Region	Accessibility increases (10^2 urban population per km) due to:				
	transport network improvements without population increase	population increase without network improvement	extra increase when both transport improvement and population increase take place	1/4 international integration	Total increase 1950–1960
02	10	5	4	38	57
03	12	5	6	37	60
04	43	8	17	46	114
05	13	75	5	52	145
06	46	29	25	47	147
07	27	24	12	43	106
08	26	12	10	38	86
09	21	8	9	36	74
10	0	2	9	23	34
11	27	25	12	33	97
12	34	15	16	36	101
13	59	27	25	43	154
14	30	39	15	35	119
15	39	32	17	36	124
16	35	37	16	35	123
17	16	79	6	42	143
18	18	119	5	44	186
19	79	53	38	43	213
20	53	29	26	43	151
21	46	32	24	48	150
22	63	37	30	44	174
23	69	37	33	40	179
24	8	128	104	49	289
26	18	23	10	35	86
27	7	21	4	27	59
28	4	12	1	20	37
29	3	8	0	16	27
30	21	16	10	37	84
31	0	10	0	68	78
34	2	1	1	46	50
35	0	30	0	94	124
37	1	3	1	36	41
38	2	5	1	38	46
39	5	4	1	33	43
40	0	1	0	0	1

Table B.2 *Accessibility increases 1950–1960 (continued)*

Region Accessibility increases (10^2 urban population per km) due to:

	transport network improvements without population increase	population increase without network improvement	extra increase when both transport improvement and population increase take place	1/4 international integration	Total increase 1950–1960
42	2	16	2	33	53
43	3	22	5	34	64
44	0	13	1	27	41
45	1	117	1	30	149
46	0	42	2	28	72
47	0	2	0	0	2
48	1	43	2	28	74
49	2	36	3	28	69
50	59	66	44	34	203
51	31	155	24	26	236
52	30	356	24	23	453
53	20	330	15	21	386
54	39	134	31	20	224
55	38	57	27	13	135
56	62	91	18	17	188
57	34	41	23	11	109
58	33	18	23	11	85
59	81	42	56	18	197
60	0	34	0	0	34
61	0	13	0	0	13
62	20	25	14	15	74
63	2	12	1	33	48
64	2	30	0	29	61
65	13	114	9	25	161
66	6	30	6	22	64
67	18	35	18	23	94
68	20	28	17	24	89
69	24	19	21	40	104
70	13	47	12	30	102
71	11	59	8	29	107
72	22	45	27	22	116
73	15	51	16	29	111
74	23	74	24	22	143
75	21	78	22	23	144
76	17	134	18	24	193
77	23	0	27	18	68

Table B.3   *Accessibility increases 1960–1980 ?*

Region	Accessibility increases (10^2 urban population per km) due to:				
	transport improve-ments +1/4 integration	3/4 effect of inte-gration without network improvement	extra increase when both trans-port improve-ment and integration take place	100 per cent population growth	Total increase 1960–80 ?
02	29	113	71	281	494
03	33	113	75	294	515
04	16	139	42	332	529
05	13	157	39	507	716
06	13	140	35	409	597
07	9	128	29	336	502
08	13	115	33	280	441
09	15	107	32	248	402
10	18	68	36	159	281
11	34	99	64	345	542
12	67	109	84	389	649
13	37	129	72	437	675
14	36	104	56	398	594
15	47	110	50	394	601
16	47	106	59	416	628
17	19	125	41	492	679
18	17	132	39	636	824
19	16	128	46	535	725
20	34	128	44	415	621
21	26	144	46	428	644
22	18	132	37	436	623
23	12	122	23	411	568
24	9	146	24	995	1,174
26	46	104	33	317	500
27	39	82	28	248	397
28	33	59	34	185	311
29	25	48	25	141	239
30	89	110	101	412	712
31	30	203	86	417	736
34	36	137	92	317	582
35	10	282	31	537	860
37	30	109	72	287	498
38	29	116	64	268	477
39	40	99	96	285	520
40	71	0	169	242	482

Table B.3   *Accessibility increases 1960–1980? (continued)*

Region	Accessibility increases (10^2 urban population per km) due to:				
	transport improvements $+1/4$ integration	3/4 effect of integration without network improvement	extra increase when both transport improvement and integration take place	100 per cent population growth	Total increase 1960–1980?
42	49	98	78	286	503
43	26	101	62	274	463
44	44	79	69	248	440
45	21	89	45	384	539
46	38	82	45	272	437
47	0	0	0	4	4
48	16	85	43	253	497
49	16	85	44	240	385
50	17	102	35	446	600
51	14	79	30	570	693
52	17	70	26	825	938
53	17	63	21	934	1,035
54	18	60	21	521	620
55	35	38	14	302	389
56	31	50	11	333	425
57	66	33	20	277	396
58	82	33	22	249	386
59	35	54	25	362	476
60	135	0	53	226	414
61	98	0	86	199	383
62	80	46	41	275	442
63	89	100	48	254	427
64	108	85	46	238	389
65	14	76	32	404	526
66	23	66	34	220	343
67	22	68	33	261	384
68	18	71	33	241	363
69	16	121	33	298	468
70	21	91	39	301	452
71	16	86	33	306	441
72	21	66	49	301	437
73	25	87	30	297	439
74	14	66	30	316	426
75	12	69	34	321	436
76	17	73	33	319	342
77	45	54	42	209	350

APPENDIX C

List of provinces, departments or states in the South American countries

ARGENTINA (AR 100):	Name of province 1960	Name of province 1947
Code No.		
CF 101	Capital Federal	
BA 102	Buenos Aires	
CO 103	Corrientes	
ER 104	Entre Ríos	
MI 105	Misiones	
CA 106	Catamarca	
JU 107	Juruy	
RI 108	La Rioja	
SA 109	Salta	
TU 110	Tucumán	
ME 111	Mendoza	
SJ 112	San Juan	
SL 113	San Luis	
CT 114	Chubut	Non-existent (125 + part of 127)
NE 115	Neuquen	
RN 116	Río Negro	
SC 117	Santa Cruz	Non-existent (126 + part of 127)
TF 118	Tierra de Fuego	
CH 119	Chaco	
FO 120	Formosa	
SE 121	Santiago del Estero	
CB 122	Córdoba	
LP 123	La Pampa	
SF 124	Santa Fe	
CT 125	Non-existent (part of 114)	Chubut
SC 126	Non-existent (part of 117)	Santa Cruz
RV 127	Non-existent (parts of 114 and 117)	Rivadavia

BOLIVIA (BO 200):	*Name of department*	
Code No.	1950	
CH 201	Chuquisaca	
LP 202	La Paz	
CO 203	Cochabamba	
PO 204	Potosí	
OR 205	Oruro	
SC 206	Santa Cruz	
TA 207	Tarija	
BE 208	Beni	
PA 209	Pando	

BRAZIL (BR 300):	*Name of state*	*Name of state*
Code No.	1960	1950
RO 301	Rondonia	Guapore
AC 302	Acre	
AM 303	Amazonas	
RR 304	Roraima	Río Branco
PA 305	Pará	
AP 306	Amapá	
MA 307	Maranhão	
PI 308	Piauí	
CE 309	Ceará	
RN 310	Río Grande do Norte	
PB 311	Paraíba	
PE 312	Pernambuco	
AL 313	Alagoas	
SE 315	Sergipe	
BA 316	Bahía	
MG 317	Minas Gerais	
SA 318	Sierre dos Aimores	
ES 319	Espírito Santo	
RJ 320	Río de Janeiro	
GU 321	Guanabara	Distrito Federal
SP 322	São Paulo	
PR 323	Paraná	
SC 324	Santa Catarina	
RS 325	Río Grande do Sul	
GR 326	Mato Grosso	
GO 329	Non-existent (327+328)	Goiás
GO 327	Goiás	Non-existent (part of 329)
DF 328	Distrito Federal	Non-existent (part of 329)

CHILE (CH 400):	*Name of province*	*Name of province*
Code No.	1960	1952
TP 401	Tarapacá	
AN 402	Antofagasta	
AT 403	Atacama	
CQ 404	Coquimbo	
AC 405	Aconcagua	
VA 406	Valparaíso	
SA 407	Santiago	
OH 408	O'Higgins	
CO 409	Colchagua	
CU 410	Curicó	
TA 411	Talca	
MA 412	Maule	
LI 413	Linares	
NU 414	Ñuble	
CP 415	Concepción	
AR 416	Arauco	
BB 417	Bío-Bío	
MC 418	Malleco	
CA 419	Cautín	
VD 420	Valdivia	
OS 421	Osorno	
LL 422	Llanguihue	
CL 423	Chiloé	
AY 424	Aisén	
MG 425	Magallanes	

COLOMBIA (CO 500):	*Name of department*	*Name of department*
Code No.	1964	1951
AN 501	Antioquia	
AT 502	Atlántico	
BL 527	Non-existent (503 + 507)	Bolívar
BY 504	Boyacá	Boyacá + Casarnare
CD 505	Caldas	
CC 506	Cauca	
CU 508	Cundinamarca	
CH 509	Chocó	
HU 510	Huila	
MA 511	Magdalena	
ME 512	Meta	
NA 513	Nariño	
NS 514	Norte de Santander	
SA 515	Santander	
TO 516	Tolima	
VC 517	Valle de Cauca	

AR 518	Arauca	
CQ 519	Caquetá	
GU 520	Guajira	
AM 522	Amazonas	
VA 528	Non-existent (523 + 525)	Vaupéz
PU 524	Putamayo	
VI 526	Vichada	
BL 503	Bolívar	Non-existent (part of 527)
CO 507	Córdoba	Non-existent (part of 527)
GN 523	Guanía	Non-existent (part of 528)
VA 525	Vaupéz	Non-existent (part of 528)

ECUADOR (EC 600):	*Name of province*	*Name of province*
Code No.	1962	1950
AZ 601	Azuay	
BO 602	Bolívar	
CA 603	Cañar	
CE 604	Carchi	
CO 605	Cotopaxi	
CH 606	Chimborazo	
EO 607	El Oro	
ES 608	Esmeraldas	
GU 609	Guayas	
IM 610	Imbabura	
LO 611	Loja	
RI 612	Los Ríos	
MA 613	Manabi	
NP 621	Non-existent (615 + 616)	Napo-Pastaza
PI 617	Pichincha	
SZ 622	Non-existent (614 + 619)	Santiago-Zamora
TU 618	Tungurahua	
MS 614	Morona Santiago	Non-existent (part of 622)
NA 615	Napo	Non-existent (part of 621)
PA 616	Pastaza	Non-existent (part of 621)
ZC 619	Zamora Chinchipe	Non-existent (part of 622)

PARAGUAY (PA 700):	*Name of province*	*Name of province*
Code No.	1962	1950
AS 701	Asunción	
CP 702	Concepción	
SP 703	San Pedro	
CO 704	Cordillera	
GU 705	Guairá	
CG 706	Caaguazú	
CZ 707	Caazapá	
IT 708	Itapúa	
MI 709	Misiones	
PA 710	Paraguarí	
AP 711	Alto Paraná	
CE 712	Central	
NE 713	Ñeembucú	
AM 714	Amambay	
PH 715	Presidente Hayes	
BU 716	Boquerón	
OL 717	Olimpo	

PERU (PE 800):	*Name of department*	*Name of department*
Code No.	1961	1940
AM 801	Amazonas	
AN 802	Ancash	
AP 803	Apurimac	
AR 804	Arequipa	
AY 805	Ayacucho	
CJ 806	Cajamarca	
CA 807	Callao	
CU 808	Cuzco	
HV 809	Huancavelica	
HU 810	Huanuco	
IC 811	Ica	
JU 825	Non-existent (812+819)	Junín
LL 813	La Libertad	
LA 814	Lambayeque	
LI 815	Lima	
LO 816	Loreta	
MD 817	Madre de Dios	
MO 818	Moquequa	
PI 820	Piura	
PU 821	Puno	
SM 822	San Martín	
TA 823	Tacna	
TU 824	Tumbes	

JU 812   Junín   Non-existent
                                                 (part of 825)

PA 819   Pasco   Non-existent
                                                 (part of 825)

VENEZUELA (VE 900):	*Name of state*	*Name of state*
Code No.	1961	1950
DI 901	Distrito Federal	
AN 902	Anzoategui	
AP 903	Apure	
AR 904	Aragua	
BA 905	Barinas	
BO 906	Bolívar	
CA 907	Caraboba	
CO 908	Cojedes	
FA 909	Falcón	
GU 910	Guárico	
LA 911	Lara	
ME 912	Mérida	
MI 913	Miranda	
MO 914	Monagas	
NE 915	Nueva Esparta	
PO 916	Portuguesa	
SU 917	Sucre	
TA 918	Tachira	
TR 919	Trujillo	
YA 920	Yaracuy	
ZU 921	Zulia	
AM 922	Amazonas	
DA 923	Delta Amacuro	

GUIANAS
GU 011   Guyana (1960 and 1946)
SU 012   Suriname (1964 and 1950)
FR 013   French Guiana (1961 and 1954)

URUGUAY
UR 001   1963

APPENDIX D

List of the 74 regions, their composition and their code numbers

Code no. region	country	Name of main city	Code numbers of administrative areas included in the region. The numbers refers to the list in appendix C
02IQ	4	Iquique	401
03AN	4	Antofagasta	402
04SE	4	La Serena	403 + 404
05SA	4	Santiago	405 + 406 + 407 + 408 + 409
06TA	4	Talca	410 + 411 + 412 + 413
07CO	4	Concepción	414 + 415 + 416 + 417 + 418
08VD	4	Valdivia	419 + 420 + 421
09PM	4	Puerto Montt	422 + 423 + 424
10PA	4	Punta Arenas	425
11SA	1	Salta	107 + 109
12FO	1	Formosa	120
13CR	1	Corrintes-Resistencia	103 + 119
14TU	1	Tucumán	110
15LR	1	La Rioja	106 + 108
16ES	1	Sant. del Estero	121
17CD	1	Córdoba	122
18RO	1	Rosario	124
19PA	1	Paraná	104
20SJ	1	San Juan	112
21ME	1	Mendoza	111
22SL	1	San Luis	113
23SR	1	Santa Rosa	123
24BA	1	Buenos Aires	101 + 102
26NE	1	Neuquen	115 + 116
27RA	1	Rawson	114

Fig. D. *Regions in South America and their code numbers*

Code no. region	country	Name of main city	Code numbers of administrative areas included in the region The numbers refers to the list in appendix C
28SC	1	Santa Cruz	117
29US	1	Ushuaia	118
30PO	1	Posada	105
31As	7	Asunción	701 − 714
34ME	7	Mcal. Estigariba	715 + 716 + 717
35MO	0	Montevideo	001
37LP	2	La Paz	202 + 205
38SU	2	Sucre	201 + 203 + 204 + 207
39SC	2	Santa Cruz	206
40TR	2	Trinidad	208 + 209
42PU	8	Puno	821
43AR	8	Arequipa	804 + 818 + 823
44CU	8	Cuzco	803 + 808 + 817
45LI	8	Lima	807 + 811 + 815
46HU	8	Huancayo	805 + 809 + 810 + 812 + 819
47IQ	8	Iquitos	816 + 822
48TR	8	Trujillo	801 + 802 + 806 + 813 + 814
49PI	8	Piura	820 + 824
50PA	3	Porto Alegre	324 + 325
51CU	3	Curitiba	323
52SP	3	São Paulo	322
53RJ	3	Río de Janeiro	320 + 321
54BH	3	Belo Horizonte	317 + 318 + 319
55RE	3	Recife	310 + 311 + 312 + 313 + 314 + 315
56SA	3	Salvador	316
57FO	3	Fortaleza	309
58TE	3	Terezina	307 + 308
59BR	3	Brasília	327 + 328
60BE	3	Belém	305 + 306
61MA	3	Manáus	302 + 303 + 304
62CI	3	Cuiabá	301 + 326
63QU	6	Quito	602 + 604 + 605 + 606 + 608 + 610 + 615 + 616 + 617 + 618

Code no. region	country	Name of main city	Code numbers of administrative areas included in the region The numbers refers to the list in appendix C
64GU	6	Guayaquil	$601 + 603 + 607 + 609 + 611 + 612 + 613 + 614 + 619 + 620$
65CA	9	Caracas	$901 + 904 + 913 + 924$
66CB	9	Cuidad Bolívar	$906 + 922 + 923$
67BA	9	Barcelona	$902 + 914 + 915 + 917$
68AP	9	San Fernando de Apure	$903 + 905 + 910$
69SC	9	San Cristóbal	$912 + 918$
70MA	9	Maracaibo	921
71BQ	9	Barquisimeto	$907 + 908 + 909 + 911 + 916 + 919 + 920$
72BA	5	Barranquilla	$502 + 503 + 507 + 511 + 520 + 521$
73BU	5	Bucaramanga	$504 + 514 + 515 + 518$
74ME	5	Medellin	$501 + 505 + 509$
75CA	5	Calí	$506 + 510 + 513 + 516 + 517 + 519 + 524$
76BO	5	Bogotá	$508 + 512$
77CM	5	Calamar	$522 + 523 + 525 + 526$
78GE	0	Georgetown	011
79PM	0	Paramaribo	012
80CA	0	Cayenne	013

Country codes

1. Argentina
2. Bolivia
3. Brazil
4. Chile
5. Colombia

6. Ecuador
7. Paraguay
8. Peru
9. Venezuela
0. Uruguay and Guyanas

International integration, 1960

The accessibility index used in chapter 7 in the regression equations for 1960 is

$$A = A_{\text{National}} + h\, A_{\text{Integration}}$$

where $h = 1/4$.

The value of h can be determined as that which results in the largest correlation coefficients between accessibility and *per capita* income and urbanization. To find the best h these correlation coefficients were computed for $h = 0$, $h = 1/4$, $h = 1/2$, $h = 3/4$ and $h = 1$. These correla-.. tions are shown in Table E. The largest correlation coefficient was in

Table E. *Correlations between urbanization, per capita income and accessibility,* $(A = A_{\text{National}} + h\, A_{\text{Integration}})$ *under different assumptions about the level of integration (h)* Only 41 consolidated regions, 1960

	Urbanization		*Per capita* income	
	Coefficients of		Coefficients of	
	correlation R	determination R^2	correlation R	determination R^2
$A = A_{\text{National}}$	0.716	0.513	0.743	0.552
$A = A_{\text{National}} + 1/4\, A_{\text{Integration}}$	0.734	0.538	0.756	0.571
$A = A_{\text{National}} + 1/2 A_{\text{Integration}}$	0.733	0.537	0.753	0.567
$A = A_{\text{National}} + 3/4\, A_{\text{Integration}}$	0.728	0.529	0.747	0.558
$A = A_{\text{National}} + A_{\text{Integration}}$	0.719	0.517	0.739	0.546

both cases found for $h = 1/4$, though the actual maximum probably is somewhere between $1/4$ and $1/2$. This indicates that the continent in 1960 as an average had reached a level of integration at about a quarter of full integration.

This result however is very inconclusive as the variation of the correlation coefficients is very small and insignificant. One of the reasons for this small variation in the correlation coefficients is that the variance of accessibility due to integration is much smaller than the variation in national accessibility.

Accessibility by the airline and maritime shipping networks

In the airline network, distances have been computed as travel times rather than travel costs. To make allowance for differences in the frequency of departures larger waiting times were added to the travel time on routes with few departures than on routes with frequent departures. (For exact computational procedures see footnote[1]). Of the 74 regions included in the analysis, three were not connected to the airline network and therefore have zero airline potential.

As the attractive power of an airline decreases rapidly with the distance from the airport only the population of the city served by the airline has been included in the mass $(u_j P_j)$.

In the rate structure for maritime transportation it is not unusual that the terminal costs (*i.e.* that part of the transport costs that is independent of the distance) make up between 50–70% of the total cost of shipment (Brown, 1966, p. 149).[2] Variations in the terminal costs are therefore much more important than variations in the distance over which goods are shipped, and the harbour with the lowest terminal costs will also have the highest accessibility. Low terminal costs will usually be found in the biggest harbours, because these will have the highest frequency of regular freight route arrivals and often also the most modern loading and unloading facilities. Exceptions to this are the specialized mineral

[1] The air travel time is computed as the sum of:

Flight time according to air schedule	= ?
+ transport time to and from airport (2×60 min.)	= 120 min.
+ waiting time due to check-in, check-out and customs	= 60 min.
+ waiting time due to low frequency of departures $(420/f)$ min.	= ?

where f = number of departures per week.

[2] This does not cover the interest loss due to waiting time and slow transportation, which is likely to be very big in Latin America where interest rates are high; nor does it include the cost of breakages and theft reflected in freight insurance rates, which in Latin America are the highest in the world.

ore and petroleum export harbours, which have very little importance outside the speciality they serve.

As a measure of maritime transport accessibility we shall therefore use the number of international, scheduled ship departures per month. Only 35 of the 74 regions are connected to international shipping routes and 39 regions therefore have zero accessibility on the maritime transport network.

Finally we have also for the airline network constructed an intercontinental accessibility index. This is defined as the weekly frequency of flight departures to destinations outside Latin America. This index has positive values for only 24 regions.

All air schedule data are taken from the *ABC Airways Guide, November 1967*. Data on maritime shipping routes are taken from the companies time tables for August, 1967. The values of the accessibility indices are shown in Table F.2.

These three accessibility indices have not been used in the regression analyses in chapter 7, because they are highly intercorrelated with road accessibility (see Table F.1). The exclusion of some of them is therefore unlikely to influence very much the correlation coefficients of the regression models in which they are to be used as independent variables.

Exclusion of the airline and maritime transportation accessibilities, however, will influence the regression equations. The three excluded accessibility indices in general have their largest value in the most urbanized regions, and their exclusion therefore will lead to an under-estimation of the accessibility of these regions, which also have the highest road accessibilities. In general we should therefore expect to find too small regression coefficients between accessibility and development.

Table F.1 *Correlation matrix for different accessibility indices* (71 regions)

	1	2	3	4
1. Maritime accessibility	–	0.60	0.76	0.51
2. Latin American airline accessibility	–	–	0.70	0.64
3. Intercontinental airline accessibility	–	–	–	0.59
4. Road accessibility 1960				–
Standard deviations	23.22	140.07	16.53	121.07

Table F.2 *Accessibilities in the airline and maritime shipping networks*

Regional code*	Accessibility in the			Region-al code*	Accessibility in the		
	Maritime transport network	Air transport network			Maritime transport network	Air transport network	
		within Latin America	out of Latin America			within Latin America	out of Latin America
024IQ	30	189	1	448GU	0	49	0
034AN	37	176	1	458LI	59	506	69
044SE	0	70	0	468HU	0	43	0
054SA	46	509	43	478IQ	3	49	0
064TA	0	0	0	488TR	2	61	0
074CO	15	69	0	498PI	5	46	0
084VD	1	52	0	503PA	17	496	0
094PM	1	152	0	513CU	25	246	0
104PA	11	138	0	523SP	88	602	36
111SA	0	231	0	533RJ	79	617	60
121FO	0	161	0	543BH	0	271	0
131CR	0	361	0	553RE	14	300	1
141TU	0	252	0	563SA	23	333	0
151LR	0	155	0	573FO	4	288	0
161ES	0	158	0	583TE	0	258	0
171CD	0	305	0	593BR	0	264	2
181RO	5	298	0	603BE	8	264	4
191PA	0	220	0	613MA	6	142	1
201SJ	0	192	0	623CI	0	133	0
211ME	0	329	0	636QU	0	264	9
221SL	0	141	0	646GU	66	367	15
231SR	0	151	0	659CA	101	381	53
241BA	77	532	70	669CB	5	43	0
261NE	0	222	0	679BA	30	59	0
271RA	0	166	0	689AP	0	36	0
281SC	0	161	0	699SC	0	56	0
291US	0	84	0	709MA	60	84	2
301PO	0	220	0	719BQ	0	75	0
317AS	4	452	5	725BA	45	166	3
347ME	0	0	0	735BU	0	108	0
350MO	68	609	29	745ME	0	126	2
372LP	0	260	3	755CA	51	260	5
382SU	0	141	0	765BO	0	401	29
392SC	0	202	0	775CM	0	27	0
402TR	0	12	0	780GE	20	29	10
428PU	0	0	0	790PM	17	29	5
438AR	29	46	0	800CA	1	5	0

*For explanation of the regional code see appendix D.

APPENDIX G

An analogy from social physics

An index similar to the accessibility measure used here has in social physics been introduced as an analogy to the potential concept in physics. In physics the potential energy of a mass m_i in the gravity field of another mass m_j is equal to the work required to move the mass towards infinity, *i.e.*

$$\int_{d_{ij}}^{\infty} -f\frac{m_i m_j}{r_{ij}^2}\, dr = fm_i\left[\frac{m_j}{r}\right]_{d_{ij}}^{\infty} = -f\frac{m_i m_j}{d_{ij}}$$

or where the gravity field of many masses are involved

$$-fm_i \sum_{\text{all } j} \frac{m_j}{d_{ij}}$$

We can extent this analogy to the energy equation, stating that the sum of potential and kinetic energy of a mass in a conservative system is constant, *i.e.*

$$E_p + E_k = -fm_i \sum_{\text{all } j} \frac{m_j}{d_{ij}} + \frac{1}{2} m_i v_i^2 = K$$

In this analogy the masses are analogous to the population of the regions, P_i, $\sum_{\text{all } j} (m_j/d_{ij})$ is analogous to the accessibility, A_i, and the velocity, v_i, is analogous to the *per capita* income per year, Y_i *i.e.*

$$-aP_i A_i + bP_i Y_i^2 = K$$

$$Y_i = \sqrt{\frac{K}{bP_i} + \frac{aA_i}{b}}$$

or, where $(K/bP_i) \ll (aA_i/b)$, with approximation

$$Y_i = a'\sqrt{A_i}$$

279

This compares favourably with the equation found empirically in chapter 7 for the consolidated regions of South America in 1960:

$$Y_{60} = 11 \, A_{60}^{0.68}$$

When the work of an active force, W, is involved the energy equation becomes

$$E_p + E_k = K + W$$

The economic analogy to W would be capital and natural resources, C_i. The equation thus becomes

$$-aP_iA_i + bP_iY_i^2 = K + C_i$$
$$Y_i = \sqrt{\frac{K}{bP_i} + \frac{C_i}{bP_i} + \frac{aA_i}{b}}$$

Only where C_i/P_i is of the same order of magnitude or larger than aA_i will capital and natural resources be important for the *per capita* income in region i. This is most likely to be the case where both accessibility and population are small, *i.e.* in the peripheral regions where the relation between *per capita* income and accessibility in chapter 7 was found to be poor.

Sectorial composition of the regional economies in South America, 1950 and 1960

In chapter 7 it was found that regional economic development could to a large extent be explained as a function of information accessibility and economic peripherality, crudely expressed as population density. To see in more detail how the two factors of growth influence the sectorial composition of the regional economies, a series of regression equations has been computed, in which the percentage of the total work force employed in each of the economic sectors is explained in terms of accessibility and population density. The results of these regressions are shown in Tables H.1 and H.2 for 1950 and 1960 respectively.

The multiple correlation coefficients obtained in these equations are not very high, but in all cases they are significantly different from zero at a 95% level.

The regression and *beta* coefficients of the equations indicate the locational characteristics of the sectors. The equations for 1960 (Table H.2) show that the first independent variable, accessibility, influences the secondary and tertiary sectors positively and the primary sectors negatively. This indicates that the secondary and tertiary sectors are concentrated in the high accessibility areas while agriculture predominates in the low accessibility areas. The second independent variable, population density, complicates this picture. It shows that:

1. Agriculture for a given accessibility tends to be more important in areas with high than in areas with low density;
2. Mining is only important in areas with low density;
3. Manufacturing and commerce primarily are accessibility oriented;
4. Services and construction in part are over-represented in areas with high accessibility, but in part also in areas with low density.

This confirms that the periphery is characterized not only by a high level of mining employment, but also by a relatively high level of service employment. The large proportion of service employment in the periphery in

Table H.1   *Regression equations for the relation between accessibility (A), population density (D), and percentage of the work force employed in each of the economic sectors*
1950: 63 regions[1]

Sector	Con-stant	Regression coefficient for log A log D		Standard error on regression coefficient		*Beta* coefficient for log A log D		Coefficient of corre-lation	deter-mina-tion
		b_A	b_D	δ_A	δ_D	β_A	β_D	R	R^2
0 Agriculture	62.6	− 10.6*	3.3	5.8	4.3	− 0.32	0.14	0.25*	0.06
1 Mining	13.7	− 5.3*	− 0.9	2.6	1.9	− 0.35	− 0.08	0.41*	0.17
2–3 Manufactur-ing	7.6	2.0	2.2*	1.7	1.3	0.19	0.29	0.44*	0.19
4–5 Construction + electricity, water, gas	1.2	2.0*	− 0.3	0.7	0.5	0.51	− 0.12	0.43*	0.19
6–7 Commerce and transport	4.0	5.4*	− 1.5	1.5	1.1	0.60	− 0.23	0.47*	0.22
8–9 Services	11.0	6.5*	− 2.8*	2.2	1.6	0.52	− 0.30	0.37*	0.14
4–9 Construction, commerce and services	16.2	13.9	− 4.6	3.9	2.9	0.59	− 0.26	0.44*	0.20

1. Data for Bolivia, Ecuador, the Guayanas, Uruguay and for Tierre del Fuego in Argentina are not included.

Regression and correlation coefficients marked with * are statistically significant at a 95% level.

The correlation coefficient between the independent variables log A and log D is $R = 0.714$.

part is a result of national governments' desire to emphasize the national identity of their peripheries, but it is also consistant with Berry's (1967, p. 33) finding, that the trade area of a service centre increases in size as density drops, but not as fast as density declines, so that the size of the populations served decreases.

A comparison of the regression coefficients in Table H.1 and H.2 indi- cates that although the general pattern is the same, one important change took place between 1950 and 1960. The manufacturing sector changed from being population-oriented (high regression coefficient for popu- lation density) to being accessibility-oriented.

Table H.2 *Regression equations for the relation between accessibility (A), population density (D), and percentage of the work force employed in each of the economic sectors*
1960: 54 regions[1]

Sector	Con- stant	Regression coefficient for		Standard error on regression coefficient		Beta coefficient for		Coefficient of correlation	determination
		log A	log D			log A	log D		
		b_A	b_D	δ_A	δ_D	β_A	β_D	R	R^2
0 Agriculture	90.8	−27.1*	6.3	7.8	3.8	−0.51	0.24	0.44*	0.19
1 Mining	7.5	− 1.0	−2.6*	2.7	1.3	−0.06	−0.30	0.34*	0.12
2–3 Manufactur- ing	−1.8	7.4*	0.6	2.2	1.1	0.47	0.07	0.51*	0.26
4–5 Construction	−0.0	3.3*	−1.5*	1.0	0.5	0.48	−0.44	0.45*	0.20
6–7 Commerce and transport	1.3	5.8*	0.3	2.0	1.0	0.43	0.04	0.45*	0.20
8–9 Services	2.2	11.7*	−3.0*	3.1	1.5	0.46	−0.28	0.46*	0.21
4–9 Construction, commerce and services	3.5	20.8*	−4.2	5.8	2.8	0.54	−0.22	0.46*	0.21

1. Data for Bolivia, Brazil, and the Guayanas are unavailable.
Regression and correlation coefficients marked with * are statistically significant at a 95% level.
The correlation coefficient between the independent variables log A and log D is $R = 0.523$.

This probably reflects the shift, which has taken place within the manufacturing sector, from traditional handicraft to more innovative manufacturing. At the same time the difference between accessibility and population density was much smaller in 1950 than in 1960 because the access to population of areas outside the local area was limited in 1950.

Dansk resumé

I diskussioner om økonomisk udviklingspolitik i udviklingslandene er de regionale problemer i de senere år kommet til at indtage en central placering. En af grundene hertil er, at en økonomis størrelse er blevet en stadig vigtigere faktor, ikke bare ved bestemmelsen af den totale produktion, men også ved bestemmelsen af produktionen pr. indbygger. I mange udviklingslande er både de sociale og de regionale forskelle i økonomisk udvikling meget store, og store dele af befolkningen i disse lande er i virkeligheden holdt udenfor den nationale markedsøkonomi. Manglen på social og regional integration er derfor en alvorlig hindring for økonomisk vækst.

Gennem 1960'erne udførtes der studier af den regionale udvikling i en række sydamerikanske lande. I mange af landene har der også været en mere eller mindre explicit regionaludviklingspolitik, f. eks. i form af støtte til industrilokalisering i udkantsområder, i form af koloniserings- og resourceudnyttelsesprojekter og i form af transportplaner. Anstrengelserne har imidlertid indtil nu kun været en begrænset succes. Dette skyldes først og fremmest at den meget stærke tradition for centraliseret styre, der findes i Latinamerika, har været vanskelig at ændre. For det andet har manglen på infrastruktur og service uden for de store byer vanskeliggjort decentralisering af de økonomiske aktiviteter. Endelig er effekten af mange forsøg på udvikling af de perifere områder blevet kraftigt reduceret, fordi planlægning ikke har kunnet finde sted på tværs af de nationale grænser.

Den politik der har været diskuteret som løsning på disse problemer er:

1. Projekter for social- og byudvikling. Mest dramatisk kommer de til udtryk i store vækstcenterprojekter, som *Brasilia* og *Ciudad Guayana*, men vigtigere er den voksende bekymring for byernes sociale problemer overalt på kontinentet.
2. Planer for transport- og kommunikationsnettenes udbygning, f.eks. planerne for *Carretera Marginal de la Selva* i Peru, det brasilianske vejbygningsprogram i Amazonområdet, og opbygningen af et overordnet telefonnetværk baseret på satellitter.
3. Planer for internationalt samarbejde og integration mellem kontinentets lande. Foruden i forsøgene på at danne et latinamerikansk fællesmarked, har

det internationale samarbejde resulteret i en række analyser af mulighederne for at lave multinationale udviklingsprogrammer for grænseområderne mellem de enkelte lande, f.eks. udviklingsprojekter for La Plata-flodsystemet og for grænseområderne mellem Colombia og dets naboer Ecuador og Venezuela.

Alle disse planer og projekter er imidlertid usammenhængende, og endnu har ingen af de sydamerikanske lande udarbejdet landsplaner, der kan danne udgangspunkt for en vurdering af udviklingsprogrammerne for de enkelte regioner. På internationalt niveau eksisterer sådanne planer naturligvis endnu mindre.

For at udvikle sådanne landsplaner vil det være nødvendigt, for det første, at kunne sammenligne udviklingen i de enkelte regioner, og for det andet, at have kendskab til sammenhængen mellem de enkelte regioner. Formålet med dette arbejde er at lave en sådan kontinental analyse af de regionale forskelle i Sydamerika.

Analysen bygger på folketællingsdata for 74 regioner, der dækker hele Sydamerika. Den består af fire dele. Første del er en beskrivende analyse af de 74 regioner (kap. 2) og sammenhængen mellem dem (kap. 3).

Kapitel 2 er en faktoranalyse af folketællingsdata (18 variable) for de 74 regioner fra omkring 1950 og omkring 1960. Der analyseres tre principale faktorer, der tilsammen beskriver 63% af den samlede varians i de 18 variable.

De første af de tre faktorer svarer stort set til den fysiske planlæggers opfattelse af urbanisering som *a place of living*. Faktor 2 svarer til sociologens opfattelse af urbanisering eller modernisering som *a way of life*, dog med den begrænsning at medens planlæggerens og sociologens urbaniseringsbegreber er indbyrdes korrelerede, så er de principale faktorer pr. definition ukorrelerede. Faktor 2 dækker derfor kun den del af sociologens urbaniseringsbegreb, der afviger fra planlæggerens. På samme måde svarer faktor 3 til den del af økonomens opfattelse af urbanisering eller industrialisering, der ikke allerede er indregnet i planlæggerens og sociologens urbaniseringsbegreber. Planlæggerens, sociologens og økonomens opfattelse af urbanisering, kan således opfattes som *oblique* faktorer i faktorrummet.

Endelig er det vist hvorledes de enkelte regioner i tiåret 1950–60 bevægede sig i faktorrummet. Det viste sig, at der er god overensstemmelse mellem strukturen af de enkelte regioner og den måde de har udviklet sig på i tiåret.

I kapitel 3 analyseres oplysninger om de interregionale strømme af varer og personer, for at få et billede af sammenhængen mellem de enkelte regioner. Analysen viser, at medens en vis integration havde fundet sted på den sydlige del af kontinentet, så var det kun i ringe grad tilfældet i den nordlige del.

I anden del er udviklingen af bysystemer opfattet som en innovationsspredningsproces. Kapitel 4 giver en beskrivelse af innovationsspredningsprocessen i et bysystem, og præsenterer nogle data for innovationsspredning i Sydamerika. I kapitel 5 analyseres sammenhængen mellem innovations- og informationsspredning og udviklingen af bysystemer.

Effektiv integration er en betingelse for hurtige spredningsprocesser. Integration kan derfor opfattes som komplementær til spredningsprocesserne. Integration er et resultat af forbedret tilgængelighed mellem flere og flere folk og aktiviteter. Tredie del præsenterer derfor en analyse af sammenhængen mellem tilgængelighed og økonomisk udvikling, målt som indkomst pr. indbygger. I kapitel 7 er det vist at et tilgængelighedsmål kan forklare ca. 50% af indkomstvariationen mellem de konsoliderede regioner (d.v.s. de regioner, der har relativ stor befolkningstæthed, og har høje faktorvægte for faktor 3 i faktoranalysen i kap. 2).

I de tyndt befolkede perifere regioner er tilgængelighed og indkomst derimod ukorrelerede. Her synes forekomsten af naturresourcer og direkte kapitalinvesteringer, ofte i form af subsidier, at spille en større rolle for variationen i indkomsterne.

I det omfang de regionale indkomstforskelle er bestemt af de regionale forskelle i tilgængeligheden vil ændringerne i indkomstforskellene kunne forklares som et resultat af ændringerne i tilgængelighedsforskellene. Ændringerne i tilgængelighedsforskellene er imidlertid delvis en funktion af ændringerne i fordelingen af befolkningen og dens socio-økonomiske udvikling. Der er således tale om en cirkulær proces. Denne proces er undersøgt i kap. 8. Det er her forsøgt at simulere, for det første, hvorledes de regionale tilgængelighedsforskelle vil blive påvirket af urbaniseringsprocessen, den internationale integration og forbedringen af kommunikationsnettene, og for det andet, hvorledes disse ændringer i tilgængelighedsforskellene kan forventes at påvirke de regionale indkomstforskelle. Resultatet af simulationen viser at de regionale indkomstforskelle kan forventes at vokse ved meget lave gennemsnitlige tilgængeligheder men aftage igen ved meget høje tilgængeligheder. Dette svarer til resultatet af de fleste empiriske studier af regionale indkomstforskelle.

Innovationsspredningsprocessen påvirker ikke bare regionernes økonomiske udvikling, men også den sociale og demografiske udvikling.

Emigranter strømmer fra områder med få økonomiske muligheder til områder med mange, og fødsels- og dødsrater påvirkes af spredningen af uddannelses- og sundhedsvæsen. De sociale og demografiske ændringer kan derfor opfattes som en feed-back fra innovationsspredningsprocesserne. Disse feedback mekanismer er behandlet i fjerde del.

References

Alkjær, Ejler and Jørn L. Eriksen (1967), *Location and Economic Consequences of International Congresses*. Copenhagen, Einar Harch.

Baerresen, Donald W., Martin Carnoy and Joseph Grunwald (1965), *Latin American Trade Pattern*. Washington D. C., The Brookings Institution.

Barbarovic, Ivo (1971), *Marginalidad Rural y Politicas de Desarollo Regional en Brazil*. Santiago de Chile, Mimeo.

Berry, Brian J. L. (1967), *Geography of Market Centers and Retail Distribution*. Englewood Cliffs, Prentice-Hall Inc.

—, (1970), 'City size and economic development: conceptual synthesis and policy problems, with special references to South and South-East Asia', *Urbanization and National Development*, edited by Leo Jacobsen, Ved Prakash and Sheilah Jacobsen. Beverly Hills, Sage Publications.

Berry, Brian and Elaine Neils (1969), 'Location, size and shape of cities as influenced by environmental factors: the urban environment writ large', *The Quality of the Urban Environment*, edited by Harvey S. Perloff. Washington D. C., Resources for the Future.

Bowers, R. V. (1937), 'The direction of intra-societal diffusion', *American Sociological Review* 2:826–836.

Brown, Lawrence A. (1968), *Diffusion Processes and Location*. Philadelphia, Regional Science Research Institute.

Brown, Robert T. (1966), *Transport and the Economic Integration of South America*. Washington D.C., The Brookings Institution.

Bruton, Henry J. (1967), 'Productivity growth in Latin America', *The American Economic Review* 57:1099–1116.

Burke, Melvin (1970), 'Land Reform and its effect upon production and productivity in the Lake Titicaca region', *Economic Development and Cultural Change* 18:410–450.

Carleton, Robert O. (1965), 'Fertility trends and differentials in Latin America', *The Milbank Memorial Fund Quarterly 43*, 4/2:15–31.

Cole, J. P. (1965), *Latin America. An Economic and Social Geography*. London, Butterworth.

Coleman, James, Elihn Katz and Herbert Menzel (1957), 'The diffusion of an innovation among physicians', *Sociometry* 20:253–270.

Chisholm, Michael (1963), 'Tendencies in agricultural specialization and regional concentration in industry', *Papers and Proceedings of the Regional Science Association* 10:157–162.

—, (1966), *Geography and Economics*. London, G. Bell and Sons.

Christ, Raymond E. (1965), 'Some aspects of centrifugal and centripetal forces at work in Andean America', *Annals of the Association of American Geographers* 55:610.

Cumberland, John H. (1971), *Regional Development. Experiences and Prospects in the United States of America*. The Hague and Paris, Mouton (Regional Planning Series, No. 2)

Dell, Sidney (1966), *A Latin American Common Market?* London, Oxford University Press.

Dennison, E. F. (1962), *The Sources of Economic Growth in the United States and the Alternatives before us*. New York, Committee of Economic Development.

Deutsch, Karl (1970), 'Integration and autonomy: some concepts and data', *Ekistics* 179:327–331.

Ducoff, Louis J. (1965), 'The role of migration in the demographic development of Latin America', *The Milbank Memorial Fund Quarterly* 43, 4/2:197–216.

Eidt, Robert C. (1962), 'Pioneer settlement in Eastern Peru', *Annals of the Association of American Geographers* 52:255–278.

Elizaga, Juan C. (1966), 'A study of immigrations to greater Santiago (Chile)', *Demography* 3:353–377.

Engström, Mats-G. (1970), *Regional arbetsfördeling*. Lund, Gleerup.

Espinoza, E. (1897), *Jeografia Descriptiva de la República de Chile*. Santiago de Chile.

Frank, André Gunder (1967), *Capitalism and Underdevelopment in Latin America*. New York and London, Monthly Review Press.

—, (1968), *Latin America: Underdevelopment or Revolution*. New York and London, Monthly Review Press.

Frederiksen, Harald (1969), 'Feed-backs in economic and demographic transition', *Science* 166:838–848.

Friedmann, John (1966), *Regional Development Policy. A Case study of Venezuela*. Cambridge, The MIT Press.

—, (1970), 'The future of urbanization in Latin America: Some observations on the role of the periphery', *Studies in Comparative International Development*.

Friedmann, John and John Miller (1965), 'The urban field', *Journal of the American Institute of Planners* 31:321–329.

Friedmann, John and Thomas Lackington (1967), 'Hyperurbanization and national development in Chile: Some hypotheses', *Urban Affairs Quarterly* 2:3–29.

Friedmann, John, *et al.* (1970), *Urbanization and National Development: A Comparative Analysis*. Mimio.

Furtado, Celso (1970), *Economic Development of Latin America*. Cambridge, Cambridge University Press.

Germani, Gino (1963), 'La movilidad social en la Argentina', *Movilidad social en la sociedad industrial Buenos Aires*, edited by Seymour M. Lipset and Reinhard Bendix. Buenos Aires.

Gould, P. R. (1967), 'Structuring information on spacio-temporal preferences', *Journal of Regional Science* 7:2–16.

Gould, P. R. and R. R. White (1968), 'The mental maps of British school leavers', *Regional Studies* 2:161–182.

Graham, Douglas H. (1970), 'Divergent and convergent regional economic growth and internal migration in Brazil. 1940–1960', *Economic Development and Cultural Change* 18:362–382.

Hagen, Everett E. (1968), *The Economics of Development*. Homewood, Ill., Richard D. Irwin, Inc.

Hägerstrand, Torsten and Antoni R. Kuklinski (eds.) (1971), *Information Systems for Regional Development – A Seminar*. Lund, Gleerup.

Haggett, Peter (1965), *Location Analysis in Human Geography*. London.

—, (1969), *Network Analysis in Geography*. London.

Herrick, Bruce (1966), *Urban Migration and Economic Development in Chile*. Cambridge, The MIT Press.

Hirshman, Albert O. (1958), *The Strategy of Economic Development*. New Haven, Yale University Press.

Isard, Walter (1956), *Location and Space Economy*. Cambridge, The MIT Press.

—, (1960), *Methods of Regional Analysis*. New York, John Wiley and Sons.

Johnson, John J. (1948), *Pioneer Telegraphy in Chile 1852–1876*. Stanford, Stanford University Press.

Karaska, Gerald J. (1969), 'Manufacturing linkages in the Philadelphia economy, Some evidence of external agglomeration forces', *Geographical Analysis* 1:354–369.

Keating, Robert B. (1967), *Regional Transport for Latin American Economic Integration*. Paper presented at a meeting arranged by the Interamerican Development Bank, Washington D. C., Oct. 1967.

Kjellström, Nils (1969), 'Sammanträden per bildtelefon-framtidsvy med frågetecken', *Industria* (Stockholm) 6/1969.

Kuznets, Simon (1966), *Modern Economic Growth. Rate, Structure and Spread*. New Haven, Yale University Press.

Larsen, Flemming (1970), Unpublished manuscript. Copenhagen.

Lasuen, J. R. (1969), 'On growth poles', *Urban Studies* 6:137–161.

Law, C. M. (1970), 'Employment growth and regional policy in North-West England', *Regional Studies* 4:359–366.

Lefeber, Louis and Mrinal Datta-Chaudhuri (1971), *Regional Development. Experiences and Prospects in South and Southeast Asia*. The Hague and Paris, Mouton (Regional Planning Series, No. 1).

Lewis, Oscar and Philip M. Hauser (1965), 'The folk urban ideal types', *The Study of Urbanization*, edited by Philip M. Hauser and Leo F. Schnore. New York, John Wiley and Sons.

Linsky, Arnold S. (1965), 'Some generalizations concerning primate cities', *Annals of the Association of American Geographers* 55:506–513.

Lipinsky, Andrew J. (1969), 'Integration of Latin American communications', *The Movement Towards Latin American Unity*, edited by Ronald Hilton. New York, Praeger Special Studies.

Lowry, Ira S. (1967), *Population Policy, Welfare and Regional Development*. Paper prepared for the Conference on Regional Development Planning, University of Puerto Rico, 29–31 March 1967.

Mansfield, Edwin (1968), *Industrial Research and Technological Innovation*. New York, W. Norton and Comp., Inc.

Marin Vicuña, Santiago (1900), *Estudios de los Ferrocarriles Chilenos*. Santiago de Chile.

Matilla, John M. and John Floncannon (1964), *A Study of ARA Designated Counties*. Area Redevelopment Administration. Research Project No. 82. Mimeo.

Matos Mar, J. (1961), 'Migration and urbanization. The "barriadas" of Lima: an example of integration into urban life', *Urbanization in Latin America*, edited by Philip M. Hauser. New York, Unesco.

Mattelart, Armand (1965), *Integración Nacional y Marginalidad*. Santiago de Chile, Editorial del Pacífico, S. A.

Meier, Richard L. (1962), *A Communication Theory of Urban Growth*. Cambridge, The MIT Press.

Metha, Surinder K. (1964), 'Some demographic and economic correlates of primate cities. A case for revaluation', *Demography* 1:136–147.

Miller, John and Ralph A. Gakenheimer (1971), *Latin American Urban Policies and the Social Sciences*. Beverly Hills, Sage Publications.

Miro, Carmen A. and Ferdinand Rath (1965), 'Preliminary Findings of Comparative Fertility Surveys in Three Latin American Cities', *The Milbank Memorial Fund Quarterly* 43, 4/2:36–62.

Montoya Rojas, Rodrigo (1967), 'La migración interna en el Perú. Un caso concreto', *America Latina* 10:83–106.

Morrill, Richard L. (1968), 'Waves of spatial diffusion', *Journal of Regional Science* 8:1–18.

Mueller, Eva, Arnold Wilken, and Margaret Wood (1961), *Location Decisions and Industrial Mobility in Michigan*. Ann Arbor, Institute for Social Research, The University of Michigan.

Myrdal, Gunnar (1957), *Economic Theory and Under-developed Regions*. London.

Nordborg, Knut (1967), 'Elit lokalisering och befolkningspotential', *Svensk Geografisk Årbok* 43:93–100.

North, Douglas C. (1955), 'Location theory and regional economic growth', *Journal of Political Economy* 63:243–258.

Olsson, Gunnar (1965), *Distance and Human Interaction. A Review and Bibliography*. Philadelphia, Regional Science Research Institute.

Pedersen, Poul O. and Walter Stöhr (1969), 'Economic integration and spatial development in South America', *American behavioral Scientist* 12:2–12.

Pedersen, Poul O. (1970), 'Innovation diffusion within and between national urban systems', *Geographical Analysis* 2:203–254.

Perloff, Harvey S., Edgar S. Dunn, Eric E. Lampard, and Richard F. Muth (1960), *Regions, Resources, and Economic Growth*. Baltimore, John Hopkins Press.

Pred, Allan (1966), *The Spatial Dynamics of U.S. Urban – Industrial Growth 1800–1914*. Cambridge, The MIT Press.

—, (1972), *Urban Growth before the Telegraph: Information Circulation and the U.S. System of Cities, 1790–1840*. Forthcoming.

Pyle, G. F. (1969), 'The diffusion of cholera in the United States in the nineteenth century', *Geographical Analysis* 1:59–75.

Rijckeghem, Willy van (1967), *Tabela de Insumo-Producto Brazil – 1959.* Mimeo.

Rogers, Everett M. (1962), *Diffusion of Innovations.* New York, The Free Press of Glencoe.

Schmookler, Jacob (1957), 'Inventors past and present', *Review of Economics and Statistics* 39:321–333.

Seebas, Jan (1969), 'Tre industriföretags externa personkontakter', *Urbaniserings-processen* No. 22. Lund.

Schakes, S. El (1965), *Development, Primacy and the Structure of Cities.* Harvard University, Ph.D. dissertation.

Soberman, Richard M. (1966), *Transport Technology for Developing Regions.* Cambridge, The MIT Press.

Solow, R. M. (1957), 'Technical change and the aggregate production function', *Review of Economic and Statistics* 39:312–320.

Sovani, N. V. (1964), 'The analysis of over-urbanization', *Economic Development and Cultural Change* 12:113–122.

Stöhr, Walter (1974), *Regional Development in Latin America. Experiences and Prospects on the Verge of the Second UN Development Decade.* The Hague and Paris, Mouton (Regional Planning Series, No. 3). Forthcoming.

Stycos, J. Mayone (1965), 'Needed research on Latin American fertility: Urbanization and fertility', *The Milbank Memorial Fund Quarterly* 43, 4/2:299–315.

Stycos, J. Mayone (1968), *Human Fertility in Latin America.* Ithaca, N.Y., Cornell University Press.

Thorngren, Bertil (1967), *Regionale Externale Economies.* Stockholm. Ekonomiska Forskningsinstituttet, Handelshögskolan.

—, (1970), 'How do contact systems affect regional development?', *Environment and Planning* 2:409–427.

Törnquist, Gunnar and Peter Gould (1971), 'Information, innovation and acceptance', *Information Systems for Regional Development – A Seminar,* edited by Torsten Hägerstrand and Antoni R. Kuklinski. Lund, Gleerup.

Valerie, Fifer J. (1967), 'Bolivia's pioneer fringe', *The Geographical Review* 57:1–23.

Warntz, William (1965), *Macrogeography and Income Fronts.* Philadelphia, Regional Science Research Institute.

Webber, Melvin (1964), 'The urban place and the non-place urban realm', *Explorations into Urban Structure,* edited by C. B. Wurster. Philadelphia, University of Pennsylvania Press.

Weber, Alfred (1929), *Theory of the Location of Industries.* Chicago, University of Chicago Press.

Williamson, J. G. (1965), 'Regional inequality and the process of national development. A description of the patterns', *Economic Development and Cultural Change* 13:3–45.

Wirth, Louis (1938), 'Urbanization as a way of life', *American Journal of Sociology* 44:1–24.

Wood, W. D. and R. S. Thomas (eds.) (1965), *Areas of Economic Stress in Canada.* Kingston, Ontario, Industrial Relation Centre, Queens University.

Wright, Maurice (1967), 'Provincial office development', *Urban Studies* 4:218–257.
Zeidler, H. M. *et al.* (1969), *Patterns of Technology in Data Processing and Data Communications.* Report No. 7379 B–4, Standford Research Institute, Clearinghouse.

Annuario de Estadístico de Chile 1871–72 (1873), Santiago de Chile.
Area Redevelopment Administration (1965), *Area Redevelopment Policies in Britain and the Countries of the Common Market.* Washington D. C., Economic Redevelopment Research, US Department of Commerce.
Centro de Estudios de Población (1969), *Condicionamientos Socioculturales de la Fecundidad en Bolivia.* La Paz.
Comité Interamericano de Desarollo Agrícola (CIDA) (1966), *Chile. Tenencia de la tierre y desarollo socio-economic del sector agrícola.* Santiago.
Centro de Investigaciones Sociales por Muestreo (1967), *Población Economicamente Activa de Lima Metropolitana. Encuesta de Hogares.* Lima, Servicio del Empleo y Recursos Humanos, Ministerio de Trabajo y Communidades.
Dirección de Estadística y Censos (1966), *Seria de Investigaciones Muestrales. Muestra Nacional de Hogares. Encuesta Continua de Mano de Obra. Julio – Octobre 1966.* Santiago de Chile.
Instituto Latinoamericano de Planification Economica y Social (ILPES) (1968), *Elementos para la elaboración de una politica de desarollo con Integración para America Latina.* (INST/S. 3/L. 3) Santiago de Chile.
ODEPLAN (1962), *Matrix de Transacciones Intersetoriales de Bienes y Servicios.* Santiago de Chile, Mimio.
OECD (1968), *Gaps in Technology between Member Countries.* Third Ministerial Meeting on Science of OECD Countries, Paris.
United Nations (1961), 'Demographic aspects of urbanization in Latin America', *Urbanization in Latin America,* edited by Philip M. Hauser. New York, Unesco.